R. Herrick

The elementary forms
of the new religious life

International Library of Sociology

Founded by Karl Mannheim

Editor: John Rex, University of Aston in Birmingham

Arbor Scientiae
Arbor Vitae

A catalogue of the books available in the **International Library of Sociology** and other series of Social Science books published by Routledge & Kegan Paul will be found at the end of this volume.

The elementary forms
of the new religious life

Roy Wallis

Routledge & Kegan Paul
London, Boston, Melbourne and Henley

First published in 1984
by Routledge & Kegan Paul plc
39 Store Street, London WC1E 7DD,
9 Park Street, Boston, Mass. 02108, USA,
464 St Kilda Road,
Melbourne 3004, Australia and
Broadway House, Newtown Road,
Henley-on-Thames, Oxon RG9 1EN, England
Printed in Great Britain by
Thetford Press

Library of Congress Cataloging in Publication Data
Wallis, Roy.
The elementary forms of the new religious life.
(International library of sociology)
Bibliography: p.
Includes index.
1. Cults. 2. Religions. I. Title. II. Series.
BL80.2.W27 1984   291   83-11092

ISBN 0-7100-9890-1

For Bryan R. Wilson,
teacher and friend

Contents

Preface

This book started life in 1977, when I began preparing an inaugural lecture on my appointment to the Chair of Sociology in The Queen's University of Belfast. Queen's took a considerable gamble in appointing a young (I have aged far more than five years since) and quite inexperienced lecturer to their vacant Chair. Whether that gamble paid off only they can judge. For my part, however, it should be said that I was honoured by the trust reposed in me by their decision, and that I have found Queen's to be a civilised and enlightened island within a sea of dogmatic intolerance, a sea which may at present lap the coasts of Ulster more fiercely than elsewhere in the British Isles, but whose tides ebb and flow far further afield. The Queen's University has been an environment congenial to scholarly endeavour, even in such exotic fields as those which have informed this book. I am grateful to it for its support of this research through many small grants and other facilities.

My interest in the new religions has persisted over some twelve years now, during which time I have conducted detailed studies of Scientology, the Children of God, the Human Potential Movement, and currently the movement of Bhagwan Shree Rajneesh, while maintaining a watching brief over the field generally, and mounting small expeditions to outposts of a great many of the movements referred to in the following pages. This is a controversial area for research. The Church of Scientology has been only one of the critics of my methods and integrity. While they have found my work biased against them, opponents of the Children of God and the Unification Church have found other grounds for objection. For some, my very willingness to engage with these groups, and to give them an open-minded hearing, has seemed reprehensible. In research of this kind, to be construed as biased by both sides is probably the only sure sign that one is getting it about right.

My studies over the years have been greatly assisted by grants from the Social Science Research Council, the British Academy, The Leverhulme Trust and the Nuffield Foundation. I wish to express my warm appreciation for these subventions, without which my research would not have been possible.

I have discussed many of the ideas in this book with Dr Steve Bruce, with whom parts of chapter four were formulated in Wallis and Bruce (1983). His willingness to drop everything and listen to a new conceptualisation has often sustained me. Other parts of this volume have had preliminary formulations in Wallis (1979b,

1982a, 1982c, and forthcoming). Dr Bryan Wilson, to whom this work is dedicated, has commented upon it in draft, and I wish to record my appreciation of his many kindnesses over the years.

Mrs Brenda Harkess and Mrs Evelyn Hunter have typed and retyped various efforts at creating and improving the text, and the final version was the joint product of Christine Clegg, Margaret Drumm, Helen McAllister, Gillian Ellis and Nicola Shearer to whom, with Miss Angela Smartt and Mrs Lorna Gold-strom who supervise the endeavours of the university Typing Centre, I am grateful for their efforts on my behalf and their unfailing good humour. My wife and children kept me sane.

1 Introduction

This essay presents a framework for conceptualising the new religious movements which have emerged in the West in the post-second world war period, particularly the extremely diverse range of movements which became prominent in the 1960s. This conceptualisation elaborates a logical trichotomy into three analytical types, and from this develops a theory of the origins, recruitment bases, characteristics, and developmental patterns which they display. Although some of the movements have been widely publicised, even attaining a certain notoriety through mass media treatment, for example: Scientology, Krishna Consciousness, the Unification Church, and the Manson Family; others such as The Process, Meher Baba, and 3-HO, are much less well known. While some became international, others remain small, local entities, or have already virtually disappeared. In multitudinous other ways too - style, ritual, belief, organisation, and so on - they exhibit enormous diversity.

While less discerning commentators have sought to describe and explain all the new religions as a unified phenomenon, or to treat each one as unique, more thoughtful and perceptive scholars such as Bryan Wilson have sought to distinguish them in terms of a limited number of types. Wilson, for example, constructs a classification on the basis of three themes which he finds to characterise the teachings of the new religions. The themes are:

> that salvation is gained by becoming acquainted with a special, perhaps secret, knowledge from a mystic source; that ultimate salvation and knowledge comes from the liberation of powers within the self; that real salvation is attained by belonging to a saved community, whose life-style and concerns are utterly divergent from those of worldly people. (Wilson, 1976: 63)

Wilson's treatment of the new religions has been one of the more interesting and enlightening, but none the less it must be said that classification is of limited utility unless linked to a theory which *explains* salient differences distinguished by the classification.

Frederick Bird (1979) distinguishes between the various new religious movements in terms of 'the relationship of followers to masters or the relationship of the religious seekers to the sacred power they revere' (1979: 336). Thus, adherents may

become '(a) *devotees* of a sacred lord or lordly truth, (b) disciples of a revered or holy discipline, (c) or *apprentices* skilled
at unlocking the mysteries of a sacred, inner power' (ibid.). In
the first category would fall Neo-Pentecostals, Divine Light
Mission and Krishna Consciousness. (Descriptions of these groups
- albeit inevitably brief and selective - will be presented in the
pages that follow.) In the *disciple* category fall some of the
smaller groups such as Integral Yoga, or the Zen Centers in the
American West. (Groups of this type have not been widely described, but on Zen, see Tipton, 1982b). Examples of *apprentice-
ship* groups would be Silva Mind Control, *est*, Transcendental
Meditation, or Scientology. Bird seeks to show that these
different types of movement provide different ways of coping
with the problem of 'moral accountability' which he believes to be
one of the factors in their appeal.

Thomas Robbins and Dick Anthony have produced one of the
best known and most influential typologies of the new religious
movements. Drawing theoretically upon Robert Bellah's (1967,
1969) conception of religious evolution and 'civil religion', they
argue that the new religious movements are to be understood as
a response to a crisis in American civil religion (Anthony and
Robbins, 1982a). I shall examine this theory more closely in
chapter four, when I consider the relationship between such
movements and secularisation. Here, however, I wish to explore
the typology which is associated with this theory.

Robbins and Anthony argue that two main types of response
to the 'decline of civil religion' can be observed in the new
religions: the emergence of '*dualistic* movements which reaffirm
elements of traditional moral absolutism in an exaggerated and
strident manner' (Robbins, Anthony and Richardson, 1978: 101),
and '*monistic* movements which affirm relativistic and subjectivistic
moral meaning systems' (ibid.). The former type are sometimes
called 'civil religion sects' by Robbins and Anthony.

DUALISTIC 'CIVIL RELIGION SECTS'

These movements articulate a protest against the ambiguity,
relativism and permissiveness of modern culture, and reaffirm a
'theocentric ethical dualism'. They also aspire to reorder the
political process and its assumptions, generally in a conservative
direction. They fall into two sub-types: 'neo-fundamentalist',
such as the Jesus People; and 'revisionist syncretic', such as
the Unification Church. Other groups within this type are the
Children of God, the People's Temple, and Synanon. In the face
of resistance to their efforts to recast the political arena, or
to initiate its transformation by supernatural means, they may
'create alternative communities as models of future American
society' (Anthony and Robbins, 1982a: 221). They may thus
become regimented 'total institutions' and sharply segregate their
members from former associations and the wider society.

'MONISTIC GROUPS'

These movements articulate a 'vision of the universe in which
there is an ultimate metaphysical unity or "oneness" which dis-
solves polarities and imparts an ultimately illusory or epiphen-
omenal quality (Maya) to the material world' (Robbins, Anthony
and Richardson, 1978: 102). They cultivate an inner spiritual
awakening and 'the exploration of intrapsychic consciousness'.
They may thus converge with psychotherapeutic preoccupations.
They tend to be ethically relativistic. Various sub-types of
monistic movement are suggested, depending on the means by
which enlightenment is secured, i.e. *technical* or *charismatic*,
and on whether enlightenment is seen as involving one or two
levels.
    Technical movements employ defined techniques and standard-
ised procedures of an instrumental kind, for example, TM, *est*,
Scientology and (surprisingly) Krishna Consciousness. *Charismatic* movements promise enlightenment 'through veneration and
emulation of leaders who are regarded as exemplars of advanced
consciousness' (ibid.: 105). Examples are Meher Baba, Guru
Maharaj-Ji, and Charles Manson. *One-level* movements see their
members as being enlightened as soon as they are converted, or
are movements in which enlightenment is seen as being attained
very rapidly. Again TM and *est* are offered as examples, along
with Scientology. *Two-level* movements view enlightenment as
'a characteristic of a rare stage of spiritual evolution' (ibid.:
106), for example, Meher Baba, Yogi Bhajan (Healthy-Happy-
Holy Organisation).
    This typology is ingenious and insightful. It illuminates the
vast plethora of movements by dividing them into a set of
categories which are economical in terms of the criteria employed,
and which appear to be strong predictors of other attributes
of the movements concerned. However, it is not without difficulties. ISKCON (Krishna Consciousness) may be monistic, as
would be expected from a movement so clearly committed to Hindu
traditional thought, yet it also possesses an aspiration to reform
the social and political order, and has developed a model of the
new world in its communal endeavours, such as New Vrndāvana.
Thus, in many ways it would seem to have more in common with the
Children of God and the Unification Church, than with *est* or TM.
It also seems somewhat curious to refer to the devotional practice
of ISKCON, notably chanting the Hare Krishna mantra, as merely
a technique for securing enlightenment.
    Frederick Bird (1979: 337) has also raised some queries about
the blanket description of the eastern-originated groups as
monistic, 'not only because of the ontological and ethical dualisms
which seem to be inter-related with Hindu Vedantism . . . but
also because the significant differences between religions arising
out of Buddhist, Muslim, Hindu and Taoist traditions are blurred.
. . .' He argues that some of the groups identified by Robbins
and Anthony as monistic are, in fact, dualistic, suggesting some

ambiguity about the correct application of these labels. Moreover, I would also argue that some of the groups in the monistic category have quite significant political aspirations - albeit not of a nationalistic kind (e.g. Scientology, and ISKCON, perhaps even TM in more recent years). On the other hand, it is not entirely clear to me that a movement like Synanon can be said to advance a political perspective which reaffirms a 'theocentric ethical dualism', as the basis for the re-invigoration of national consensus, and thus that it qualifies as a 'civil religion sect'. Therefore, not all dualistic movements would seem to qualify as 'civil religion sects'. Some seem to have no political orientation at all to speak of (e.g. the followers of Brother Evangelist, see Martin, 1979).

The Robbins and Anthony typology has achieved a substantial measure of descriptive validity, and its dimensions do appear to have some value in predicting further features of the movements in question. It must be recognised, however, that any given body of phenomena is susceptible to classification in terms of an infinite number of typological schemes. Thus, ultimately, the test of a typology lies not in its components, but rather in the uses to which it can be put, particularly that of identifying the significant characteristics of the phenomena in terms of a theory which turns out to be able to bear the heat of critical appraisal. It is at this point that the adequacy of the Robbins and Anthony schema falls most into question, but discussion of their theory, and that of Frederick Bird, will be reserved for a later stage, when I take up the issue of the role of secularisation, in chapter four.

These various typologies, then, all have considerable value in providing insight into the beliefs and structure of the new religious movements. However, in the pages that follow I shall advance an alternative typology which seems not only to provide some leverage on the divergent forms of the new religious movements, but which is also linked to an analysis of their sources of support, and of their developmental patterns.

A TYPOLOGY OF NEW RELGIONS

The typology I wish to present requires the construction of a *conceptual space*. This conceptual space is formed by the components of a logical trichotomy, the elements of which constitute an exhaustive set of ways in which a new religious movement may orient itself to the social world into which it emerges. A new movement may embrace that world, affirming its normatively approved goals and values; it may reject that world, denigrating those things held dear within it; or it may remain as far as possible indifferent to the world in terms of its religious practice, accommodating to it otherwise, and exhibiting only mild acquiescence to, or disapprobation, of, the ways of the world. A visual representation of this is presented in Figure 1 (see page 6).

I contend that there are definite *types* of new religion associated
with these orientations, and in the two principal cases (rejection
of the world and affirmation of the world), knowledge of the
dominant orientation is an excellent predictor of a wide range of
further attributes. These will be presented as ideal types, *not*
as mutually exclusive empirical categories. Empirical instances
will therefore only *approximate* to these types, of course, often
combining elements of more than one orientation. None the less,
some actual cases approximate extremely closely to these constructs and will be drawn upon frequently as sources of appropriate illustrative material.

The third orientation, accommodation to the world, is not
associated with an analytical type of new religion comparable in
scope to rejection of the world and affirmation of the world. While
the two latter orientations seem to create imperatives of, and
constraints upon organisation, belief and behaviour over a very
wide range, accommodation to the world seems compatible with a
broad spectrum of forms and ideologies. Nevertheless it is possible
to say something of the features and sources of such a religious
movement and this will be briefly essayed.

The world-accommodating type of new religion will be treated
more briefly than the other two, since it is less significant for
the purpose of characterising those new religions which predominantly emerged in the post second world war period. Movements closest to this type often emerged in an earlier period than
is our focus here, and are of little numerical significance (see,
for example, Wallis 1974 on the Aetherius Society), or they are
an 'added blessing', an adjunct to an existing religious attachment (as in Neo-Pentecostalism), rather than a complete alternative to it as a path to salvation. The only important exception
to this is the western branch of the Japanese-originated
movement, Soka Gakkai. The type is principally important,
however, as a possible developmental path for the two main
movement types, as they move away from an initial stage of
zealous purity. Hence it is of importance also, as a source of
insight into the developmental tensions and internal strains in the
beliefs and life-style of actually existing cases.

As a final preliminary, it must be observed that this analysis –
the conceptual scheme and theoretical observations – are designed
to meet only a limited purpose. There is no claim advanced here
that the analysis is of universal applicability, relevant to all new
religious movements in no matter what historical or cultural
circumstances. The aim of this work is a more modest one,
essentially involving an attempt to make some sense of the forms
and dynamics of new religious movements in the West in the
period since the second world war. I would be the very first to
admit that the range of movements which emerged in this historically and culturally specific period differed in a number of ways
from those appearing in other times and places. The restricted
nature of the case being advanced must be borne in mind throughout.

I thus entirely agree with Dr Bryan Wilson's recent observations on this matter:

> Perhaps the time has come to recognise the impossibility –
> in any terms that are not unduly vague – of any *general*
> theory of new movements. Certainly we should not aim –
> as sociologists have sometimes been wont to do – at a theory
> that seeks to be outside time and space, even though we wish
> our concepts to apply outside and beyond the confines of any
> one culture or historical epoch. If sociology is not to abandon
> the real world for purely theoretical artifacts, then, we are
> always likely to be in some degree captive to the empirical
> circumstances of given cultures, of geography, and of history.
> (Wilson, 1979: 194-5)

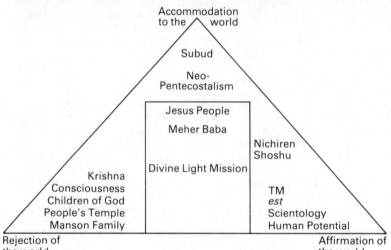

Figure 1 Orientations of the new religions to the world

Figure 1 is intended to provide a broadly representational visual configuration rather than an exact mapping. The latter would not be possible, except for an extremely narrow time span, because a movement may shift around considerably during the course of its development. The representational convention employed places groups and movements which closely approximate the analytical types in the appropriate angles of the conceptual space. In the rectangular central section are located examples of more clearly 'mixed' cases.

A superficial appraisal of this construct by those possessing a passing acquaintance with the work of J. Milton Yinger may suggest a similarity with his conceptualisation of types of sect (Yinger, 1970: 278). There is, indeed a similarity – although

this typology was not based upon his in any way, deriving
rather from an earlier formulation in terms of a continuum
between the base types (see Wallis, 1978; 1982a) - in that both
employ a triangular visual configuration, and both are attempts
to conceptualise types of new religious movement in terms of an
attitude toward 'the world'. There is even some broad overlap
in types.

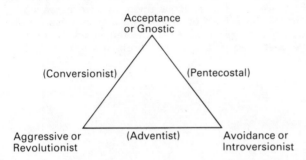

Figure 2 Yinger's typology of sects (Source: Yinger, 1970:278)

Yinger speaks of 'Acceptance' sects, by which he refers to
what Wilson has termed 'Gnostic sects', and this category is
clearly very similar to my 'world-affirming' category (see Yinger,
1970: 275). However, his 'Aggressive' sects are not at all cotermin-
ous with my 'world-rejecting' category, in that he has in mind
here what Wilson has called 'Conversionist' and 'Adventist' sects
(Yinger, 1970: 275-6). While the latter *would* be included in my
'world-rejecting' type, the former certainly would *not*. Moreover, my 'world-rejecting' type *also* includes Yinger's 'Avoidance'
(Wilson's 'Introversionist') sects which thus do not form a
separate type for my purpose here. Yinger's typology has nothing approaching my world-accommodating type. Hence my construct is neither derived from that of Yinger, nor does it seek to
supplant it, since its purpose is solely to help illuminate a
particular range of new religious movements, i.e. those emerging
in the West in the last quarter century or so. Yinger's construct
aims at far broader descriptive utility, particularly in historical
coverage and it is not my intention to dispute its general useful-
ness. Indeed the convergence of Yinger, Wilson and myself in
approach and conceptualisation - in so far as it occurs - suggests
that there *really is something there*, which we each articulate in
different ways for our separate purposes.
    In endeavouring to show the utility of my conceptualisation
of the new religions and the theoretical insight which it makes
possible, I shall need to draw upon a very broad range of available descriptive material and I am fortunate, therefore, to undertake this task at a stage when a considerable number of case
studies of particular movements have appeared. Although some

reference will be made to primary sources, it is upon this extant body of studies - by sociologists, anthropologists, theologians, journalists and even by former members - that I shall primarily draw. My use of any particular reference is not necessarily an endorsement of it as a whole, merely the utilisation of a particular point in such a work normally perfectly well available in other sources, but perhaps most conveniently, dramatically, or succinctly stated in the reference or quotation chosen. At some points, however, I shall draw upon my own research materials - in the form both of interviews and movement documents - which I have gathered over the ten years or so during which I have been engaged upon research into various of these movements.

2 Three types of new religious movement

In this chapter I propose to provide a characterisation of the three types of new religion, illustrating the characteristics of each type from actual movements which appear to approximate them particularly closely, or to embody features of the type in a sharply visible form.

THE WORLD-REJECTING NEW RELIGION

The world-rejecting movement, no matter what religious tradition it draws upon, is much more *recognisably* religious than the world-affirming type. It possesses a clear conception of God as at the same time a *personal* entity but yet radically distinct from man and prescribing a clear and uncompromising set of moral demands upon him. For example, in the International Society for Krishna Consciousness (ISKCON) - the saffron-robed devotees of Swami Bhaktivedanta (also known as Prabuphāda), an Indian guru who travelled to America in 1965 to spread devotion to Krishna and the ecstatic practices of his worship, such as chanting the Hare Krishna mantra - Krishna 'is not an idea or abstract principle but a person not unlike every human, however unfathomably greater, more magnificent, opulent and omnipotent he may be' (Reis, 1975: 54).

The Children of God derive from a quite different tradition, that of American fundamentalism, adapted to the counter-cultural youth revolt of the 1960s. Founded in 1968 by David Brandt Berg (later known as Moses David, or Mo) in California among the youthful rebels and drop-outs of the West Coast, it subsequently spread nomadically throughout the world. The deity of the Children of God is a variation upon the traditional Judeo-Christian God, highly personalistic even when referred to more impersonally as 'Love' and possessed of the same whims, emotions, arbitrariness, and tendencies to favouritism as any human being.

The Unification Church, whose followers are popularly known as the 'Moonies', also emerged from within the Judeo-Christian tradition. But in this case fundamentalism was syncretised with Asian religious conceptions in Korea where the Reverend Sun Myung Moon, its founder, was born. Although missionaries of the church arrived in America late in 1959, it was not until the late 1960s and early 1970s that it began to expand significantly and to attain an almost unrivalled public notoriety. For all its novel features, however, the deity of the Unification Church is a

Heavenly Father, to whom conventional attitudes of prayer and supplication are taken.

The world-rejecting movement views the prevailing social order as having departed substantially from God's prescriptions and plan. Mankind has lost touch with God and spiritual things, and, in the pursuit of purely material interests, has succeeded in creating a polluted environment; a vice-ridden society in which individuals treat each other purely as means rather than as ends; a world filled with conflict, greed, insincerity and despair. The world-rejecting movement condemns urban industrial society and its values, particularly that of individual success as measured by wealth or consumption patterns. It rejects the materialism of the advanced industrial world, calling for a return to a more rural way of life, and a reorientation of secular life to God.

Moses David, leader of the Children of God, observed in disappointment after a visit to Israel, that it:

> reminds us more of America than any country we visited with all its busy materialism, its riches, power, and armaments, its noisy traffic and air pollution, and its increasingly materialistically-minded younger generation. (Moses David, 'The promised land?', 4 February 1971)[1]

> God's government is going to be based on the small village plan. . . . Each village will be virtually completely self-contained, self-controlled and self-sufficient unto itself, like one big happy family or local tribe, just the way God started man out in the beginning. His ideal economy, society and government based on His own created productive land for man's simple necessities.

> We're going to go back to those days with only the beautiful creation of God around us and the wonderful creatures of God to help us plow and power and transport what little we have to do to supply our meagre needs (Moses David, 'Heavenly homes', 21 October 1974)

These sentiments are echoed by the Krishna Consciousness movement in its references to New Vrndāvana, its model agricultural community established in West Virginia, to

> show that one need not depend upon factories, movies, department stores, or nightclubs for happiness; one may live peacefully and happily with little more than some land, cows, and the association of devotees in a transcendental atmosphere of Krishna Consciousness. (*Back to Godhead*, 60, 1973: 14)

Jonestown in the Guyana jungle was viewed as a potential rural paradise by Jim Jones's followers in the People's Temple. The prospect of a communist agrarian idyll where food would be plentiful, prejudice and discrimination non-existent, and all

would share as they had need, was attractive indeed for under-
privileged black ghetto-dwellers in northern California, and for
white middle-class radicals alike.

Rather than a life pursuing *self-interest*, the world-rejecting
sect requires a life of *service* to the guru or prophet and to
others who likewise follow him. Through long hours of proselytising on the street or distributing the movement's literature,
through an arduous round of devotional ritual before the deities
or unpaid domestic duties for leaders or other members, the
devotee will suppress his own desires and goals in expression
of his commitment to the greater good of the movement, or love
of God and His agent. Reis observes of the Krishna Consciousness
devotee that:

> Although one has a duty to provide financial support for the
> maintenance and expansion of the organisation, this is not done
> for the self, the fragile illusionary ego, but out of love for
> Krishna and his personal representative, Prabhupāda (Reis,
> 1975: 159-60).

Such a movement may anticipate an imminent and major
transformation of the world. The Children of God, for example,
expect a progressive movement toward the prophesied End Time
with the rise of the Anti-Christ shortly to occur or even now
under way, the confirmation of the Covenant in 1985 and the
inauguration thereby of the final seven years of world history.
In 1989 the Tribulation will begin as the Anti-Christ demands
to be worshipped as God, turning against the saints; and in 1993
Jesus is to return. Many members of the Unification Church, too,
regard themselves as living in the Last Days (Edwards, 1979:
80-9) in which the Lord of the Second Advent is destined to
take up the task which Jesus failed to complete because of his
crucifixion. Jesus was able only to establish God's spiritual
kingdom on earth when his mission had been to establish both a
spiritual *and* a physical kingdom. The Christian tradition has
held - in some of its varieties - to a conception of the physical
return of Christ at the Second Coming to establish his millennial
reign after defeating the forces of evil. Members of the Unification
Church see the Reverend Sun Myung Moon as occupying the
role of Christ (rather than being Jesus returned), and engaged
in a God-directed mission to establish the basis for the physical
kingdom of God, and the restoration of the world to His dominion
after wresting it from Satan.

The world-rejecting movement expects that the millennium will
shortly commence or that the movement will sweep the world, and,
when all have become members or when they are in a majority,
or when they have become guides and counsellors to kings and
presidents, then a new world-order will begin, a simpler, more
loving, more humane and more spiritual order in which the old
evils and mistakes will be eradicated, and utopia will have begun.
These examples illustrate the close link between religious and

political aspirations among world-rejecting sects. Their rejection
of the world clearly embraces secular institutions. Since their
aim is to recover the world for God, they deny the conventional
distinction between a secular and a religious realm, the secular
must be restored to its 'original' religious character. Their
tendency to reject a distinction between the religious and the
political also follows from a conception of mundane events as
implicated in a cosmic plan, one based on a struggle between God
and evil, truth and illusion, now near culmination. Political
differences thus mirror cosmic positions in this struggle, with
communism typically seen as the Satanic representative on earth.
It also follows from this that, with the final struggle so close,
the faithful cannot hope to change the world sufficiently one soul
at a time. Thus, although they seek to convert among the world's
masses, they also address themselves to the influential, who are
in a position to affect a much wider range of people and events
and thus to meet the pressing cosmic timetable more effectively.
Hence, a number of such movements have cultivated the company
of the powerful. Judah quotes a Krishna devotee on the benefits
of such a policy:

> So the idea is that the politicians . . . take advice from Krishna
> Consciousness. . . . Just try to conceive for a moment the
> potency of a political candidate running for office having
> spiritual advisers who are telling him that his only goal should
> be to serve Krishna. (Judah, 1974: 119)

The Unification Church, too, has sought to gain a role for some
of its members as advisers to, and confidantes of, prominent
American politicians. The Children of God have also seen themselves as aides and counsellors to rulers and, more especially,
to the world-ruler they believe to be about to rise. After
Armageddon and the return of Christ, they believe that 'we, the
Children of God, shall rule and reign with Him . . .' (Moses
David, 'Daniel 7', May 1975).
  So active have some groups been in this direction that their
claim to a *religious* mission comes to be regarded as little more
than a front for political aspirations. Such accusations have been
levelled against Sun Myung Moon and the Unification Church, who
have been vigorous in their opposition to communism, and their
support for anti-communist figures and regimes such as Richard
Nixon, and successive South Korean military dictatorships. Jim
Jones, founder of the People's Temple, was courted by many
Californian politicians. Manson's gory group are not perhaps
readily conceived as 'religious', but it appears that Charles
Manson did view himself as a composite of Christ and Satan,
returned to earth in preparation for the imminent cataclysm of
Armageddon (Bugliosi, 1977: 581), which would largely consist
of a terrible violent revolution of the blacks against the whites
in America. Thereafter his political role would emerge. He is said
to have believed that the American blacks, having vanquished the

whites, would eventually have to turn to him to guide them.
Meanwhile, in such movements, characteristically the faithful
have come out of the world until Armageddon or the millennium
transpires, setting themselves apart from it, anticipating utopia
in the communal life wherein they can keep themselves separated,
uncontaminated by the worldly order, able to cultivate their
collective spiritual state unmolested. The religious involvement of
members is thus a full-time activity. The committed adherent will
need to break completely with the worldly life in order to fulfil
the movement's expectations, and separation may result in a
rift with family and former friends, with conventional education
and career. The movement is a 'total institution', regulating all its
adherents' activities, programming all of their day but for the
briefest periods of recreation or private time. Not only will the
member live in the community, normally he will also work for it.
Although this may sometimes mean taking a job 'in the world', the
risks of this are quite high for a movement that so heartily condemns the prevailing social order. Usually an economic base for
the movement will be devised which limits involvement in the
world. Often this can be combined with proselytising, as in the
case of the Krishna Consciousness devotees who offer copies of
their magazine, books, or flowers, or the Children of God who
offer copies of their leader's letters printed in pamphlet form,
in return for a donation. Contact with non-members can then be
highly routinised and ritualised. It is, anyway, transient; it can
be interpreted in terms confirmatory of the movement's beliefs
as, for example, when a hostile response is received from someone approached on the street, which serves only to confirm the
evil nature of the world; but such forms of fund-raising do
provide the opportunity for contact with people who may show
some interest in, or sympathy with, what they are being offered,
and thus provide occasions for conversion.

An alternative approach is to separate economic activity and
proselytism, or to establish an independent source of income,
for example, farming, as in the case of some Jesus People groups,
or various manufacturing activities such as those conducted by
the Unification Church. Most movements tend to have multiple
economic bases often also deriving income from the possessions
of new members handed over to the collective fund on joining;
donations from sympathetic or unwary businessmen; and remitt-
ances from parents of members; as well as the street sales and
manufacturing enterprises. Despite their rejection of the world
and its materialism, members are often encouraged to collect
state welfare payments, rent subsidies, child allowances, etc.
Two hundred of the Jonestown, Guyana residents were receiving
social security benefits.

Street solicitation became a major initial economic resource for
many of the youthful world-rejecting new religions (Children of
God, Unification Church, ISKCON, The Process) for a variety of
pressing reasons. Unlike the world-affirming movements they
had no commodity or service to purvey. Unlike earlier generations

of world-rejecting movements, this cohort emerged into a world
where readily available, cultivatable land for producing their
own subsistence had virtually disappeared. What remained was,
at best, marginal land impossible to farm satisfactorily without
agricultural expertise lacking among the primarily urban-raised
membership (Whitworth, 1975). While they could support themselves for a time through handing over their resources to a
communal fund, most of those recruited were economically marginal
and thus had few resources and little capital to offer. Working
at conventional jobs for support entailed a consequent loss of
time for spreading the word, for proselytising others. They
lacked funds initially for investment in other income-producing
enterprises such as forms of manufacture. Hence, what they
required was an economic base which needed little capital investment; made use of their only resources - people and enthusiasm;
and which, if possible, brought them into contact with potential
members. Street solicitation - seeking donations in return for
some low cost item such as leaflets, magazines, candles, or
flowers - met this need. Later, when investment capital had
been secured by this means, some of these movements invested
in viable agricultural land and book publishing (ISKCON), fishing
and manufacture (Unification Church), etc., which supplied some
of their resources. The Children of God continued to combine
witnessing and fund-raising through the practice of 'flirty
fishing': demonstrating 'God's love' through sex, and encouraging the beneficiaries of their favours to provide financial and
other assistance in return (Wallis, 1979a: ch. 5).
   The People's Temple illustrates the pattern of severe economic
self-renunciation characteristic of such movements, particularly
in their early years:

> Finances for People's Temple members were fairly simple:
> everything went to Jim Jones. Families signed over homes,
> property, and pay-checks to the temple. To raise additional
> money for the cult, some members occasionally begged on street
> corners.
>   Members who did not live in the church had to tithe a mini-
> mum of 25 percent of their earnings. Those living on church
> property gave everything to Jones, who returned to them a
> two dollar weekly allowance. (Kerns, 1979: 159)

The life-style to be found in world-rejecting movements - despite its deviant appearance - is characteristically highly organised
and controlled. The need to generate adequate financial support
often imposes severe rigours on members, particularly when
combined with an ascetic ethic. Thomas Robbins *et al.* (1976:
115) argue of the Unification Church, for example, that, 'Life
in a communal center is disciplined and most of the day is
devoted to activities such as "witnessing" on the street, giving
and listening to lectures, and attending other functions.'
   The rigours of fund-raising in the Unification Church have been

described by Christopher Edwards, a former member:

> I had been flower selling for a week now. At the end of each
> afternoon, we would return to the van, exhausted. For dinner
> - if lucky, we would receive a generous donation of unusable
> burgers someone had begged from the McDonald's franchise
> down the road by telling the manager we were poor mission-
> aries. If we weren't so lucky, we might dine on donated stale
> doughnuts and cold pizza.
> Our group was collecting over a thousand tax-free dollars
> daily.
> Each morning we picked up our order of roses from the San
> Francisco flower district. We slept in vans at night, eight in
> a row, brothers at one end, sisters at another. When Family
> members were on the road for several days, we couldn't change
> clothes or shower. To even change a shirt in this crowded,
> smelly vehicle could tempt the sisters to fall again, might stir
> and excite the sexual drives now buried deep within our uncon-
> scious.
> Night after night we worked until two in the morning, doing
> bar runs - blitzing, as we called it, coaxing drunks to buy
> wilted roses for the angry wives awaiting them at home. At 2.30,
> we would drive to a local park, praying in unison in the dark-
> ness. . . . After the gruelling ritual ended, we settled down
> for a night's sleep, a full hour and a half, for we must soon be
> up for pledge service Sunday morning. (Edwards, 1979: 161-2)

Success in fund-raising becomes an indicator of the member's
own spiritual condition rather than of his worldly skills. Fund-
raising is interpreted by members less as an economic necessity
than as a method of spiritual growth (Bromley and Shupe, 1979:
123). A Unification Church member reports that:

> Fund-raising was a powerful experience for me. I was out on
> my own and had to make a decision: do I believe in the *Divine
> Principle* and am I willing to go through this? To me, fund-
> raising was a very spiritual experience in that it reaffirmed my
> faith. Every day I had to question what I believed. (Bryant
> and Hodges, 1978: 62)

Daner (1976: 77) asserts that in Krishna Consciousness too,
'A devotee must be prepared to give his entire self to lead a
life of day to day obedience and service.' Indeed, in the face of
the increasing competition from groups and movements offering
forms of 'easy' enlightenment, ISKCON'S magazine, *Back to
Godhead* has laid *increasing* stress on the necessity of spiritual
discipline (Reis, 1975: 133).
The disciplined character of the communal life may extend to
the use of physical sanctions to encourage the achievement of
movement requirements. When 'litnessing', i.e. the distribution
of literature in return for donations, was a major aim of the

Children of God, members who failed to reach the quota set for
them were, at times, sent out again after a day on the streets
and forbidden to return to the colony (i.e. the commune) until
the quota target in literature distributed, or daily financial
quota, was met. Synanon is a movement that began life as a
communal drug-rehabilitation programme in California, which
developed a religious self-conception and philosophy only subsequently. It has thus undergone considerable changes during
the course of its development which I shall discuss later, but,
during its most explicitly world-rejecting phase, physical
violence was occasionally inflicted on deviant members. As the
People's Temple, too, became more world-rejecting over the
course of its development, so physical violence became more
normal as a means of social control (Kerns, 1979: 157, 185). This
was also, of course, the case in Manson's Family. None the less,
the demand for discipline only rather infrequently issues in
the routine use of violence in new religious movements. The
reason is not far to seek. These movements are voluntary
communities living usually in densely populated societies with
strong central state authorities. They cannot effectively coerce
those who can make their wish to dissent or abandon membership known; they cannot normally hope to isolate effectively
members who rebel or resist authority; nor can they compete
with the means of violence available to the state if they infringe
upon the liberties of members to the degree where they call upon
its aid. They must retain their following by persuasion - albeit
some may see such persuasion as entailing forms of blackmail -
or by the instilling of fear at the prospect of departure. Followers
must be given reasons to remain when they cannot in general be
coerced. And since *enthusiasm* is normally a prerequisite for the
survival and growth of the movement, love, rather than fear, is
much the more frequent means of persuasion.

The communal life-style of the world-rejecting movement
exhibits a high level of diffuse affectivity. Members of such
movements kiss each other and hug in greeting, hold hands with
other members, or call endearments and offer constant encouragement. Typically, this highly visible affectivity is coupled with a
strongly puritan moral code which permits it to go no further
than public display. Or, when sexual relationships are permitted,
it is normally primarily for the purpose of reproduction. Married
members of the Krishna Consciousness movement, for example,
are allowed to engage in sexual intercourse only at the wife's
most fertile point in the monthly cycle, and even then only after
extensive ritual preparations. Sexual relationships are subordinated to *collective* rather than private, *personal* ends, so
that, in the Unification Church and the early Children of God,
members were willing to have marriage partners chosen for them
even from among complete strangers. In the Unification Church,
moreover, members will normally lead lives of rigorous chastity,
often for a number of years before marriage.

Married members of Synanon and the People's Temple, on the

other hand, were prepared to divorce their mates and take new spouses at their leader's direction. But even when, as in the later Children of God, the movement has become sexually antinomian, such apparent self-indulgence may in fact itself be largely a matter of service. The liberal sexuality of the Children of God is employed at least in part to win converts and to increase the solidarity and commitment of members, and personal pleasure therefore remains a *secondary* consideration to helping others and serving God.

In this quotation, Moses David stresses the use of sex as a means of 'saving souls' and serving God:

Who knows? - When all other avenues of influence and witnessing are closed to us this may be our only remaining means of spreading the Word and supporting the work, as well as gaining new disciples and workers for the Kingdom of God.
What better way to show them the love of God than to do your best to supply their desperately hungry needs for love, fellowship, companionship . . . affection, a tender loving kiss, a soft warm embrace, the healing touch of your loving hands, the comforting feeling of your body next to theirs - and yes, even *sex* if need be! (Moses David, 'King Arthur's nights: chapter one', 29 April 1976).

Even earlier he had indicated that monogamous marriage was by no means sacrosanct in the Children of God, and could not be permitted to endanger the solidarity of the movement:

We do not minimise the marriage ties as such. We just consider our ties to the Lord and the larger Family greater and more important. And when the private marriage ties interfere with Our Family and God ties, they can be readily abandoned for the glory of God and the good of the Family! . . . partiality toward your own wife or husband or children strikes at the very foundation of communal living - against the unity and supremacy of God's Family and its oneness and wholeness. (Moses David, 'One wife', 28 October 1972)

Moses David is quite explicit about the role sexual relationships can play in generating solidarity in the Children of God, as in his letter reflecting on 'The real meaning of The Lord's Supper!' (Moses David, 1 October 1978):

Boy, there's a hot one for our Family!: One in the flesh, one body, and one in spirit! . . . in our Family we are one body, all the way! Sexually as well, really one Bride of Christ, One Wife, One Body! How much more could you be one body than *we* are, amen? PTL! *We're one all the way!* . . .
Thank God, in our Family . . . we are not only one in spirit but one in body, both in sex and sacrificial service to others.

The Manson Family – to take a yet more extreme case – also employed sexual promiscuity as a means of eliminating the individual ego and subordinating all individual personality and goals to those of the collectivity, as formulated by Charles Manson:

> The lack of sexual discrimination among hard-core Family members was not so much gross animalism as it was simply a physical parallel to the lack of emotional favoritism and attachment that Charlie taught and insisted on. As long as we loved one person more than the others, we weren't truly dead [to self] and the Family wasn't one. (Watson 1978: 70)

Manson's Family also employed sexuality instrumentally as a means of attracting converts (Zamora, 1976: 79). Through sexuality the Children of God believed they showed God's love, and the Manson Family the love of Charlie (Watson, 1978: 68-9).

The life of the world-rejecting movement tends to require considerable subordination of individual interest, will, and autonomy in order to maximise collective solidarity and to eliminate disruptive dissent. Naranjo (1979: 27) reports from her observations that 'members are expected to learn that Synanon places the explicit needs and demands of the community over and above the needs of any individual.' A common theme in world-rejecting movements is that of having been *reborn* on joining the group. A complete break with past desires, interests, statuses, with any past identity, is made by dating one's birth from the moment of joining (as, for example, in the Love Israel movement, a small Seattle based, counter-cultural, communal, religious group). A new identity will be acquired incorporating as its central features the beliefs, norms and values of the collectivity joined. Typically this nascent identity is signified by the convert taking a new name as in the Children of God, Love Israel, Krishna Consciousness, The Process, and the Manson Family.

The ego or former self must be completely repudiated. The Children of God employ the term 'forsake all' to mean not only the process of handing over all worldly possessions to the movement on joining, but also the renunciation of the past and of all self-interest. Enroth reports from some reflections of a COG 'lit shiner' (i.e. a distributor of the largest number of MO Letters in her area at a time when members were encouraged to maximise their output), her aspiration to do even better: 'I'm sure it's possible to hit 12,000 a week. I know it. *I have to die more to myself* and put more hours in' (Enroth, 1977: 51, my emphasis). Even the exclusiveness of the marital bond must be abandoned for the collective good. As Moses David, leader of the Children of God put it in one of his letters to his disciples: 'it's the last vestige of forsaking all to forsake even your husband and wife to share with others' (Moses David, 'One wife', 28 October 1972; on sex and marriage in the Children of God, see

Wallis, 1979a: ch. 5). Giving up any exclusive claim upon particular others was an important part of abandoning the self. In
similar vein, Watson recounts the beliefs of the Manson Family:

> True freedom means giving up ourselves, letting that [sic] old
> ego die so we can be free of the self that keeps us from one
> another. . . . 'Cease to exist', Charlie sang in one of the
> songs he'd written. 'Cease to exist, come say you love me'.
> The girls repeated it over and over – *cease to exist, kill your
> ego, die* – so that once you cease to be, you can be free to
> totally love, totally come together, (Watson, 1978: 54)

Abnegation of personal identity, or self-renunciation to this
degree renders more comprehensible the awesome mass suicide
of People's Temple members in Jonestown, Guyana. When the
cause and the movement are everything, and the self is nothing,
giving one's own life may be a small price for what one has had,
or for what may be achieved by the gesture.

When individual identity is so thoroughly tied to a collective
identity and subordinated to the will and authority of a leader
personifying that collective identity, any threat to the leader or
the community is a threat to the self. Life is far less important
than protection of the leader, defence of the movement's ideal, or
indictment of its enemies. The logical extreme of 'forsaking all'
for the common good is not – as Moses David supposes – the
abandoning of an exclusive sexual claim upon a spouse, but
rather it is the *suicidal act*. Members of the Unification Church
and the Children of God are warned that they may have to die
for their movement or their faith:

> We know that some will suffer and some will have to die for
> Thee and Thy Gospel. You promised it, Lord, but you said
> 'Great is your reward in Heaven, for so persecuted they the
> prophets which were before you! (MT 5: 12).' (Moses David,
> 'The happy ending', February 1979)

The deindividuation, subordination of self, and the correlated
sense of rebirth, of complete break with the past are highlighted,
in the case of the Manson Family, by a recollection of Tex Watson.
A prolonged intimate relationship normally results in the partners
acquiring substantial background knowledge of each other, yet
Watson observes of the girl specially assigned to him by Manson
that, 'During the months that Mary and I were more or less
together, I learned practically nothing about her past. The past
was non-existent for the Family, something to discard along
with all the materialistic middle-class programming and the ego
that it had built' (Watson, 1978: 61).

A collective identity may be fostered by various means as
Rosabeth Kanter (1972) has shown, including a common mode of
dress and appearance. This is seen at its clearest in Krishna
Consciousness, wherein temple residents wear Indian dress and

men shave their heads but for a topknot. Observers often
commented on the similarity in dress and appearance of members
of the Unification Church in its early years of notoriety. To a
considerable extent this was also true of the Children of God who
might not all look precisely alike, but for whom there was a
considerable commonality in style. Another expression of this
deindividuation is to be seen in the practice in the Manson
Family of keeping all the clothes not in immediate use in one large
pile on the floor (see e.g. Watson, 1978: 29). This is echoed in
Edwards's (1979: 97) account of induction to the Unification
Church:

> I left the shower room house, wearing the crumpled old clothes
> I had pulled out of the collective laundry hamper. . . . All
> our clothes were thrown together and we dressed on a first-
> come, first-serve system, those newest in the Family choosing
> the shabbiest clothes to show humility and Family leaders
> picking out the finest as a sign of their status.

Another typical means of fostering and marking collective
identity, so usual as almost to be a defining characteristic of the
world-rejecting movement, is that of new members handing over
on joining all belongings (Unification Church, Children of God,
Krishna Consciousness, Manson Family, etc.), or major assets
and income (People's Temple). Equally general is the conceptualisation of the movement as a family in which other members are
closer than any physical brothers and sisters, and in which the
leader occupies the status of father with an appropriate authority
over his 'children'. By this means movements as diverse as the
Love Family (in Seattle), the Unified Family - a designation
employed by the Unification Church; the Manson Family, and
the Family of Love - a later name taken by the Children of God,
have sought to describe the close, emotional bonding and
corporate loyalty felt by members of the group.
Movements such as these, mandated by God through the
medium of a messiah, prophet or guru to fulfil His demands, tend
to be highly authoritarian. The resulting constraints of the
communal life and an authoritarian leadership provide a basis
for the claim by hostile outsiders that the youthful members
have lost their identity, personality, and even their 'free will'
in joining. Such claims have formed a major part of the rhetoric
of the 'anti-cult' movement (Shupe, Spielmann and Stigall, 1977;
Wallis, 1977. This issue is discussed further below).

THE WORLD-AFFIRMING NEW RELIGION

The other end of the continuum presents a sharp contrast. The
style of the world-affirming movement lacks most of the features
traditionally associated with religion. It may have no 'church',
no collective ritual of worship, it may lack any developed theology

or ethics (in the sense of general, prescriptive principles of human behaviour and intention - although see Tipton, 1982b[1] on *est*). In comparison to the world-rejecting movement, it views the prevailing social order less contemptuously, seeing it as possessing many highly desirable characteristics. Mankind, too, is not so much reprobate as needlessly restricted, containing within itself enormous potential power which, until now, only a very few individuals have learned to utilise effectively, and even then normally only by withdrawing from the world, and subjecting themselves to the most rigorous disciplines. Silva Mind Control is a training involving techniques of self-hypnosis and visualisation, which is transmitted in 40-48 hours and which:

can train anyone to remember what appears to be forgotten, to control pain, to speed healing, to abandon unwanted habits, to spark intuition so that the sixth sense becomes a creative, problem-solving part of daily life. With all this comes a cheerful inner peace, a quiet optimism based on first-hand evidence that we are more in control of our lives than we ever imagined. (Silva and Miele, 1977: 12-13)

The method - which brings one 'into direct, working contact with an all-pervading higher intelligence' (ibid.: 17) - was invented by a Mexican American, Jose Silva in the 1950s. An advertising leaflet for Silva Mind Control avers that:

In 48 hours you can learn to use your mind to do *anything* you wish. . . . There is no limit to how far you can go, . . . to what you can do, because there is no limit to the power of your mind.

Transcendental Meditation (TM) involves - as its name makes clear - a meditational technique taught to those who are initiated in a relatively brief ceremony in which the initiator conveys to the new meditator a 'personal' mantra, in fact selected according to the new meditator's age, on which the individual meditates for twenty minutes each morning and evening. The technique was brought to the West by the Maharishi Mahesh Yogi in the late 1950s, but achieved celebrity mainly as a result of the Beatles becoming initiated and visiting the Maharishi in India in 1968. Although their interest shortly waned, numbers undertaking initiation into TM increased dramatically in the late 1960s and 1970s. (For data on the expansion of TM in the USA, see Bainbridge and Jackson, 1981.) A pamphlet published by one of the organisations of Transcendental Meditation announces the supernormal powers to which it provides access:

The TM-Siddhis programme . . . creates the ability to function from the level of . . . unbounded awareness. Any thought consciously projected from that unbounded awareness will be so powerful, will be so supported by all the laws of nature,

that it will be fulfilled without problems, without loss of time.
(Mahesh Yogi, 1977)

Movements approximating the world-affirming type claim to
possess the means to enable people to unlock their physical,
mental and spiritual potential without the need to withdraw from
the world, means which are readily available to virtually everyone
who learns the technique or principle provided. No arduous
prior period of preparation is necessary, no ascetic system of
taboos enjoined. No extensive mortification of the flesh nor
forceful control of the mind. At most, a brief period of abstention from drugs or alcohol may be requested, without any
requirement even of continued abstention after the completion of
a training or therapy period.

est (the italicised initial lower case form is used even at the
beginning of a sentence) is the commonly used designation for
Erhard Seminar's Training, an organisation which provides a
60-hour training, the purpose of which is 'to transform your
ability to experience living so that the situations you have been
trying to change or have been putting up with, clear up just in
the process of life itself'. While it is one of the less transcendental
of the new world-affirming salvational movements, *est* is clearly
part of the same domain as its more overtly religious counterparts
among movements of this type. As will be argued subsequently,
movements of this type tend to possess a more secularised and
individualised conception of the divine. Moreover, they offer
access to supernatural, magical and spiritual powers and abilities
which legitimise the attribution to them of the label 'religious'.
Participants in the *est* training are not expected to submit to any
severe preparatory trials or rigours. They are required merely
to observe a series of rules during the 60 hours the training
involves (normally spread over two weekends in four approximately 15-hour days). They may not smoke in the training room,
eat except at the specified meal break, drink alcohol or take any
drug (except as medically prescribed) during the training period
and the intervening week. The 'asceticism' involved in securing
enlightenment through *est* goes no further than being permitted
breaks for smoking or the lavatory only three or four times
during each 15-16 hour day; being required to sit in straight-
backed chairs during much of the training with the consequent
mild physical discomfort; and being obliged to raise one's hand,
be acknowledged, and stand to use a microphone before speaking.
Persons wishing to be initiated into Transcendental Meditation
are asked to cease drug use for fifteen days beforehand.

Just as no rigorous discipline is normally involved, so, too, no
extensive doctrinal commitment is entailed, at least not at the
outset. There may even be no initial insistence that the adherent
believe the theory or doctrine at all, as long as he is willing to
try the technique and see if it works. Examples are readily available in Transcendental Meditation and in *est*:

No one is required to declare a belief in TM, in the Maharishi,
or even in the possible effects of the technique in order for it
to work. *It works in spite of an individual's disbelief or
skepticism.* (Robbins and Fisher, 1972: 7)

Q. Do I have to believe the training will work in order for the
   training to work?
A. No. *est* is not a system of beliefs or techniques to be learned
   and practised. Some people approach the training with
   enthusiasm, and some with skepticism - and some with
   both. Your willingness to be there is all you need.
   (*Questions People Ask About The est Training*, 1977, no
   pagination)

Nichiren Shoshu, also known as Soka Gakkai, is a movement of
Japanese origin which - although formed prior to the second
world war - only flourished with the return of religious liberty
to Japan under the post-war American administration. From 1951,
it began an aggressive programme of proselytisation which led to
rapid expansion in Japan and the conversion of some American
service men, often married to members of Soka Gakkai. It was
largely as a result of their return to America, bearing their new
faith, that it spread to the West (Dator, 1969). From interviews,
I understand that it was by a similar process that the movement
was brought to Britain. Soka Gakkai members believe that by
chanting the Lotus Sutra, believed to be the highest and most
powerful scripture, and the mantra *Namu Myoho Renge Kyo*
('Adoration be to the Sutra of the Lotus of the Wondrous Law'),
before the *Gohonzon* (a copy of a scroll representing the
Buddha, the original of which was inscribed by Nichiren, the
thirteenth century monk, founder of this branch of Buddhism)
(White, 1970: 30), kept in a household shrine, they can attain
personal happiness, economic improvement, and other this-
worldly goals as well as spiritual rewards. Individuals drawn into
an initial discussion meeting by Nichiren Shoshu proselytisers
are customarily told:

These meetings are to get you to experiment with the practice,
not to believe in it. The reason for having you come to this
meeting is to get you to try and test the practice. We don't
expect you to believe in it right away, but we do want you to
give it a try. (Snow, 1976: 236)

While followers of such movements may object to some limited
aspects of the present social order, the values and goals which
prevail within it are normally accepted. They have joined such a
movement not to escape or withdraw from the world and its values,
but to acquire the means to achieve them more easily and to
experience the world's benefits more fully. Snow (1976: 67) argues
that, for most rank and file members, the philosophy of Nichiren
Shoshu of America is:

usually interpreted and defined in terms of the various things which collectively yield a sense of personal satisfaction and well-being in one's everyday life in the immediate here and now. For most, happiness or value creation is thus constituted by the attainment of a semblance of material well-being, family harmony, friends, good health, inner security, and a sense of meaning, purpose and direction.

In world-affirming movements, the social order is not viewed as entirely and irredeemably unjust, nor society as having departed from God as in the world-rejecting case. The beliefs of these movements are essentially individualistic. The source of suffering, of disability, of unhappiness, lies within oneself rather than in the social structure. This view is stated for TM by Forem (1973: 235), but could be duplicated for many movements of this type:

When individuals within a society are tense, strained and dissatisfied with life, the foundation is laid for conflict in its various forms: riots, demonstrations, strikes, individual and collective crimes, wars. But a society composed of happy, creative individuals could not give rise to such outbreaks of discord.

Hence, it follows that producing social change is dependent upon producing individual change. The individual must 'take responsibility' for the circumstances around him and for transforming them:

While it does not as yet provide them with political power, NSA [Nichiren Shoshu of America, the corporate name in America for Soka Gakkai] philosophy does teach that responsibility lies with the individual . . . rather than despairing or complaining, individuals are encouraged to think about and discuss solutions to the problems they see, chant for them and work in any capacity then can, where they are, to bring about better societal conditions. (Holtzapple, 1977: 138)

Transcendental Meditation articulates its version of this theory through the notion of the 'Maharishi Effect', which refers to the social consequences of the practice of TM by a significant proportion of the population (once 10 per cent was aspired to, but, more recently, as the following quotation shows, the movement has lowered its recruitment expectations):

The phenomenon known as the Maharishi Effect is the basis of Maharishi's prediction that every nation will soon become invincible in the growing sunshine of the Age of Enlightenment. This phenomenon has been verified in about 1,100 cities around the world, where it was found that crime, accidents, sickness, and other negative trends fell sharply, as soon as just one per cent of the population began the Transcendental Meditation technique. The Maharishi Effect on a global scale results in ideal societies everywhere and invincibility for every nation. (*World Government News* No 8, August 1978: 4)

Leading Transcendental Meditators, called 'Governors of the Age of Enlightenment', have been despatched in large numbers to areas of civil crisis. There they in no way participate in relief programmes or in providing physical assistance, but rather engage in meditation and the 'Siddhi programme' (a more advanced set of practices which produce magical abilities, such as levitation), and thus:

Without going out of their comfortable hotel rooms, the Governors of the Age of Enlightenment enliven the ground state of natural law deep within themselves and produce the gentle impulses of coherence which neutralize turbulence and disorder in collective consciousness. . . . Violence naturally calms down. (*World Government News*, issue No 2, Nov/Dec 1978, Jan 1979: 6)

The 'Governors' then educate local leaders in the virtues of TM and the 'Siddhi programme', and secure their assistance in teaching these in that locale. By such means world peace is ensured.

Similarly the Hunger Project sponsored by *est* engages in promotional activities connected with ending starvation in the world, and raises money for that purpose. However, the Hunger Project does not send money to feed the starving, nor otherwise directly provide aid to the underdeveloped world, nor even advocate any particular social or economic remedy:

It is not the purpose of The Hunger Project to feed hungry people . . . but rather to speak to the world on behalf of hungry people. . . . Your contribution to the Hunger Project goes directly to generate the most important process on our planet - creating the end of hunger and starvation as an idea whose time has come. (*A shift in the wind* [The Hunger Project Newspaper], 4, February 1979: 15)

The Hunger Project exists to convey to the world that hunger can be ended within twenty years. Its purpose, that is, is to change our *consciousness* about the possibility of ending starvation. World hunger is inevitable only because we believe it to be inevitable. The Hunger Project therefore exists 'to create a context of commitment among a critical mass of people, to create the elimination of death due to starvation as "an idea whose time has come"' (Babbie, 1978: 16).

This should not be taken to mean that world-affirming movements never have genuinely reformist aims. A number of groups within the Human Potential tradition have aspirations which combine the personal and the political. Human Potential enthusiasts often see

a need for action to effect liberation at the level of social structure as well as that of personal psychology. Such issues as
feminism, the ecology, peace, siting of nuclear power stations or
nuclear weapons facilities, race, and community action are often
part of the agenda of such groups as Re-evaluation Counselling
which devotes resources to publicising precisely these issues
and educating its members and others in their implications. Even
a movement such as Scientology has undertaken campaigns for
the protection of the civil rights of mental patients, although, as
in so much of the activity of this group, it is sometimes difficult
to disentangle a disinterested desire for social reform from the
pursuit of enhanced power and security for Scientology.

However characteristically in world-affirming movements, the
individual is responsible not only for the environment around him
but for everything he is and does. The individual's nature and
behaviour is not viewed as a composite of predispositions, situations, and a psychological biography, but simply in terms of
free choice at the point of performance. *est*, for example, even
views stories about predispositions, situations and psychological
biographies as part of the individual's 'act', by means of which
he avoids experiencing what is happening to him. The individual
is the only one who experiences (for him) what is happening to
him, and hence he is responsible for (his experience of) life's
vicissitudes for him; even his disasters and his illnesses. The
individual therefore chooses his (experience of his) circumstances,
his illnesses, etc. And as one chooses to be and to behave, so
one can choose to change. Linda Dannenberg (1975: 20) observes
from a Silva Mind Control lecture: 'You are free to change . . .
and can make anything of yourself that you wish. You will be
as happy, sad, beautiful, ugly, rich or poor, relaxed or nervous
as you make up your mind to be.'

The spiritual dimension in particular is a matter of individual
experience and individual *subjective* reality rather than social
reality or even social concern. Moreover, God is not perceived
as a personal deity imposing a set of ethical prescriptions upon
human society. If God is referred to at all it is primarily as a
diffuse, amorphous and immanent force in the universe, but
present most particularly within oneself. Mind Dynamics, for
example, encourages its followers to bring their minds into states
where they produce alpha waves. Its founder argues that 'when
you are working dynamically in Alpha you are in touch with
Higher Intelligence. . . .' (Silvá and Miele, 1977: 37), although
Higher Intelligence may be less than God Himself. For many of
these groups and movements, the self is the only God there is,
or at least the only one that matters. One observer of the Human
Potential Movement notes that, rather than 'God', adherents are
likely to refer to 'my ground of being, my true nature, the ultimate energy'; and that, 'The most common image of God is the
notion of cosmic energy as a life force in which all partake'
(Stone, 1976: 102). He also relates the experience of one
follower: 'A psychiatric social worker said she formerly used

terms like *God* to explain suffering and the source of happiness
and love. Subsequent to the *est* (Erhard Seminars Training)
training, she did not use these terms so often, sensing that she
is god in her universe and thus creator of what she experiences'
(Stone, 1976: 103). Maharishi Mahesh Yogi, founder and leader
of Transcendental Meditation and the Spiritual Regeneration
Movement, makes the same point, that 'the inner man is Divine,
is fully Divine. . . .' (Mahesh Yogi, 1962: 7), although he may
not always know it consciously (Mahesh Yogi, 1962: 14). John-
Roger, the American founder of the Movement of Spiritual Inner
Awareness, associated with the Insight training, announces to
his followers that 'we are the Holy Spirit, we are Gods in manifestation' (John-Roger, 1976: 18). According to Ellwood (1974:
107), in Nichiren Shoshu (Soka Gakkai), 'All the promises of
religion are made to apply to this world. All divine potential is
within man, it is said, and can be unleashed.'

These movements, then, share a view of man as inherently
perfectible. People possess a potential far beyond their current
level of functioning. The key to attaining the level of their
potential lies not in modification of the social order or the structure of social opportunity, but in facilitating the transformation
of *individuals*. Moreover, such a transformation is believed to
be possible on the basis of techniques and theories which can be
rather quickly transmitted and learned.

The world-affirming movements emphasise the *present*, what
Kurt Back (1972) refers to as the 'mythology of the here and
now'. They are often hostile to intellectualisation and rational
evaluation, seeing these as a defence against, or barrier to,
feeling and experience. Understanding, Werner Erhard observes
of the *est* training and of life in general, 'is the booby prize'.
The world-affirming movement offers immediate and automatic
benefits of a concrete kind through the practice of some formula
or recipe: chanting 'Namu Myoho, Renge Kyo' (Soka Gakkai);
fifteen minutes' meditation on a mantra morning and evening (TM);
or merely by 'keeping your soles in the room and taking what you
get' (*est*). Holtzapple summarises these characteristics in the
case of Nichiren Shoshu of America (Soka Gakkai):

> The emphasis within NSA is on practice, i.e. 'doing', 'acting',
> not theorizing. The 'benefits' which can be achieved are not
> just in the future. They are here and now, because any goal
> can be accomplished through the universal mystic law of cause
> and effect. The right attitude and right effort automatically
> lead to the right effect. (Holtzapple, 1977: 139)

It follows from this ethos of individual self-realisation that
collective activities have little or no sacred quality and indeed
are likely to have only a small place in the enterprise unless it is
particularly centred upon some group-based or interpersonal
technique, such as encounter groups; and even here the group is
of importance only as a means to self-liberation. *est*, for example,

is presented to 250 trainees at a time yet requires minimal interpersonal contact, and indeed develops a thoroughly subjective
idealist theory of knowledge and of the world. So subjective is
its epistemology that it appears at times to verge on solipsism.
Its ontology, as noted above, rests on the claim that 'You're god
in your universe. You caused it.' (Erhard, 1973: n.p.) Scientology, one of the most notorious of the world-affirming new
religious movements, was developed by L. Ron Hubbard in
America from his lay psychotherapy Dianetics – presented to the
public in 1950 – which briefly attained the proportions of a craze
in the USA. Scientology, although it describes itself as a church,
has only the most rudimentary of religious practices in any conventional sense. So, too, its activities are principally of an
individualistic character, with little value placed upon collective
or communal enterprise. Its central activity, 'auditing', is undertaken between an 'auditor' and 'pre-clear' on a one-to-one basis,
or even by the pre-clear auditing himself; and even training in
the theory and practice of Scientology is organised in such a
fashion as to enable the student to pursue his course quite alone.
Moreover, involvement in Scientology, too, is oriented primarily
to the pursuit of individual goals of success, greater power and
ability and personal spiritual attainment (Wallis, 1976b). Such
developments in therapy and spiritual search have been characterised as a 'new narcissism' (Marin, 1975; see also Tom Wolfe's
amusing essay deflating many of the pretensions of such movements as *est* in Wolfe, 1977).

It follows that the world-affirming movement rejects the
dualism of the world-rejecting movement, with its concrete conception of the transcendental realm and of the coming transformation of the earth in a physically tangible millennium. Indeed, it
rejects the materialist assumptions upon which such a view is
predicated. Its philosophy is idealist to the degree that perfec-
tion is merely the result of realising that everything is *already*
perfect. John Weldon quotes Werner Erhard from an *est* seminar,
expressing a sentiment which, with minor modification, could be
found in many other cases:

> Life is always perfect just the way it is. When you realize that,
> then no matter how strongly it may appear to be otherwise, you
> know that whatever is happening right now will turn out all
> right. Knowing this, you are in a position to begin mastering
> life. (John Weldon, n.d.: 5)

Three themes can be identified which seem, albeit in varying
degrees, to be central to the beliefs and ethos of the world-
affirming movement. Although these can be distinguished analytically, they none the less sometimes co-occur empirically, perhaps
as major and minor themes within the same movement. There is
first the theme of coping with the demands made upon us to
succeed in modern capitalist societies, of coping with the dilemmas
of *individual achievement*. Underlying much of the rhetoric of

'awareness' and 'realising potential' is the theme of personal success in securing the valued goals of this world: improved income and personal relationships, greater confidence and self-esteem, enhanced ability to cope with life's vicissitudes (Wallis, 1979b). Intelligence will be increased, social capabilities immeasurably improved, psychosomatic illnesses and psychological disabilities eliminated. The Inner Peace Movement, founded in 1964 by Francisco Coll, provides methods for spiritual and psychological growth through the medium of a pyramid sales corporation which encourages recruits to move into leadership roles marketing the movement's product of spiritual growth and inner peace (Scott, 1980: 24). Scott argues that 'Success and its achievement . . . are emphasised repeatedly in IPM programs and songs' (1980: 73).

> To achieve success, the IPMer is encouraged to develop certain personality attributes, such as being positive, enthusiastic, hard working, assertive, dynamic, motivated, committed, confident and organised. . . . Given these success concerns, many IPM classes center around success, such as an ALC [American Leadership College] class entitled 'Success, Goals, and Motivation'. Many techniques are designed to show participants what they need to do to obtain success . . . , (Scott, 1980: 74-5)

A small sample of Scientologists completed a questionnaire in Wallis's (1976b) study, which included a question asking them what kinds of problems they hoped Scientology would solve for them. Twenty-five of the twenty-nine who answered this question indicated a wide range of problems to which they had been seeking solutions (they could indicate more than one):

Problem	No.
(a) Loneliness	8
(b) Financial	4
(c) Marital	5
(d) Other interpersonal relationships	14
(e) Psychological	15
(f) Physical illness	11

(Adapted from Wallis, 1976b: 170)

Re-evaluation Counseling was founded in the early 1950s by Harvey Jackins, a one-time associate of L. Ron Hubbard. Re-evaluation Counseling appears to lean heavily upon Dianetic theory and to develop central features of its practice, notably co-auditing - or, as it is called in Re-evaluation Counseling, 'co-counseling' - by lay peers. A member of Re-evaluation Counseling, interviewed by the author, presents this achievement theme in somewhat lower key:

People who come into Counseling are functioning quite well,
but they know they could be functioning better. They know
they're just not achieving their potential; they're not doing
things as well as they could do; they're not behaving to other
people as well as they could. Things aren't just quite right.
But to all external intents and purposes, they're doing very
well.

In some movements this theme of coping with the expectations of
individual happiness and achievement prevailing in the western
world appears in the form of its converse, i.e. the dominant
theme is one of the *reduction of expectations* from life to a
realistic level. This has its clearest embodiment in *est* which
encourages participants to make the most of their present experience, to live for the present rather than future aims or past
aspirations. *est* assures its adherents that 'This is all there is,'
and they might as well enjoy it rather than constantly compare
their present condition unfavourably with some other, non-
existent state of affairs. Even if they did achieve the new job,
wife, home, image they want - *est* informs them with considerable,
if mortifying, realism - they would only be happy with it for a
couple of days before they began to feel as dissatisfied with that
as they are with what they have now. Werner Erhard assures his
followers that 'Happiness is a function of accepting what is.'
Moreover, 'Life is a rip off when you expect to get what you want.
Life works when you choose what you get.' (Erhard, 1973: n.p.)
   A second theme, clearly closely related to the desire to achieve
one's full potential, is that of coping with our sense of constraint,
of facilitating the desire for liberation from social inhibitions, of
breaking free from the bonds of social roles to reach the 'real'
person beneath. The individual will be released from conventional
ritual; from habitual modes of speech or interaction; from inhibitions acquired in childhood; from repressions of instinctual life;
or from a learned reserve. He will thereby be enabled to 'get in
touch with' his feelings, his emotions; and encouraged to express
the 'authentic' self beneath the social facade; to celebrate
spontaneity, sensual pleasure and the indulgence of natural
impulse.
   The shifting congeries of groups, organisations and activities
which form the Human Potential Movement take this to be a
fundamental assumption. Human beings possess vast potential by
way of ability, awareness, creativity, empathy, emotional
expressiveness, capacity for experience and enjoyment, and the
like. The pristine human being possesses these characteristics
and qualities, but is believed to lose or to repress them as a
result of the impact of society and the constraining structures it
imposes upon the individual. Oscar Ichazo, founder of Arica,
a gnostic school drawing much upon Gurdjieff, but eclectic in its
synthesis of concepts and practices, has said that:

A person retains the purity of essence for a short time. It is

lost between four and six years of age when the child begins
to imitate his parents, tell lies and pretend. A contradiction
develops between the inner feelings of the child and the social
reality to which he must conform. Ego consciousness is the
limited mode of awareness that develops as a result of the fall
into society. (Interview with Sam Keen, see Keen, 1973.)

Arica provides practices, exercises, ritual and a conceptual
system which will enable the individual to transcend mere 'ego
consciousness', and thus to recover some of his capabilities
from before the fall. Bernard Gunther, author of two best-selling
books on the topic of sensitivity training and a major teacher in
the Human Potential Movement, has commented on his own
approach as follows:

> I guess largely I feel that most people in our culture tend to
> carry around a lot of chronic tension, and that they tend to
> respond largely on the basis of *habit* behavior . . . what I
> call sensory awakening is a method to get people to . . . let
> go their tension and focus their awareness on various parts
> of the body. And of experiencing the *moment*, experiencing
> what it is they are actually doing, as opposed to any kind of
> concept or conditioned kind of habit behavior. (Back, 1972: 81)

In his book, *The Human Side of Human Beings*, Harvey Jackins
provides an illustration of the inter-related themes of a desire to
achieve one's full capacity, held to be vastly greater than is
manifested at present, and a belief that this achievement is to be
gained through liberation from those constraints upon our powers
which society has imposed upon us. Reminiscent of early
Dianetics, Jackins (1978: 19-20) argues that,

> if any of us could preserve in operating condition a very large
> part of the flexible intelligence that each of us possesses
> inherently, the one who did so would be accurately described
> as an 'all round genius' by the current standards of our culture.
> This is not, of course, the impression that most of us have
> been conditioned to accept. We have heard, from our earliest
> age, that 'Some have it and some don't,' 'Where were you when
> the brains were passed out?', 'Don't feel bad, the world needs
> good dishwashers, too', and similar gems. These impressions
> and this conditioning, however, seem to be profoundly wrong.
> Each of us who escaped physical damage to our forebrain began
> with far more capacity to function intelligently than the best
> operating adult in our culture is presently able to exhibit.

Successful adults, Jackins calculates, are operating on only about
10 per cent of their 'original resources of intelligence, ability to
enjoy life and ability to enjoy other people' (Jackins, 1978: 59).
Re-evaluation Counseling offers a method which will enable its
practitioners to recover this enormous inherent capacity.

Arianna Stassinopoulos, a recruit to Insight, an American self-realisation movement which she subsequently introduced to Britain, represented particularly sharply the theme of liberation at a public presentation in London in 1979, when she announced that the purpose of Insight could be summarised as 'getting free'. It offered, she said, freedom from the melodrama which goes on in many of our heads most of the time, the fear, anxiety, guilt and recrimination; the burden of the past which continues to dominate our present responses, and produces exaggerated or inappropriate reactions to current circumstances. Freedom from 'self-limiting images and beliefs' which make us feel we are not terribly worthwhile; which sabotage us at points of crisis, by making us feel we simply cannot do whatever the situation requires. But also, from contrary images of ourselves as perfect, leading to self-judgment, guilt and a burden of blame. It offered freedom from the sense of oneself as victim, as the passive recipient of life's circumstances. Thus, like *est* on which it is substantially based, the Insight training purveys the view that we are 'totally responsible for our lives'. Finally, the training offers, it was claimed, freedom from the limitations imposed by a rationalistic and cerebral culture; realisation that the heart is equally in 'energy centre', and thus the opportunity to celebrate one's emotional nature.

A third theme is that of coping with the pervasive loneliness of life in modern society. The desire for liberation, therefore, readily shades over into that of attaining a sense of *intimacy*, of instant if highly attenuated community. In a safe, secure environment - or at least one sufficiently separated from the normal world and normal routine so that rebuff or failure can be effectively isolated from everyday reality - individuals seek not only to discover *themselves*, but to make contact with others, to open themselves to relationships which have hitherto seemed threatening. The activities of these movements may provide opportunities wherein with barriers lowered, participants may find it possible to make contact with others without elaborate and socially sophisticated preliminaries, and indeed without any necessary long-term commitment or enduring responsibilities. Kurt Back (1972: 33) has argued, for example, that 'Encounter groups have become a respectable "lonely hearts club" for new-comers or those without roots in a community.'

Many 'graduates' of the *est* training undertake voluntary work for the movement and Adelaide Bry (1976: 76), a sympathetic commentator, describes how intimacy forms at least one reward of such continued participation:

Working at est means instant friends, confidants, and people who sincerely are interested in one another. . . . Someone would burst into tears and immediately find both a sympathetic ear and assistance in getting whatever the tears related to. The problems shared were intimate ones - a bad trip with parents, a lover, a boss. Nothing seemed too private, too embarrassing, too crazy to [have to] hide.

As the world-affirming movement does not reject the world and
its organisation, it will quite happily model itself upon those
aspects of the world which are useful to the movement's purpose.
The salvational commodity includes a set of ideas, skills and
techniques which can be marketed like any other commodity since
no sense of the sacred renders such marketing practice inappropriate (as it might, for example in, say, the idea of marketing
the Mass, or Holy Communion). The logic of the market is wholly
compatible with the ethos of such movements. Thus the salvational
product will be tailored for mass-production, standardising content, instructional method, and price, distributing it through a
bureaucratic apparatus which establishes or leases agencies, just
as in the distribution of Kentucky Fried Chicken or Ford motor
cars. Scientology, for example, possesses a substantial bureaucratic structure which invests a great deal in the collection of
statistics, maintenance of records and the implementation of a
considerable body of rules. Professional practitioners may operate
as employees of the central organisations of the movement, as
'Field Auditors', i.e. relatively independent practitioners teaching
and auditing the lower levels of Scientology, or they might
establish 'franchises', expected to send a proportion of their
receipts to the central organisation in return for assistance,
preferential discounts and other concessions (Wallis, 1976b:
127-56).

The Inner Peace Movement is organised on the model of the
modern multinational corporation. Like Scientology, it possesses
an elaborate fee structure, offering introductory courses as 'loss-
leaders' at rates as low as $1.00 per hour, but moving up to as
much as $600 for advanced courses. Like Scientology too, it
employs modern methods of marketing:

> Besides soliciting business from those already committed, the
> group makes a major effort to recruit newcomers through news-
> paper, TV and radio promotions. . . . This kind of hard-
> driving promotional push draws heavily from the corporate
> business model and systematises the selling of spiritual growth.
> (Scott, 1980: 38)

The methods of mass instruction employed in universities or
mail-order colleges are drawn upon for pedagogic technique by
world-affirming movements. The outlets are situated in large
cities where the market exists, rather than reflecting an
aspiration for a return to the rural idyll. And, as with the sale
of any commercial service or commodity, the normal round of life
of the customer is interfered with as little as possible. Courses
of instruction or practice are offered at weekends or in the
evenings, or during periods of vacation. *est* offers its basic
training over two consecutive weekends, albeit at the rate of
15-16 hours for each of the four days. TM is transmitted on the

basis of an initial lecture, a talk with the initiator explaining it
in more detail, an initiation and practice session lasting perhaps
a couple of hours, and brief checking sessions thereafter, a
total of probably no more than 12-15 hours. Encounter and other
forms of human potential training are usually programmed to take
place over a maximum of a fortnight at a time, in the evenings.
Although clients may sometimes subtly be encouraged to engage
in further participation, full-time involvement and complete
commitment are not normally required. Membership is a leisure
activity, one of the multiple role-differentiated pursuits of the
urban dweller. His involvement will be partial and segmentary
rather than total.

Such movements tend to employ quite normal, commercial means
for generating income. Their followers are mostly in orthodox
employment, and the movement simply sells them a service or
commodity for an established price plus local taxes, sometimes
even with facilities for time-payment or discounts for cash! Only
for the staff of full-time professionals employed by the organisation will life normally approximate to any degree the 'total
institution' setting of the contemporary world-rejecting religions.

It is evident, then, that in the context of a Christian culture,
the world-rejecting movement appears much more conventionally
religious than the world-affirming movement. Christianity has
tended to exhibit a tension between the church and the world,
based in part on the institutional differentiation of Christianity
from society, which leads us to expect religious institutions to be
distinct in form. This differentiation is much less evident in
Hindu and Buddhist culture, where, too, the more immanent
conception of God, the idea of each individual as a 'divine spark',
and that of the existence of hidden wisdom which will lead to
salvation, are also familiar. Many of the world-affirming movements
have been to some extent influenced by Hindu and Buddhist
idealist philosophies. But they have also drawn substantially
upon developments in modern science and psychology for their
beliefs and practices - or at least for the rhetoric of their presentation - and, marketing a soteriological commodity in quite highly
secularised surroundings, the tendency has been to emphasise
the *scientific* character of their ideas and techniques, and to
suppress the more overtly religious aspects, although an attitude
of pragmatism has informed their practice in this regard.
Transcendental Meditation, for, example, was first presented in
the west in much more explicitly religious terms than it is today
(see e.g. Mahesh Yogi, 1962), the religious rhetoric being
dropped largely on marketing grounds. Robert McCutchan (1977:
146) makes the observation that:

> Publications dating from the late fifties are overtly religious
> and spiritual. . . . Other early publications such as *Love and
> God, Commentary on the Bhagavad-Gita, The Science of Being*
> and *Art of Living*, are overtly Hindu and religious. After about
> 1970, however, the movement focused entirely (at least in terms

of its public face) on the scientific verification of psychological, physical, and social benefits of TM. None of the more recent publications even mentioned God, much less Hindu cosmology. Simply, one could say that the Hindu cosmology remained, but expressed in more 'sanitized' language. God became cosmic creative intelligence; *atman* became the pure field of creative intelligence within; *karma* became the law of action and reaction; *brahman* became the ground state of physics.

Scott (1978: 217) presents evidence of the rationale behind this shift. He reports a conversation between Professor Robert Bellah and an official of the Maharishi International University in which the latter replied to Dr Bellah's inquiry concerning why TM denied its religious nature, by stating that this was for 'public relations reasons'. He also reports a public lecture by Charles Lutes, a leading figure in TM, in which Lutes declared: 'The popularisation of the movement in non-spiritual terms was strictly for the purpose of gaining the attention of people who wouldn't have paid the movement much mind if it had been put in spiritual terms.' (See also Spiritual Counterfeits Project, 1976, for a report of the affidavit from which this evidence derives. See also Woodrum, 1977 for an analysis of the phases through which the TM movement has passed.) TM has even unsuccessfully fought a legal action to defend itself from being declared a religion in New Jersey, since this would inhibit its presentation in public schools. Scientology, on the other hand, was made more explicitly religious when it seemed this would be a useful public-relations device in the face of government hostility and intervention (Wallis, 1976b; see also the case of Synanon discussed later).

The world-affirming movements could perhaps be conveniently called 'quasi-religious' in recognition of the fact that, although they pursue transcendental goals by largely metaphysical means, they lay little or no stress on the idea of God or transcendent spiritual entities, nor do they normally engage in worship (Soka Gakkai is an exception here, since for this movement worship at the sacred shrine of the *Gohonzon* is a very significant element of its practice). As Donald Stone notes, these movements tend to prefer the term 'spiritual' to 'religious' as a self-description. They straddle a vague boundary between religion and psychology, and which side they are held to fall upon will depend entirely on the nature of the definition of religion employed.

THE WORLD-ACCOMMODATING NEW RELIGION

The world-accommodating new religion draws a distinction between the spiritual and the worldly in a way quite uncharacteristic of the other two types. Religion is not construed as a primarily social matter; rather it provides solace or stimulation to personal, interior life. Although it may reinvigorate the individual for life

in the world, it has relatively few implications for how that life
should be lived, except that it should be lived in a more religiously
inspired fashion. Any consequences for society will be largely
unintended rather than designed. While it may strengthen the
individual for secular affairs and heighten his enjoyment of life,
these are not the justifications for its practice. The benefits it
offers are not of the thorough-going instrumental variety to be
found in world-affirming movements. Michael Harper, a leader in
Charismatic Renewal, has said that:

> Its main strength, and for many its attractiveness, lies in its
> spontaneity, and in the fact that it is so far comparatively
> unstructured. It is not basically a protest movement, but a
> positive affirmation of faith in God and His power to change
> people and institutions. It is a new style of Christian life.
> (Quoted in Quebedeaux, 1976: 71)

Neo-Pentecostalism, or the Charismatic Renewal Movement,
comprises a wide range of bodies, organisations and groups both
within and beyond the major denominations (including the Catholic
Church), which have flourished since the early 1960s. They
typically consist of individuals who, although committed
Christians before joining the Renewal Movement, felt something to
be lacking in their spiritual lives, particularly an active *experience* of God's power working within them and within the church.
Involvement in the Renewal Movement was often motivated by the
desire for experience of the power of the Holy Spirit, the most
obvious and characteristic sign of which was normally glossolalia,
the 'gift of tongues'. It would also be accompanied by enthusiastic
participation in worship - other religious activities of a less
formally structured and more fully participatory kind than the
normal religious services - which they would often also continue
to attend, perhaps even more zealously than before. Fichter,
speaking of the Catholic Pentecostal movement on the issue of its
social consequences, argues that:

> The goal of the renewal movement is personal spiritual reform
> not organized social reform, but this does not imply the absence
> of social concern. The movement's basic conviction is that a
> better society can emerge only when people have become better,
> yet it would be completely erroneous to interpret this as an
> individualistic and self-centred attitude. (Fichter, 1975: 144)

Nevertheless, while its beliefs and the benefits of practice are
personalistically oriented, the form of practice in worship or ritual
will characteristically be collective.

At a conscious level at least, the innovatory religious movement
with a world-accommodating orientation will be seen not so much
as a protest against the world or society, but as a protest against
prevailing religious institutions, or their loss of vitality. These
are seen to have abandoned a living spirituality, to have eschewed

experience for an empty formalism. The new movement restores
an experiential element to the spiritual life and thereby replaces
lost certainties in a world where religious institutions have
become increasingly relativised. The membership of such movements is drawn from the 'religiously musical' middle and 'respectable' working classes, firmly integrated into the prevailing social
order, who are not entirely unhappy with it, but who seek none
the less some experiential reassurance of their general spiritual
values. Movements approximating this type are likely to draw
their associational forms from traditional social models of churches
or other religious voluntary associations. Religious activities will
tend to be regular and frequent but none the less leisure-time
commitments.

As I indicated earlier, all actual cases are likely to be mixed in
some degree, but the Charismatic Renewal or Neo-Pentecostal
Movement embodies this orientation to a significant extent.
Meredith McGuire (1975), for example, argues of the former
that:

> pentecostal Catholics can be considered a cognitive minority
> relative to the rest of American society in general because of
> their insistence on a religion which over-arches all spheres of
> every-day life. With the rest of society, however, the pente-
> costal Catholics tend to accept most of the prevailing social and
> political system, but interpret it within their religious frame-
> work. Nevertheless, the pentecostal belief system, with its
> emphasis upon interior spiritual concerns, has an inherent bias
> toward accepting the status-quo in 'worldly' affairs.

Fichter's survey of American Catholic Pentecostals showed them
to be predominantly strongly attached to the church before
becoming charismatics and for the most part *even more so* after-
wards. Eight out of ten affirmed the Pope to be the infallible
Vicar of Christ (Fichter, 1975: 25); 76 per cent reported that
they attended mass, and 77 per cent that they received Holy
Communion *more* than before joining the Charismatic Renewal
(ibid.: 30). Fichter argues that the movement originated in the
middle classes and that there has been a gradual spread down into
the working classes. His sample showed the following distribution
(ibid.: 49)

	%
Professional-Managerial	40.5
White collar	29.4
Blue collar	30.1

Bradfield (1975: 98) found 65 per cent of his sample of members
of the Protestant Neo-Pentecostal Full Gospel Businessmen's
Fellowship to be in professional-managerial occupations (on
Catholic charismatics, see also Hammond, 1975).

Such movements need not be of Christian origin. Subud, for

example - a Muslim mystic movement introduced to the West by an
Indonesian, Pak Subuh - seems to fit this category. A slightly
greater admixture of world-rejection produces a group like the
Aetherius Society (Wallis, 1974). The Aetherius Society is a
movement founded by a Londoner, George King, in the mid-1950s,
on the basis of an eclectic synthesis of ideas drawing heavily
upon the Theosophical tradition but modified to the degree that
the Masters were now to be found not in the Himalayas, but in
space craft. Members engage in rituals designed to transmit
energies for the good of humanity, and undertake - at set times
of the week and in special pilgrimages and ceremonials - a cosmic
battle against the forces of evil. The rest of their time, they, by
and large, conduct themselves conventionally as accountants,
shop-keepers, housewives, and the like (Wallis, 1974). This
movement is world-rejecting to the extent that it advances a
critique of contemporary greed and materialism which have led to
violence and ecological despoliation, and mobilises its efforts to
produce social, political and environmental changes, albeit by
magical means. But the world is ameliorable. Its ills can be
remedied if treated in time, and thus the followers of the
Aetherius Society do not cut themselves off from the world
around them. Their response to the world is one of accommodation,
while they pursue their mission of striving to save it from its
self-inflicted fate.

An interesting contrast is formed by the western supporters
of the Japanese movement, Soka Gakkai, called in America
Nichiren Shoshu of America (NSA), and in Britain Nichiren
Shoshu of the United Kingdom (NSUK). In this movement, transition to western, particularly American, culture has led to
substantial changes in style which render it an apparently stable
combination of world-accommodating and world-affirming types.
While its main message is one of individual self-improvement
through the chanting of the movement's *mantra*, it began during
the late 1960s to recruit larger numbers of American followers
and to undergo considerable adaptation as a result. The early
membership of the movement in the USA was among Japanese-
Americans, many of whom were GI brides, and in some cases
their converted husbands. Proselytisation was predominantly
among the Japanese community. During the late 1960s, the
movement attracted a large number of Caucasian Americans,
mostly single, under thirty, and often students or lower white-
collar workers (Snow, 1976: 133-4).

In the course of this revolution in its social composition, the
movement sought self-consciously to accommodate to American
society and to ingratiate itself with Americans. The Japanese-
born president of the movement in America became a United
States citizen, and changed his name to George Williams.
Members are encouraged to dress in a respectable middle-class
fashion. English is now used, rather than Japanese as formerly
at meetings. The American flag is prominently displayed in
movement buildings. NSA participated actively in the American

bicentennial celebrations. Thus, by every possible means, it
seeks to foster 'the impression that its values, aims, and conduct
are in conformity with, or at least not incongruent with certain
values, traditions, and normative standards within its community
or society of operation' (Snow, 1976: 190).

While much of the discussion will be devoted to the analytical
types and cases which best exemplify them, a later section will
focus further on some of the more clearly mixed cases variously
located within the conceptual space I have delimited, to show the
theoretically predictable properties resulting from conflicting
orientations. I shall argue that incompatibilities of this kind are
significant causal factors in producing characteristic changes
which many new religions have undergone.

3   Social change and the new religions

Undoubtedly the major long-term trend underlying the emergence
of the new religions, as indeed of many features of the world as
we know it in the industrial West, is, as Max Weber recognised,
that of *rationalisation*. Rationalisation is the process whereby
life has increasingly become organised in terms of instrumental
and causal considerations; a concern with technical efficiency,
the maximising of calculability and predictability; and the subordination of nature to human purposes. Rationalisation thus
tends to bring *secularisation* in its wake, since transcendental
values and absolute moral principles find it hard to survive
this increasing preoccupation with causal efficacy and utilitarian-
ism (Wilson, 1982: 148-79). Rationalisation thus tends to produce
what Max Weber has called the 'disenchantment of the world',
a loss of our sense of magic, mystery, prophecy, and the sacred
(Wilson, 1975).

Rationalisation also produces major changes in the relationship
of individuals to each other and to social institutions. In particular, as Peter Berger has noted, it produces a differentiation
and pluralisation of life-worlds or institutional domains (Berger
and Berger, 1976; Berger, Berger and Kellner, 1974). The social
world becomes ever less an organised whole for each person,
and more a series of discrete segments. For example, industrialisation created a separation between work and the family. In
contemporary western societies there is a high degree of differentiation between institutional arenas in which individuals live
out their lives: where they live is separate from where they
work, which is separate from where they play (Wilson, 1970a).
The world of the child is separated from that of the adult.

Unlike his forebears then, modern man cannot so readily identify
himself with his public institutional roles because their very
variety may make it impossible to gain more than a fragmented
conception of self from them, and none quite captures or embodies
the person as a whole. Moreover, as rationalisation has led to
ever greater routinisation and mechanisation of work, to an ever
greater division of labour in the interest of efficiency, so a
major focus of identification for earlier generations, the occupational role, has tended to become less attractive for all but a
privileged few in prestigious or intrinsically satisfying occupations.
Identity for the majority becomes *de-institutionalised*, and
individuals begin 'to assign priority to their private selves, that
is, to locate the "real me" in the private sphere of life' (Berger,
1965). The public institutions of education, the state, and the

economy tend to be viewed by many as agents of a baleful and
dehumanising constraint on the realisation of the 'authentic self'
and the 'good society'.

Rationalisation of production has the further effect of creating
a shift from ascription to achievement (not *who* you are, but
what you can *do*) as the basis for selection into adult occupational
roles. Status and a sense of worth thus come to rest on the level
of achievement which has been attained in the course of one's
life. But where achievement is viewed as an end in itself, such a
sense of worth and of status is inevitably precarious since there
are no clear guides as to when *enough* has been achieved, and
the chances are that comparison with others will lead the individual always to feel a *relative* failure.

De-institutionalisation of identity has been accompanied and
enhanced by another consequence of rationalisation and industrialisation, that is by the *attenuation of community*. Industrialisation
destroys traditional forms of community and inhibits the creation
of new forms due to the levels of mobility – both geographical
and social – which become characteristic, and due to the differentiation among people which tends to follow from an increasing
division of labour and a consequent divergence of life-styles.
This attenuation of community is experienced as a lack of close
ties with a group of persons outside the family with whom the
individual has a relationship of more than a role-oriented kind;
of a group of persons with whom he can 'be himself', who will
accept him as, and for what, he is rather than as the producer of
a particular performance. In practice most interactions are with
individuals with whom lack of prolonged acquaintance has not
permitted an easy, slowly growing intimacy, and which are
inevitably therefore somewhat fragile and threatening.

The new religious movements have – in substantial measure –
developed in response to, and as attempts to grapple with the
consequences of, rationalisation (Wilson, 1976: 99, 104-8). But
having identified three analytically distinct types which have
emerged in this context, it is clearly important to distinguish
the more specific factors which have led to their distinctive
forms of salvational message and of organisation.

THE SOURCES OF SUPPORT FOR THE WORLD-REJECTING
NEW RELIGIONS

The world-rejecting new religions of the past have characteristically been composed of the poor and the oppressed. In the
form of millennialist movements anticipating the imminent total
transformation of the world and the supernatural establishment of
a heaven on earth, new religions have often formed in circumstances of great adversity. Defeat in war, colonisation, natural
disaster or economic collapse have often been heralds of millennialist movements (Wilson, 1970b). Supernatural forces, or even God
himself, will come down to earth, transforming and purging it,

banishing pain, evil and indignity, and ousting the oppressor.
Introversionism, the pursuit of salvation by gathering in a tight
community of the elect, withdrawn from the taint of the world 'to
preserve and cultivate their own holiness' (Wilson, 1970b: 39),
has often been a further development from millennialism. Continued oppression, repeated defeat, or failure of the millennial
prophecy, may lead to the postponement of hope, transcendentalising it and projecting it into the distant rather than the
immediate future.

Millennialism and introversionism represent respectively the
active and the passive response to a world seen as beyond reform.
Both indicate the failure of, or the perceived unavailability of,
secular solutions to the problems by which various individuals
and groups see the world, or themselves, beset. Some of the
contemporary new religions have an explicitly millennialist
character, for example the Children of God who anticipate
Christ's return in 1993, and the Unification Church which once
expected the onset of the millennium in the 1980s. Others, such
as Krishna Consciousness, are more introversionist in their form.

The new groups and movements which fall into the world-
rejecting category sometimes pre-dated, but scarcely flourished,
before the late 1960s. The Unification Church, for example, had
a tiny following in California in the 1960s, and the miserable
failure of its efforts to recruit any substantial following until
late in the 1960s is well documented (Lofland, 1966). The Jesus
People, who in their more radical manifestations displayed world-
rejecting features, did not make an appearance until about 1968.
Krishna Consciousness, although established in America from
1965, only rather gradually built a following.

The principal early following of each of these movements was
drawn from among the hippies, drop-outs, surfers, LSD and
marijuana users among the American and European young, and
many more from those who sympathised with, and shared aspects
of, the same sub-culture as these groups. Robbins *et al.* for
example, argue that 'Unification Church members in America are
practically all between 18 and 35 and usually in their twenties'
(1976: 115).

J. Stillson Judah says of the sample of Krishna Consciousness
members interviewed for his study that, 'All devotees interviewed
have shown some sympathy with countercultural ideas' (1974: 81).
Eighty-five per cent were twenty-five years old or younger, and
only 3 per cent were over thirty at the time of the survey
(ibid.: 111). But it can scarcely be said that the world-rejecting
new religions recruited principally from among the poor and
oppressed. Judah (1974: 111) found that Krishna Consciousness
devotees were largely drawn from among 'upper-middle-class
youth'. Ellwood points out that, 'Most Jesus people are between
the ages of fourteen and twenty-four. Their backgrounds usually
include some exposure to the "youth culture", including drugs.
Like the "hip" society, they are generally of middle or upper-
middle-class white background' (1973: 58).

A recruit to the Children of God displays these themes in his testimony. Born in 1950 to a wealthy Lima (Peru) business family,

> I was sent to the best schools in Lima. . . . Most of the time we were given what we wanted. . . . After I finished High School . . . my father decided it would be best if I went to the United States to get trained in Business Administration so that one day I could take over his business. . . . [At the University of Texas] I met some people involved in smoking marijuana which got me started in that world . . . I started to experiment heavily with drugs. . . . But by 1972 I had become disillusioned with what was becoming of the Youth Revolution in the States. . . . By this time I had met a very young and pretty high society girl. . . . Together we got into dealing drugs, which proved to be very profitable, and we became very rich in just a short time. (*Family Education Book of the Month*, No. 1, May 1982: 19-20)

Subsequently he and his wife decided to abandon this materialistic life-style and to live a simple life in the Peruvian Andes, and to order their lives according to the Bible. They found this difficult to accomplish on their own. On meeting the Children of God they were greatly impressed by their success at living a biblically oriented life, and by the 'spirit of love' in the Home, and they joined up.

Often the conversion of these young people was so sudden, the transition so abrupt and dramatic, that parents and friends would argue that only *brainwashing* or *hypnosis* could account for it. A circular issued by one movement devoted to opposing the new religious movements, the Committee Engaged in Freeing Minds (Arlington, Texas), composed mainly of hostile parents of current members of the movements and of former members who have since turned against the source of their erstwhile salvation, stated the case as follows:

> Tens of thousands of our youth are being manipulated by leaders of cults for personal power and wealth; these victims have been coerced into a 'master-slave' relationship through mind-control. (21 June 1976)

The mechanisms have been specified by Ted Patrick, a man professionally occupied in undoing their alleged effects:

> The way they get them is by on-the-spot hypnosis. Once they get them they brainwash them. The technique is the same as the North Koreans used on our prisoners of war (Patrick, 1976: 20)

Such a theory readily legitimates the infringement of normal civil liberties to 'rescue' 'kids' who have been thus 'psychologically kidnapped'.

Once they had been programmed . . . there was no longer any
question of their exercising anything that could be called free
will. They stayed with the cults because they had been programmed to stay, brainwashed into believing that it was Satan
who was tempting them to go. (ibid.: 65)

Hence it is not inappropriate to engage in systematic deception to
bring the movement member into a position of vulnerability,
which will permit him to be persuaded or forced into a vehicle,
and transported against his will to some secluded location. There
the movement member is denied freedom of movement or of
contact with former associates or their legal advisers, and is
subjected to an emotional and intellectual barrage aimed to persuade him that the movement to which he belongs is a confidence
trick designed to enrich and glorify an exploitative leader who
has succeeded in duping his youthful following. He may be kept
in captivity for a period of some days unless escape or acquiescence
earlier intervene. This process, known as 'deprogramming' has
given rise to a new profession, and to a number of organisations
devoted to its practice. (For discussions of the anti-cult movement and 'deprogramming' see Wallis, 1977; Shupe, Spielmann
and Stigall, 1977; Le Moult, 1978; Shupe and Bromley 1980,
1981; Sage, 1976).

Although 'deprogrammings' have been carried out upon members
of all manner of new religious movements (and indeed members of
some old religious movements, and even upon people with no
particular religious attachments at all), they have been a weapon
deployed most frequently against world-rejecting movements to
which conversion often seems to be a sudden and dramatic
thing, and which cut the new recruit off from former associations
and involvements much more sharply than movements of the other
types.

The 'brainwashing' and 'hypnosis' hypotheses were clearly an
attempt to grapple with the dramatic character of the conversion.
Such ideas seemed plausible enough if the reasoning was that
the convert had had insufficient time and contact *prior* to joining
to gain any clear grasp of the movement's beliefs. But this was
entirely to misunderstand the nature of the conversion. What led
these young people to abandon their friends, family, education
or career in this impulsive way was not the promise of some future
spiritual reward, nor any extensive initial doctrinal comprehension, but the actuality of the way of life which they observed,
and its immediate consequences for the follower. Although they
might 'parrot' statements of belief in a mechanical way, this was
less a result of brainwashing than of the fact that commitment to
these *ideas* in the early stages was largely a matter of *commitment
to memory*. The conversion was typically not to a body of doctrine,
but to the quality of life and social relationships which they
found in the movement.

Moses David recognised this in the first large colony of the
Children of God in Texas in 1970:

What we are doing is more important than what we're saying.
People don't come out to hear what we're saying. They come to
see what we're doing. The don't even want to hear what we
have to say. They want to see how we live. (Moses David, 'Not
a sermon, but a sample', 3 July 1970).

The new converts might offer a memorised statement of belief
to uncomprehending parents as a 'vocabulary of motives', but
this was not why they had joined. What attracted them to the
movement characteristically was the warmth and affection with
which they were treated, the sense of purpose and meaningful-
ness exhibited by the adherents, their openness and apparent
sincerity, their joy or serenity. David Taylor, who observed
prospects being drawn into the Unification Church during
'weekend training sessions' to which they were invited, argues
that in the dilemma of whether to go or stay, 'The overwhelming
kindness and attention members have extended to them frequently
is the strongest factor influencing their decision' (Taylor, 1977:
13; see also Taylor, 1982). J. Stillson Judah observes that, 'The
chanting of the Hare Krishna *mantra* and the friendliness and
close fellowship with the devotees are the two factors that most
devotees said were the initial attractions to the Movement' (Judah,
1974: 165). Tex Watson recounts that it was the love apparently
emanating from Charlies Manson that drew him in (1978: 50).
Enroth's informant on the Unification Church, discussing the
approach to new recruits says: 'We wanted to communicate that
they had nothing more to fear, that they were among friends.
. . . All the love that they had ever wanted was now theirs '
(Enroth, 1977: 103).
    A member of the Children of God again represents the experi-
ence of many in that movement in this respect, if not in the
particular circumstances of her biography. Born in 1941 to a
devoutly Catholic family, Lydia became a nun after completing
high school:

But even after taking final vows, inside I felt there was something wrong, and I began to feel more and more disillusioned,
empty, without direction and mostly just lonely and looking for
real love. . . . Finally in the fall of 1971 I made the decision
that I simply had to leave. . . . But after 3 or 4 months I
realised I was lonelier than ever. . . . On that life-changing
Saturday in March I rode my bicycle to the park and was
relaxing under a tree watching the people when I noticed a
tall young man with a guitar. . . . He . . . walked straight
over to me and without saying a word began singing a song,
looking intently into my eyes. . . .The song and the love so
touched me that tears came to my eyes . . . 'How long you
been [sic] waiting for somebody to love you? How long you
been waiting for someone to show you the way . . .?' I soon
found myself surrounded by about 5 more young men all smiling
down at me with the same radiant look of love shining on their

faces. I was so taken by the love and totally new spirit of
these boys that when they invited me to come home and
eat supper with them I readily agreed. (*Family Education
Book of the Month*, No. 1, May 1982: 280-3)

Salvation for the convert to the world-rejecting religions, then,
was principally salvation from the loneliness and impersonality
of the world. Salvation lay primarily in *community*, in the existence of a group which would provide an enduring, warm, supportive environment in which the individual would be treated as a
person rather than a role-player, and in which his idealism
would be mobilised and given concrete meaning in terms of
spreading the salvational message to the world. Robbins *et al.*
have made this point clearly: 'The need for communal solidarity
and expressive warmth in an impersonal bureaucratic society
has frequently been cited as an explanation for the current
upsurge of relatively non-political mystical, occult, and pentecostal groups' (Robbins *et al.*, 1976: 122). However, in the past
such efforts to locate the causal antecedents of these movements
have tended too little to discriminate what are quite clearly
distinctive types, with distinctive social sources. Communal
solidarity plays a relatively small part, for example, in the
activity of such world-affirming movements as Scientology or
Transcendental Meditation. The world-rejecting movements provided a repository, and a vehicle, for the awakened idealism of
many members drawn to them, and this fact explains in large
measure why they were often able to continue as members even
in the face of corruption or harshness, contradiction and
deception. They simply pushed these things to one side, ignored
them, and concentrated on the *good fruit*, the things that *were*
being achieved, the people who actually had been *helped* by
contact with the movement. Focusing on the good, the positive,
the ways in which their ideals *were* being fulfilled enabled them
to ignore or to downplay the bad, the negative, the ways in
which they were not.
   These sentiments appear in two accounts of involvement in the
People's Temple and the Unification Church which are worth
citing at length:

With hindsight, it is hard for me to justify why I stayed
around. The degeneracy of People's Temple stood in sharp
contrast to the good it was doing for the poor, the elderly, the
sick, and the misunderstood. All I can say is that at this point
in my life, Jim Jones was the only game in town. I had shut
off Christianity once and for all. The society at large was
thought to be hostile, racist, and dangerous. So I stayed,
trying to suppress the degrading aspects and think mostly
about what was admirable. (Thielmann, 1979: 82)

Most of my life in the Family, I hadn't ever closely examined
the *Principle* [i.e. *Divine Principle*, the primary doctrinal text

of the Unification Church]. Four years before, after a precult
conversion experience, I had precipitously determined that my
life was to be given to God and had joined the first group I'd
encountered which seemed to share this great emotion. I then
lived it out, pressing myself to fit in. From the first weeks I
tried . . . to make connection with those beliefs which I felt
right, while suspending doubt about other matters that, I was
led to believe, would become clear as I grew spiritually. . . .
Finally I just threw away my critical faculties on the assumption
that question and search was faithless. (Underwood and
Underwood, 1979: 224)

In many ways the appeal of the world-rejecting movements
almost exclusively to the young at that time is readily understandable. The 1960s represented a peak in the history of youth
culture. This phenomenon of a youth culture is itself of recent
provenance, a consequence of the development of an industrial
technology which freed the young from productive activity, and
established the need for extensive and often specialised education
covering an increasing period of the life-cycle. Youth thus
became the ambiguous status between childhood and the adult
world of work, a status without any clear social place which
nevertheless became the repository of ever larger sections of
the population, many of whom were segregated into separate
youth 'ghettoes', such as advanced educational institutions.
There they possessed much freedom and few responsibilities, but
at the same time little power and few immediate rewards in terms
of income or status.

Some measure of the scale of this development can be secured
through statistics on higher education. Between the academic
years 1962 and 1967, the number of students in full-time higher
education in Britain grew from 217,000 to 376,000, an increase of
73 per cent (Layard and King, 1969: 13). In the USA between
1960 and 1970, 'the number of people in college more than
doubled' (Howard, 1974: 163). Thousands and thousands of
young people, most of them middle class in social origin, were
flooding into institutions where they had relatively little contact
with anyone other than their age-peers. The affluence of the
period provided not only resources for the emergence of
industries directed towards the construction and sale of symbols
of youth, such as the popular music recording industry, but
also a sense of the imminence, and indeed the necessity, of
progress. Technology, it was believed, had resolved the problem
of scarcity, and hence peace, plenty and social justice could
now prevail for all, were it not for the reactionary forces or
structures preventing them. Everything was possible, every
problem resolvable where there was a will to do it. Affluence
encouraged idealism, and it also created a sense of security that
entry into the world of work could wait, that something would
turn up, that one would be provided for, if only by welfare,
assistance from home, or through petty or illicit trading, as in

craft-work or drugs. Robert Ellwood makes the point that:

> It was largely an affluent, middle-class family life which offered
> the leisure and confidence of security which made disdain of
> material goods and middle-class values possible. Few blacks or
> really poor people were found in the counter culture, just as
> few were people of rural background. (Ellwood, 1973: 15)

Wider political and social events conspired to give this new
social category an identity and a solidarity as persons of a
distinctive type. The Civil Rights Campaign in America and the
Campaign for Nuclear Disarmament in Britain began to create that
solidarity which was symbolised and enhanced in new styles of
music and dress promoted by industries eager to exploit this
new market. The Vietnam War, particularly among American youth
where the draft created a heightened sense of urgency, was a
major phenomenon leading to the alienation of the young from the
structure and culture of adult society. Its impersonality, bureau-
cratisation, and dehumanising division of labour were already
rejected in preference to a way of life closer to the warmth,
intimacy and integration of childhood. This rejection was cele-
brated in the hippie life-style, the norms and values of which
embodied an opposition to the Protestant Ethic dominating the
world of work and adult responsibility. Hippie values comprised
an emphasis on spontaneity against restraint, hedonism against
deferred gratification, ego expressivity against conformity to
bureaucratic rules, and a disdain for work against its elevation
as a virtue (Young, 1971: 126). The hostility which this rejection of dominant values, life-styles and career-patterns provoked
against them, helped to weld this new social *category* into a social
group in opposition to the structure and culture of the environ-
ing society; into a counter-culture. They 'dropped-out' of that
wider society in varying degrees, seeking to found a better
way of life in its interstices or at its margins, in Haight-Ashbury
or the rural commune.

At the same time, the young had begun to develop a political
consciousness, opposed, as one might expect, to the prevailing
social order. In student political movements, and anti-war
protest movements, through sit-ins and demonstrations, the
young sought to transform aspects of their society. Robert
Wuthnow (1978: 126) had argued that the distinctive life
experience of those reaching adulthood in the 1960s was such as
to create a 'generation unit' in Karl Mannheim's terms.

But these attempts to recreate the world by secular means
largely foundered. The hippie vision of love, peace, community,
and everyone 'doing his own thing' had been found to lead to
disorganisation, entropy, mental illness, exploitation, and the
victory not of the meek, but of the most insensitive. Youthful
political activism resulted in bloody confrontations on the
campuses; in Chicago at the 1968 Democratic Convention; in
Grosvenor Square, London; in Paris; and elsewhere. The utopian

vision had become a rather sordid reality. (For an alternative
evaluation see Foss and Larkin, 1976).
It was in this context that many world-rejecting new religions
began to find their converts. . . . In some cases they represented the fulfilment of radical youthful ideas, as for example in
this case of a recruit to the Unification Church:

> I joined the Unification Church . . . in 1972. In the years
> before that, I had been a college student, a participant in
> Martin Luther King's 1963 March on Washington, a New York
> City taxicab driver, an Army draftee, and then a conscientious
> objector sentenced to Leavenworth for willful [sic] disobedience
> during the Vietnam War. Finally, in 1970, I completed my
> bachelor's degree at Berkeley, amid rock-throwing rioters and
> tear-gas throwing police. I saw that my idealism had reached
> a dead end.
> Like thousands of others, I became a mellow dope-smoking
> longhair trying to live off the land in the California mountains.
> At times I felt like a cop-out, taking it easy while the world
> went to hell. I thought back to the sixties and wondered what
> went wrong. I realized that our Movement had lacked something
> spiritual. . . . I visited an old friend who had joined the
> Unification Church. . . . The more I found out, the more
> interested I became. (Wells, 1978)

A further account illustrating a number of the elements referred
to so far is drawn from the case of the People's Temple. It is
particularly poignant in being the reflection of Larry Layton,
indicted for conspiracy to murder Congressman Leo Ryan and
defectors from the Temple at the Kaituma airstrip in Guyana:

> Having failed the third grade, I was always tormented with
> feelings of inferiority as a child. Despite this, once I learned
> to read in the third grade I became very much interested in
> the news, current events, politics, and race relations. I was
> an outcast among the children at Indian Head and this furthered
> identification with blacks, peasants in South America, and so
> on. I thought I might become a great political reformer. I
> admired men like FDR and Stevenson. I followed the civil rights
> movement avidly. By the time we reached Berkeley I was
> involved in politics and hoped someday to run for office. But
> with the assassination of Kennedy and the events that followed
> I lost hope, little by little, in the ability of politics to right
> the world's wrongs which weighed so heavy on my prematurely
> adult mind. . . . With college came alcohol, and interest in
> psychology, sociology, and unfortunate experimentation with
> pharmacology. That caused me to see pot and LSD as the answer
> to my problems. I became further separated from society with
> its race for money, its power, and lack of brotherhood. The
> draft was on my heels so I always had to study enough to stay
> in school, but I really was looking for a happy existence, and

this after graduation led me . . . to head to Ukiah in search
for utopia. . . . There is a lot I will never know about People's
Temple. The only thing I can say is that it started out looking
like a civil rights movement, and Jim Jones started out looking
like Martin Luther King. Obviously things turned out differ-
ently. (Yee and Layton, 1981: 343-5)

Proclaiming that they offered a 'high that never lets you down',
or claiming to be 'Spiritual Revolutionaries' or the 'Revolution
for Jesus'; displaying their opposition to prevailing social
institutions and playing rock music, a number of world-rejecting
movements possessed many cultural continuities with the counter-
culture. Since secular change efforts had failed, many young
people were open at this point to the idea, sometimes encouraged by the drug experience, that a supernatural realm existed,
and that salvation could now come from it alone. Robert Ellwood,
in his discussion of the Jesus People, argues that at this time,
'what was needed was a religion for a situation of failure' (1973:
18). But equally significant was the fact that the youth culture
vision of creating a functioning, meaningful, loving, sharing
society appeared to have been realised in the communalism of the
Children of God, the Unification Church, and other such movements. Since the way of life seemed so successful, many young
people were prepared to take the movement's beliefs on trust.
It seemed to offer much that the drop-outs and hippies had been
trying to achieve: a stable, warm community; a rejection of
worldly materialism, competition and achievement; a structured
setting for the experience of ecstasy or mystical insight. Gregory
Johnson found that, 'the Krishna temple successfully generated
what the larger counter-culture had failed to accomplish: the
establishment of a unified community based on the non-coercive
authority of love' (Johnson, 1976: 47). Ellwood argues that the
'psychedelic' culture possessed many characteristics which were
carried over into the the Jesus movement. They shared a stress on
subjectivity as the key to reality; the 'high' as a goal; the
importance of musical expression; an idealised view of the rural
past; a tension with science and technology; and a suspicion of
history and the intellect (Ellwood, 1973: 18-20). Since individualism and voluntarism had proven unsuccessful in attaining any of
their ideals for long, they were often willing to subordinate their
autonomy for the benefits of this new way of life when it was
offered. Not all who joined, of course, had experienced the
hippie culture, but all identified with its aspirations for a more
idealistic, spiritual, and caring way of life, in the context of
more personal and loving social relationships.

THE SOURCES OF SUPPORT FOR THE WORLD-AFFIRMING NEW RELIGIONS

The world-affirming new religions also gained members to some extent from the failure and disintegration of the counter-culture. Hashimoto and McPherson (1976) argue, for example, that membership of the Japanese-originated new religion, Nichiren Shoshu (Soka Gakkai), grew very rapidly in America in the second half of the 1960s, slowing down into the early 1970s. There is some evidence of a similar pattern for Scientology (Wallis, 1976b: 221-2), while *est*, which began in 1971, had been delivered to 185,000 customers by 1979. Many young people, faced by their inability to change the world, decided to accommodate to it to a greater or lesser extent. For some, the world-affirming movements were to provide the recipe or the anodyne for this accommodation. None the less, these movements did not depend for their development upon so transient a phenomenon as the youth-culture of the 1960s. Rather, they have their origins in pervasive features of advanced capitalist societies.

Their main source undoubtedly lies in the unequal distribution of various resources in society: power, status, self-confidence, personal attractiveness, interpersonal competence, etc. But rather than transforming the world or creating an alternative to it, these movements offer recipes, techniques and knowledge to reduce the gap between aspiration and actuality: either to ensure their possessor an improvement in his access to these resources, or to enable him to restrict his desires the better to fit his circumstances. Edward Moody claims that members of the Church of Satan desire successes denied them - money, fame, recognition, power . . . (Moody, 1974: 358). Those who join want 'the rewards, the monetary successes and sexual conquests, that are the symbols of social adequacy in our culture' (361); and 'They are people troubled by a lack of self-esteem, by failure and doubt' (362). James Dator, analysing testimonials of American converts of Soka Gakkai (Nichiren Shoshu) published in the movement's magazine, found that:

> Almost all of the testimonials centred on accounts of the subjects' troubled lives before entrance into Soka Gakkai, the events which led them to join that organization, and subsequent 'divine benefits' that they had received. Generally, the problems that the members encountered before joining were in one (or all) of three areas: *sickness* (including both mental and physical distresses) was mentioned by 57% of the (American) members, *financial problems* were cited by 28%, while problems of *human relations*, especially domestic squabbles and the lack of friends, were mentioned by 18%. (Dator, 1969: 33)

These testimonials emphasised that, 'This religion does work here and now, and not in some possible after-life' (ibid.: 35). In like

manner, a recent study found that a major factor in recruitment
to Scientology is the expectation of relief from problems of
physical illness and disability, psychological difficulties, or
problems of a social or interpersonal kind. Like its forerunner,
Dianetics, Scientology offered to improve the individual's
chances of social mobility; of achieving his aspirations; of dis-
covering his 'true self' and realising all the potentialities
inherent in it; of eliminating the discrepancies between this
idealised identity and the one confirmed in day-to-day interaction
(Wallis, 1976b: 65). Transcendental Meditation makes similar
offers:

> 'Here comes a process suited for the present time. Meditate . . .
> and . . . not only unfold the consciousness of God, but begin
> to supplement and reinforce the material glories of life; com-
> plete growth of spirituality, Self-Realization, God-Realization
> in the end, and the supplementation of material glories of life
> in the beginning.' (Mahesh Yogi, 1962: 10)

Their main attraction lies in their provision of facilities for
exploring and cultivating the self within a social structure which
is largely taken-for-granted. The contrast with the world-
rejecting sects is sharp in this respect. James Beckford illustrates
this in a discussion of one world-rejecting movement, the Unification Church, in which, he suggests:

> it is important to cultivate and refine one's spirituality to the
> point of . . . perfection. But this is no part of a programme of
> self-discovery for its own sake. Human potential is deliberately
> realized for the sake of 'Father', that is, the founder/leader.
> Nearly everything is dedicated to him or done in his name. . . .
> Consequently, the self is conceived as an inferior, subordinate
> entity that can only achieve perfection in and through the
> recognition of its necessary dependence on Father. (Beckford,
> 1978: 234)

The contrasting ethos of the world-affirming movements on the
other hand, is closer to this characterisation by Christopher
Lasch:

> Love as self-sacrifice or self-abasement, 'meaning' as submission
> to a higher loyalty - these sublimations strike the therapeutic
> sensibility as intolerably oppressive, offensive to common
> sense and injurious to personal health and well-being. To
> 'liberate' humanity from such outmoded ideas of love and duty
> has become the mission of the post-Freudian therapies and
> particularly of their converts and popularizers, for whom mental
> health means the overthrow of 'inhibitions' and the nonstop
> celebration of the self. (Lasch, 1976: 5)

Movements approximating to this type form part of a progressively unfolding tradition in American culture, where
individualistic instrumentalism has been a major ideological theme
(Bellah, 1976; Schur, 1976: 3). As a study of best-selling
religious literature in America has shown (Schneider and Dornbusch, 1958), popular religion over the last hundred years has
increasingly stressed the this-worldly, instrumental benefits of
religion, for the relief of anxiety, the increase of self-esteem
and self-confidence, the improvement of health and welfare.
Organised movements offering access to these goals have been a
constantly renewed accompaniment to the development of industrial
America. In the late nineteenth century, Christian Science and
New Thought focused particularly on the instrumental goals of
providing physical healing at a time when medicine had made
only limited progress in achieving routine efficacy. But to these
traditional magical elements of religion have been added new
concerns, deriving rather more from the problems produced by
an advanced industrial society than from the universal concern
for physical health.

North America has tended to lead the world in its support for
self-improvement movements, providing a home more conducive
to the growth of psychoanalysis, for example, than even its
native Europe, and, since then, exporting to the rest of the
world a varied range of therapeutic cults and self-exploration
and self-improvement systems: Primal Therapy; Scientology;
Pelmanism; Encounter Groups; Gestalt Therapy; Sensitivity
Training; and Biofeedback, plus dozens of lesser known systems
and practices. Many of them began to develop soon after the end
of the second world war, and their following until the late 1960s
was characteristically middle-aged and even then continued to
draw from this age group, in contrast to the world-rejecting
movements which were all but exclusively youthful. The average
age of those in the San Francisco 'Bay Area New Religious
Consciousness survey for 1973' who had participated in one or
another of the Human Potential Movements was thirty-five years
(Stone, 1976: 107). This is far higher than would have been the
case at the time in the world-rejecting movements. Relatively few
young persons were members of the Church of Satan during 1968-
69 according to Randall H. Alfred (1976). Nichiren Shoshu of
America (Soka Gakkai) is reported to have had an age composition
in 1970 which located only 17 per cent as twenty or under, 40 per
cent between twenty-one and thirty, and 43 per cent as thirty-
one or older (Ellwood, 1974: 101). (These figures show a slightly
smaller proportion of the young as members of Nichiren Shoshu
of America than in the survey conducted by John Kie-chang Oh
(1973: 172), but even this showed over 30 per cent to be
thirty-one years of age or older which would entail a higher
mean age than is characteristic of world-rejecting movements).
Babbie and Stone (1977: 124) found that the median age of
graduates of *est* 'as of 1976, was around 33 years of age'. A later
survey by the organisation of a sample of *est* graduates showed

the average age to be thirty-six years (*The Graduate Review*, September/October 1980: 4).

While the world-rejecting religions offer an alternative to the anonymity, impersonality, individualism, and segmentalisation of modern life, the world-affirming religions and their secular counterparts take these things for granted. They offer salvation for those who already have firm attachments to the modern industrial world, or those who, like former American youth radical, Jerry Rubin, subsequently a Human Potential teacher, had decided that there were no viable alternatives to it. (For Rubin's pilgrimage through the world-affirming movements both secular and spiritual, see Rubin, 1976.)

The paradox of the world-rejecting new religions is that, like the radical movements which preceded them, they drew their support primarily from those who had apparently most to gain from the world as it was currently structured. The paradox of the world-affirming new religions is that they offer means of coping with a sense of inadequacy among social groups which are, by the more obvious indicators, among the world's more successful and highly rewarded people. Actualizations is yet another movement to have developed the principles and methods of *est*, having been founded by a former *est* trainer, Stewart Emery. A participant in an Actualizations training is reported to have said:

> I've always felt that I've been given the best of everything that life can offer. . . . I've got a perfectly wonderful husband who just absolutely *worships* me; a family, and many good friends. Everything just about that anybody could want. Yet I still feel . . . well incomplete . . . somehow. (Martin, 1977: 86-7)

A survey of *est* graduates in 1980 showed them to have an average of 15.5 years of education, and almost three-quarters of them earned $15,000 or more a year. Nearly 50 per cent earned $25,000 a year and over (*The Graduate Review*, September/October 1980: 4). Edwin Schur alleges that:

> the popularization of awareness is but another version of the quasi-religious dogma of optimistic individualism that has always sold so well in America. It appeals almost exclusively to the middle and upper classes, it is politically innocuous and socially complacent, and it is being promoted and marketed in the best Madison Avenue tradition. (Schur, 1976: 77)

Support for the world-affirming new religions is thus generated by central characteristics of an advanced capitalist society. In a society where the allocation of rewards depends upon achievement rather than upon inheritance for most of the population, success in terms of status and income and upward social mobility is still highly sought after. But the opportunity

for such successes inevitably falls short of aspiration for many,
who may therefore be in the market for assistance in their
endeavours, even if the techniques offered have some metaphysical or supernatural overtone (Luckmann and Berger,
1964). But they are more than just a modern form of magical
technology. Even the few who are fortunate enough to fulfil
their mobility aspirations may be disappointed to discover that
rationalisation has denuded public institutions of the power to
provide most of those engaged in them with a completely satis-
factory identity, forcing them to seek personal meaning and a
sense of worth in their private, rather than their public, lives.
While the bulk of the enterprises competing in this market offer
techniques and resources for meeting the disparity between
aspirations and achievement by increasing individual achieve-
ments, as I argued earlier, some seek to resolve this disparity
by the *reduction* of *expectations*.

The dominance of the achievement ethos produces a major
contradiction in modern western life. Success in a rationalised
public arena often rests in large part on behaviour and attitudes
derived from the Protestant Ethic and its stress on deferred
gratification, the virtue of hard-work, conformity to rules,
repression of instinctual desires, and the reduction of activities
to a routine. The worlds of leisure, play and the private sphere
of life generally tend to rest on behaviour and attitudes quite
antithetical to the Protestant Ethic; that is, on short-run
hedonism, the virtue of pleasure, spontaneity, and the pursuit
of excitement (Young, 1971). Hence, at the same time as the
emergence of a market for recipes for worldly success, there
has emerged a need for methods of escaping the constraints and
inhibitions usually required in order to achieve that success.
Methods are sought for overcoming the effects of a lengthy
socialisation into the Protestant Ethic, in order to explore the
private self, to buttress a deinstitutionalised identity, and to
indulge hedonistic impulses in an affluent, advanced industrial
society in which consumption has become as much an imperative
as production. Martin (1977: 92-3) reports a participant in an
Actualizations training:

> A handsome junior executive type who has come to the workshop
> with his equally smart wife, then goes to the dais and says,
> 'All my life, I've been an achiever; I've always won all of the
> "Best of Everything" awards. . . . I've been rising fast in the
> corporation that I work for, looking forward - somewhat
> uneasily - to the day when they make me president of the
> company. It's a goal that I have absolutely no doubt that I'll
> achieve . . . . There's just one drawback. I feel the closer I
> get, the less human I am. It's robbing me of my humanity.'

A relatively secure and comfortable middle class now sees itself
as possessing a right to some measure of indulgence, enjoyment
and self-expression. As Bryan Wilson has put it:

Producer societies are consonant with ideologies of post-mortem benefits, but consumer society demands gratification now. . . . Consumer society demands the rejection of the 'culture of postponement', and in its place it offers a cult of present realization. Human suffering, and even human waiting, are rejected together with those elaborate roundabout procedures of capital formation and production that have been essential for the development of the advanced industrial society. (Wilson, 1976: 100)

On the other hand, many middle-class social groups face the problem that the self-control and repression which enabled them to achieve or to maintain their secure and comfortable position has often destroyed their capacity for guilt-free relaxation and pleasure. Hence a range of movements, some religious and some secular, have arisen to meet this complex of demands. (For parallel thoughts on this topic, see Howard, 1974: 188-9).

Similarly, urban industrial life is a mode of life articulated through the performance of *roles*, rather than direct, diffuse interaction of persons intimately known to each other. Negotiating adult life through the accomplished performance of diverse social roles may leave individuals with a sense that these performances create barriers to the expression of a 'self' lying beneath them. Constantly acting in partial capacities before distinctive audiences may create the dissatisfaction that none of these audiences ever make contact with a complete and integrated self unmasked by a social persona; and the performer may come to fear that he is losing contact with that underlying self believed to be his most authentic expression; that he has become the prisoner of social convention, of situational performance.

Moreover, of course, an advanced industrial society is one in which mobility is extensive in pursuit of economic efficiency. Hence large numbers of individuals, particularly in the mobile middle classes, find themselves relative strangers as they move about in the furtherance of their educational and occupational careers. More and more people live in *urban* surroundings in which high levels of anonymity and impersonality prevail. Close acquaintance tends to be limited to rather few others, and intimate contact has to be made in the absence of broad background knowledge and a traditional etiquette. Hence developing intimate relationships is a threatening enterprise. Agencies or movements offering an easy intimacy and rapidly achieved community with others can be extremely attractive in such circumstances.

4 Secularisation and the new religions

Theories advancing arguments for a relationship between secularisation and the new religious movements have been of two basic
types:

(1) Where the new religions are viewed as primarily a *mani-
    festation* of secularisation with little prospect of halting
    its course.
(2) Where the new religions are viewed as a *response* to
    secularisation which seeks to - and may in one or another
    instance - reverse the trend.

The latter has a variety of particular forms sharing a common
ancestry in Durkheim's functionalist conception of religion and
society. At its simplest, Andrew Greeley (1972) argues that the
very existence of new forms of supernaturalist interest and
enthusiasm contradict the notion that secularisation has become a
dominant and persisting feature of advanced industrial societies.

Emile Durkheim argued that religion was a reflection of prevailing social structure, and a source of solidarity and collective
identity. As the social structure changed, so too, therefore,
would the dominant form of religious expression. Robert Bellah's
paper on 'Religious evolution' (1969) originally published in 1964,
touched on this issue, pointing to the collapse of the traditional
dualism of historic religion, the emergence of a situation where
groups explicitly labelled religious no longer exercised a monopoly
over 'the symbolisation of man's relation to the ultimate conditions
of his existence', and the appearance of increasingly fluid types
of organisation. He argued that:

> Rather than interpreting these trends as significant of indiffer-
> ence and secularisation, I see in them the increasing acceptance
> of the notion that each individual must work out his own ultimate
> solutions and that the most the church can do is provide him
> with a favourable environment for doing so, without imposing on
> him a prefabricated set of answers. (Bellah, 1969: 289)

The number and diversity of answers that was to emerge, was not
perhaps clear in the early 1960s when Bellah's paper was written.
In the late 1970s, clearer expression was given to this view by
Frances Westley (1978) in the light of the proliferation of salvational enterprises. Westley draws attention to Durkheim's prediction in *Suicide*, that increasing social differentiation would

result in a situation where the only remaining common element among people in advanced industrial societies would be their humanity: 'Since human personality is the only thing that appeals unanimously to all hearts, since its enhancement is the only aim that can be collectively pursued, it inevitably acquires exceptional value in the eyes of all. It thus rises far above all human aims, assuming a religious nature.' (Durkheim, 1952: 336). Westley, following Durkheim, argues that people need 'an arena in which to express and ritually enact [their] relationship to society' (1978: 137). Thus, the form of religious expression appropriate to contemporary individualism, is the 'cult of man', celebrating and worshipping an idealisation of the individual.

That a highly differentiated individualistic society is likely to generate a multiplicity of religious forms, some of which celebrate and encourage the full realisation of the self, is scarcely at issue. What is more problematic, of course, is a feature of Durkheim's theory of religion which has *always* been questionable, namely that a complex differentiated society requires a common set of values as the basis for social integration. Moreover, it is far from being self-evident that the diverse – and often mutually hostile – forms of contemporary individualistic movement provide any substantial basis for widespread social solidarity. They may *reflect* the society which generated them, but that they function to enhance its social integration seems altogether more doubtful. Finally, it is arguable whether the individualistic groups to which Westley refers would have been recognised by Durkheim as exemplifications of the 'cult of man' or 'religion of humanity' (cf. Lukes, 1969).

Colin Campbell has advanced a somewhat similar argument, drawing more upon Ernst Troeltsch than Emile Durkheim. He argues that the new religious movements display a resurgence of what Troeltsch has called 'spiritual and mystical' religion, in the face of secularisation, i.e. the 'decline of church religion' (Campbell, 1978: 149-50). Campbell argues that:

> Clearly from this perspective, the evidence of a turning away from churchly religion could be given a very different meaning from that presented by the proponents of the secularisation thesis. Indeed, it would be seen to imply its very denial. (ibid.: 150)

He sees the individualism of spiritual and mystical religion as peculiarly well adapted to modern industrial societies, along with its tolerance and syncretism. However, although it is undeniable that mystical and spiritual forms of religion have emerged, it is by no means clear that they are either the largest or the most significant. Many of the major new religious movements have a decidedly *sectarian* rather than mystical character in Troeltsch's sense: Unification Church, Children of God, ISKCON, etc., and these are far from being *individualistic* or tolerant. Campbell does not demonstrate that mystical and spiritual forms of religion

are numerically dominant among the new religions, nor does he
show - as, indeed, it would be very difficult to show - that they
can account for anything more than a tiny fraction of those who
have turned away from churchly religion, and thus that they do
effectively represent a 'denial' of secularisation.

The idea that secularisation is somehow a 'self-limiting'
phenomenon, the reversal of which is manifested in the new
religious movements is a theme vigorously argued also by Rodney
Stark and William S. Bainbridge.

THE STARK-BAINBRIDGE THEORY[2]

The theory begins from the premise that people seek to gain
rewards, that is, things they are prepared to expend costs to
secure. Some rewards which people seek are scarce or unavailable.
When highly desired rewards seem not to be available directly,
they are prepared to accept *compensators* instead. Since this
term is crucial, we should be clear about its meaning:

(1)   Compensators are a form of I.O.U. They promise that in
      return for value surrendered now, the desired reward
      will be obtained eventually. (Stark, 1981 p:161)

(2)   Compensators postulate the attainment of the desired
      reward in the distant future or in some other unverifiable
      context. Compensators are treated by humans as if they
      were rewards. (Bainbridge and Stark, 1979 p: 284)

(3)   Compensators are postulations of reward according to
      explanations that are not readily susceptible to unambigu-
      ous evaluation. (Stark and Bainbridge, 1980 p. 121)

(4)   . . . compensators are intangible substitutes for a desired
      reward. (Stark and Bainbridge, 1980 p: 121)

Compensators may be specific, such as a cure for warts, or
general, such as a means of securing immortality, a greatly transformed world, or a meaning to life. Some desired rewards are 'of
such a magnitude and scarcity that only by assuming the existence
of an active supernatural can credible compensators be created.'
(Stark 1981 p: 162) Hence, as long as people seek such rewards,
naturalistic systems of belief will be unable to compete with
religious ones in the production of credible compensators.

Two things follow from this. First secularisation is a self-
limiting process, and where major religious denominations succumb,
they will be replaced by new faiths of a more supernaturalistic
kind offering more credible compensators. Second, organisations
that address themselves to the 'biggest and most persistent
human desires' will tend to 'shift from naturalistic to supernaturalistic premises' (Stark, 1981 p: 170). The failure of rewards
to materialise will lead to the substitution of compensators and the

introduction of the supernatural as their credible source:

> in pursuit of goals of immense value which cannot be obtained
> through direct means, humans will tend to create and exchange
> compensators. . . . Not only do naturalistic organisations lack
> the resources for great compensators which are present in
> religions, but when they get too close to the matters with
> which only religion can deal, they tend to become religious
> too. (Stark, 1981 p: 173)

The cases of Synanon, The Process and Scientology are analysed
in these terms (Stark, 1981), and elsewhere (Bainbridge and
Jackson, 1981), that of Transcendental Meditation. This aspect
of the theory will be considered in chapter six. Here I wish to
examine critically the evidence advanced for the 'self-limiting'
nature of secularisation and the role of new religious movements,
and to offer some general criticisms of the theory.

Stark and Bainbridge regard secularisation as a constant
feature of the life-cycle of religious organisations. Religious
organisations, particularly those which are successful, fail to
maintain a high level of tension with the surrounding society
and drift towards churchly accommodation. A high incidence of
such transitions within a religious tradition will tend to undermine its credibility (Stark, 1983). But secularisation stimulates
revival through the emergence of sectarian schisms within the
tradition, and *innovation* of new faiths drawing upon sources
outside the prevailing tradition. Such innovations, Stark and
Bainbridge define as 'cults'. While the *sources* of religion may
vary within a society, on this theory the *amount* of religion will
remain relatively constant, due to the persistence of desires for
unavailable or scarce rewards of such magnitude that only
religion can provide credible compensators.

Stark and Bainbridge marshal a diverse range of evidence in
support of their claim that secularisation is limited by the
emergence of new religions offering more credible compensators.
They show that the number of sects, i.e. schismatic movements
within a religious tradition, tends to be high where churches are
relatively strong, but that lower rates of church involvement tend
to be associated with higher rates of cult formation and growth.
Thus, they argue that a decline in church religion gives rise
to revivalism and religious innovation in reaction, i.e. that as a
religious tradition begins to go into decline it first gives rise to
revivalist sectarianism in an effort to salvage that tradition.
However, after a certain point the tradition becomes unsalvageable,
at which time cults emerge with unprecedented vigour.

Stark and Bainbridge argue that from among these cults will,
in time, emerge a new religion which will establish a new tradition,
restoring a constant amount of religion in the society, albeit
now focused on a new dominant source. But the evidence advanced
is not, at the end of the day, entirely persuasive. To show that
new faiths may arise when old ones decay is not at issue. It is,

after all, no more than could be expected simply in terms of *availability* for recruitment. Where old faiths are strong - as in Ulster - there is no market at all, or at best only a very limited one, for new faiths. New movements will take the form, as Stark and Bainbridge predict, of more sectarian variants of prevailing traditions. Where many are unchurched, however, *some* will doubtless be available for recruitment to new faiths. What is important here - as in the case of Colin Campbell and others who claim that the new religions replace churchly decline - is not *how many cults* there are per million of the population and the like, but the *ratio of those recruited* to new religious movements *relative to the total lost* by the old faiths. Outside the Bay Area of California, the evidence suggests that the new faiths have made negligible inroads into the mass of the unchurched, who remain indifferent to organised religion of any sort. The scale of the decline in the major denominations and that of the growth of the new religious movement is simply not comparable. Church attendance in Britain appears to have dropped from around 40 per cent in the mid nineteenth century to around 10 per cent in the mid-twentieth century (Wilson, 1969). New religious movements can claim to have made little impression on such decline. The Protestant churches in Britain lost over half a million members between 1970 and 1975 alone, during which time the conservative churches that were growing gained about 14,000 new members, making no impression on the overall decline (Brierley, 1978; Currie, Gilbert and Horsley, 1977). In 1975, less than 20 per cent of the United Kingdom population claimed church membership (Brierley, 1978), leaving approximately 34 million adults available for recruitment to new religious movements. In these circumstances, the suggestion that the new religious movements - with, for example, 588 resident British Moonies in 1980 (Barker, 1981: 64), or 536 British Children of God in 1981 (*Family Education Book of the Month*, No. 1, May 1982: 12) - are an effective response, making an impact upon any substantial number of the unchurched, is scarcely compelling.

It is, of course true that numbers of those who have some contact with the world-affirming movements can range up to the hundreds of thousands, but in these cases some account needs to be taken of the character and extent of that contact. While many thousands may be initiated into TM or take the *est* training, the effect of these activities, lightly taken up and just as lightly dropped, is relatively slight for most of those concerned. Enduring impact and involvement is a relatively rare phenomenon. Many people will sample sequentially among a range of the movements and activities of a world affirming kind - signifying the transient character of the impact of each particular practice. They thus offer little support - even on the most generous estimation - for the thesis of the self-limiting nature of secularisation.

Stark and Bainbridge may claim that new religions appear as more or less random mutations, and that the one most adapted to the present circumstances, due to grow into a vast new faith and tradition, has not yet appeared or taken off into rapid growth, *although it will* do so before too long. But that is of course, to do no more than express a pious hope, to engage in prophecy rather than prediction. Some of the more general difficulties with this theory can be shown through a consideration of its key concepts of *compensator* and *reward*.

The concept of compensator is a slippery one. It is contrasted with that of reward, which is anything someone is prepared to expend costs to obtain, but seems not entirely comparable in scope. A compensator is not only something which people are prepared to expend costs to obtain (and thus a subset of rewards), it is also the *promise* of a future reward, and an *explanation* of how such a reward may be secured. A compensator is a form of reward not only because people are prepared to expend costs to obtain it, but because, according to Stark and Bainbridge (1980: 117), 'explanations are rewards of some level of generality.' This would appear to introduce a significant element of tautology into the claim that when rewards are not immediately available, people will often be prepared to accept compensators instead. It certainly undermines any force in the claim that people 'treat' compensators as rewards, or that they 'mistake' the former for the latter. Since explanations *are* rewards by definition, people cannot merely 'treat' them as such, nor be 'mistaken' about this.

But part of the difficulty of having a concept like compensator with its three elements of reward, promise of future reward, and explanation of how to achieve future reward, is that the force of the argument advanced may derive from slipping between one meaning and another. That being unable to secure scarce rewards now we will be likely to accept mere promises for the future (compensators) seems somehow a more telling point than that being unable to secure scarce rewards now we may be likely to accept explanations of how we can secure them at some time in the future after following appropriate procedures. But in the latter case, how useful - or alternatively, how misleading - is the label of 'compensator'? Explanations are not substitutes for rewards, nor can they be compared with them. Whether rewards are plentiful and immediately present, or scarce and distant, they will have explanations as to how they may be obtained. It is *explanations* of how to secure proximal rewards that should be compared with *explanations* of how to obtain scarce and distant rewards, not rewards on the one hand and explanations on the other. A description of how to achieve something can hardly be a substitute for something difficult of attainment. The reward is not abandoned as impossible to secure and the explanation accepted *instead*; rather the reward is actively sought in a new location and an account of how one is to acquire it is adopted.

It may be, of course, that if one reward is not available or difficult to obtain, we may aspire to some other reward instead. If we cannot be loved by our spouses, perhaps we can be respected by our colleagues. If happiness in this life is not obtainable, then we might be prepared to look for it elsewhere. In that sense, one reward may substitute for another or provide some compensation. In the second case, we may be prepared to accept the promise of a reward in a future life for what we cannot have now, but the promise does not substitute for the tangible this-worldly reward. It may make present misery easier to endure while we wait to secure that reward in the future, but it is only the future *reward* itself that can substitute for what we cannot have here and now.

The problem lies, however, not only in the Stark-Bainbridge notion of compensators but also in their view of rewards. Rewards seem to be acceptable to Stark and Bainbridge under that label only if they are (1) tangible, (2) concrete, and (3) immediate. Anything else somehow becomes merely symbolic, unreal and thus a substitute for some present gratification. But such a view is not sustainable. Interest on a bank deposit may not be immediate but it is none the less tangible, when, in the future, it arrives. Some rewards are not sought immediately. A long life may be highly desirable and even scarce but it is not sought *now*. Rather it is a desired future increment to what one might otherwise expect, and the advice of brokers on investments, of doctors on smoking, are thus not compensators, substitutes for future rewards, but only sound guidance on how to secure them. Moreover, intangibility does not render something a spurious reward. There may or may not be good evidence for life after death, but it may be sought by people who have an abundance in this world simply as another valuable asset worth securing if it is going and thus not as a substitute for anything at all.

Stark and Bainbridge have implicitly assumed too simple a model of reward. They draw a sharp contrast between the concrete and immediate as opposed to the distant and intangible. It is clear that what they really believe is that rewards comprise only the former, and the latter are thus only something that people will accept if the concrete and immediate gratifications cannot be secured. Their conceptualisation of human desires is a highly materialistic one. They fail to see that rewards may fall anywhere within the range defined by their poles of the immediate and the distant. What they identify as firmly opposed and sharply distinct are, at best, distinguished only as a matter of degree. If we desire wealth, we desire it not only today but tomorrow and next year. Similarly, the desire for immortality is a desire not only to live forever, but to live today and tomorrow as well. Stark and Bainbridge assume that the promises of religion cannot be desired for their own sake, rather than as substitutes for something else. In their assumption that there is something inherently faulty or unsatisfactory in religion, that it could never be desired except as compensation for something better (because this-worldly and immediate), Stark and Bainbridge build into their theory premises which are *substantively atheistic* (rather than merely methodologically atheistic in Berger's sense). They thus repeat the reductionist errors of Durkheim, Marx and Freud in construing religion as reducible to mundane considerations. (For a more extended critique of this theory, see Wallis and Bruce, 1983.)

'CIVIL RELIGION' AND NEW RELIGIOUS MOVEMENTS

Another approach to the relationship between secularisation and the new religious movements emerges from Robert Bellah's notion of 'civil religion', first advanced in the 1960s:

> there are . . . certain common elements of religious orientation that the great majority of Americans share. These . . . provide a religious dimension for the whole fabric of American life, including the political sphere. This public religious dimension is expressed in a set of beliefs, symbols and rituals that I am calling the American civil religion. (Bellah, 1970: 171)

In subsequent writing, Bellah (1975) has alleged that 'today the American civil religion is an empty and broken shell.' Undermined by the Vietnam War, Watergate, repression of the civil rights and anti-war movements, and the like, consensual civil religion in America has broken down, leading to a situation of crisis:

> The new religions that flourished in the seventies are survivors of the crisis of meaning that characterised the sixties. They articulate variations of countercultural values of spontaneity and 'love', while sometimes evolving composite symbol systems that accommodate these values to resurgent utilitarian individualism. (Anthony and Robbins, 1982a: 217)

Dick Anthony and Thomas Robbins have been the principal exponents of the view that the new religious movements have their origins in a reaction to the crisis in American civil religion. They 'represent systematized responses to the moral ambiguity that arose from the decline of traditional civil religion and the moral system of implicit legitimation' (Anthony and Robbins, 1982a: 231). Their recent formulations of this idea – as the last quotation demonstrates – link the decline of civil religion to Habermas's conception of a 'legitimation crisis'.
Essentially Anthony and Robbins argue that the crisis of civil religion has led to a need for new moral meaning systems: 'Contemporary new religions . . . can . . . be viewed as putative public theologies attempting to formulate new approaches to civil religion and the meaning of America' (Anthony and Robbins, 1981: 10). They argue that the new religious movements take two forms, embodying distinct strategies, 'for coping with the decline of civil religion' (ibid.: 17). *Dualistic* movements 'reaffirm elements

of traditional moral absolutism in an exaggerated and strident manner', while *monistic* movements 'affirm relativistic and sub-jectivistic moral meaning systems' (Robbins, Anthony and Richardson, 1978: 101). Dualistic movements, such as the Unification Church, People's Temple and Synanon, are referred to as 'civil religion sects' which 'promise a revitalised synthesis of political and religious themes as the basis for crystallising personal identities. Such groups look toward the restoration of a national convenant and the recreation of a virtuous republic. . . .' (Anthony and Robbins, 1981: 17). 'On the other hand, privatistic mystical religions - Yoga [sic] Bhajan and Tibetan Buddhism - and quasi-mystical therapeutic movements - *est* and Scientology - implicitly reject the insertion of nationalistic or political themes in spiritual life' (ibid.).

This theory has a number of problems at a variety of levels. First, it displays too little close acquaintance with the aims and aspirations of a number of the groups thus described. Scientology may not manifest any enthusiasm for nationalism, but to say that it rejects the insertion of political themes in spiritual life is entirely to disregard its proclaimed intention to 'bring the whole world under the Org board', i.e. to run the whole world on Scientology lines. Second, none of the advocates of this theory appear to feel the need to produce any evidence for their claim that the movements are a response to a crisis of civil religion. One can see some sense in such a claim in the case of movement like the Unification Church which so explicitly presents a message of America's divine mission and the need for integration around traditional moral values and political principles. But how can those movements displaying *no* such themes be said to constitute a response to the decline in civil religion independent of other evidence? No such evidence has been presented, and what remains to be demonstrated is simply assumed to be true.

Third, even the cases of the alleged 'civil religion sects' present difficulties. It is far from clear that a movement such as Synanon aspired to provide a 'public theology' as the basis for a renewed consensus around American traditions and institutions. It is equally unclear that movements such as Synanon or the People's Temple arose out of moral ambiguity or were in any way a reaction to it. Certainly no evidence to that effect has been presented. Indeed, the term 'civil religion sect' seems to be applied to any new religious movement that incorporates political themes in its ideology, to the effect that spiritual victory will entail social structural transformation. The term 'civil religion sect' simply imports as fact a theoretical premise that must be demonstrated, namely that such movements have any relationship to American civil religion.

However, the most fundamental problem lies in the fact that this usage assumes the validity of the underlying theory of civil religion as articulated by Bellah and others. Bellah claimed to be able to identify an institutionalised collection of beliefs and symbols embodying the common elements of all major creeds in

America, and providing the basis for integration around a common system of beliefs and symbols, and a set of rituals such as Memorial Day, Thanksgiving, Veterans' Day, etc. through which common identities and commitments could be reaffirmed. Political and public life in America, Bellah argues, is – at its best – organised around 'a genuine apprehension of universal and transcendent religious reality as seen in, or one could almost say, as revealed through the experience of the American people' (Bellah, 1967: 12).

Now while the bulk of American commentators have endorsed this theory wholeheartedly, some at least appear to share my doubts as to the adequacy of Bellah's formulation. John Wilson, for example, is perfectly clear as to the presence of religious themes in public ritual and the like, but argues that Bellah's accounts display an equivocation as to whether

> public religion is to be understood as a separate and differentiated religion, identifiable by means of comparison with and contrast to other positive religious cults in the society. Alternatively, it may be conceived as a dimension or aspect of the society which is present 'in, with, and under' the whole, possibly including the specific religious traditions conventionally identified as such. (John F. Wilson, 1979: 144-5)

He argues that Bellah's (1967) essay 'seems to have embodied, or may even have been constructed upon, systematic ambiguity' (ibid.: 148). But further problems arise when one inquires how such rituals and symbols are to be explained. Following the lead of Durkheim, proponents of the civil religion thesis appear to hold that they emerge from the functional prerequisite of a society for a system of common values and sentiments, and of rituals to reaffirm and re-evoke those values and sentiments. Such a theory asserts more than that such rituals have these effects – which may or may not be true – but that it is *because* they have these effects that they are performed.

Bellah and his followers produce no evidence that such rituals do in fact have the effect of social integration, but that is not crucial. In a self-regulating system, such as a central heating system, it is still the *function* of the increased fuel supply fed to the burner to produce a temperature of 65 degrees fahrenheit on a cold day, whether or not it actually achieves that goal (Ryan, 1970: 172-96). What is more crucial is that in a feedback system like that of central heating, we can see how failure to achieve its goal generates increased fuel supply through the operation of the thermostat. What Bellah and others fail to offer is any account of the way in which the system operates to generate increased ritual when its goal of social integration is not achieved, or the way in which such feedback might be accomplished.

Lest it be claimed that the feedback mechanisms of the central heating system are less analogically appropriate than the functioning of the biological organism, it should be said that the problem nonetheless remains. The operation of the lungs are explained in terms of the need to provide oxygen for the operation of the muscles. We explain the increased activity of the lungs by reference to the increased activity of the muscles, creating an oxygen deficit. First, it must be said that although for purposes of economy we may use functional language to explain the increased activity of the lungs, this statement could be unpacked in terms of causal statements specifying the feedback chain – quite unlike Bellah's claims regarding civil religion. Moreover, we are able to specify quite precisely what will happen to the system should the function not be fulfilled. At the social system level this can never be achieved beyond the vaguest metaphor and prophecy. Not only do we have no conception of the feedback mechanisms involved, but we lack any objective specification of system malfunction and 'death' arising from the failure to perform the functions attributed to civil religion.

My own view is that there need be no single explanation of civil ritual and religious themes in public ceremonial pronouncements at all. I see no reason to believe that we need any further explanation of Memorial Day services and the like in America than those offered by the participants themselves, which are likely to take the form: these services are held to enable us to remember the sacrifices of those who died during the two world wars; unless that further explanation is also purposive in character, for example: Memorial Day services are held in this church because the minister sees it as a good way of getting people into church who otherwise rarely attend. Coronation services (cf Shils and Young, 1953; Birnbaum, 1955) and Presidential Inaugurations (Bellah, 1976) seem in need of no more mysterious explanation than that provided by a purposive formulation: such rituals are performed because in the light of tradition, people regard them as legitimating the status transitions which they serve to mark. They form part of a class of rituals, such as marriages, funerals and the like, which whilst often born as religious ceremonials, have become increasingly secularised, and in common with them, have as their primary purpose the marking of status passage. There is, of course, a further sense in which ceremonial can sometimes serve a function, but again a function for certain individuals, not for society (except in so far as those individuals see the two as being the same thing – as in 'What's good for General Motors is good for America'). That is, it may very well be the case that the initiators of the ceremonial may believe that civic rituals have integrating effects for society. They see them as achieving goals which they, possessing vested interests in the established order, value highly. Thus, if heightened integration does result, the ritual can be said to have functioned to achieve their goals. Since at least some prime ministers and presidents and other political personages do indeed see civic rituals (along with other activities such as military conflict) as promoting, however transitorily, social harmony and collective enthusiasm for the established order, and foster them for that reason, then

it would appear that they thereby show themselves more sceptical
and self-aware than the sociologists who analyse them.

In the same measure, the civil religion hypothesis to explain
religious references by American presidents at Inauguration, or
in State of the Union addresses, seems rather less plausible than
the claim that politicians are wont to dignify their often self-
interested motives for pursuing or retaining office, their often
sordid and immoral political behaviour while in office, and otherwise to legitimate expediency, in terms of whatever rhetoric
lies to hand. The more traditionally respectable the rhetoric, the
more likely it is to be employed.

The dependence of the Anthony and Robbins theory upon the
deeply flawed civil religion formulation must inevitably, and
fatally, undermine its persuasive potential.

Robert Bellah's theme of a breakdown in civil religion leading to
'moral ambiguity', rehearsed by Anthony and Robbins in numerous papers (once again, for example in Anthony and Robbins,
1982b), is also developed by Steven Tipton. Tipton's argument is
that, 'Youth of the sixties have joined alternative religious movements of the seventies and eighties basically . . . to make moral
sense of their lives' (Tipton, 1982a: 185). (This is a claim
advanced more cautiously in Tipton, 1979: 286, and in his book,
Tipton, 1982b). Tipton's proposal is well taken, that various
types of new religious movement articulate in different ways with
the expressive ethic of the counter-culture and the prior ethical
systems of biblical religion and utilitarian individualism, and thus
provided a range of means of accommodating with the wider society
in the face of the disintegration of the counter-culture. Something of this argument is represented by the 'integrative
hypothesis' to be considered in the next chapter, which sees
a movement such as the Jesus People as providing a road back to
accommodation with the wider society for 60s and early 70s
dropouts. Neo-Fundamentalism clearly involves a reaffirmation of
traditional moral certainties in the face of contemporary relativism;
just so, also with a movement such as the Unification Church, with
its clear, and largely traditional, moral prescriptions. Moreover,
the guilt-alleviating thrust of ideological themes in *est* and the
Human Potential Movement are evident enough. Yet, to point
to those consequences of belief in such movements is not to
demonstrate that these 'latent functions' provide the motivation
for membership, and while Tipton is convincing in his demon-
stration that the movements he examines do promote such
consequences, he offers little conclusive evidence that it was in
virtue of these reasons that people joined them. Moreover, there
are many movements for which the argument might be hard to
defend. Scientology has no substantial concern with moral issues,
nor Transcendental Meditation, and an authoritarian movement
such as the Children of God scarcely eliminates moral ambiguities,
but rather constantly thrusts the convert into new ones.
Unfortunately, Tipton has accepted too narrow a conception of the
causal background to recruitment to the new religions. While

making 'moral sense of their lives' may sometimes have played a part in the recruitment of some members, and perhaps more so in some movements than in others, it is evidently only one among a wide range of motives, and Tipton would have to adduce rather more apposite evidence to demonstrate that it was even one of the most important among the available reasons for joining.

A related theory has been advanced by Frederick Bird (1979), who argues that the new religions, 'tend to encourage among their adherents a reduced sense of moral accountability . . . and it constitutes for participants one of the appealing aspects of these new religions' (ibid.: 335). This theory seems susceptible to the same sorts of criticism as that of Tipton. While it may be true for some converts and especially true for certain movements, the theory overgeneralises a limited and particular feature into a universal explanation. The rigorous moral lives of Unification Church members or ISKCON devotees scarcely seem designed to reduce a sense of moral accountability. Indeed 'Moonies' are particularly prone to articulate a sense of intense moral responsibility, not only for their own sins and behaviour, but that of the whole world. I find no obvious way in which life is less morally accountable for the 'Moonie', or the disciple of Brother Evangelist (Martin, 1979) after, as compared to before, his conversion. Nor do I find the evidence compelling that such considerations predominate among those which lead individuals to join the new religions. It is undoubtedly one consideration to emerge on occasion, but the evidence simply will not support its elevation to the status of sole explanatory factor.

THE 'WILSONIAN' PERSPECTIVE

A somewhat different approach to the relationship between secularisation and the new religious movements is to be found in the work of Bryan Wilson. Wilson regards secularisation as a major trend in western societies, echoing Max Weber on this point. Routinisation and rationalisation affect all of us, although to differing degrees, and those most actively implicated in the bureaucratic, technical, industrial structures and processes of our society, are likely to be more resistant than those marginal to such institutions and processes, to counter-secularising innovations (Wilson, 1976: 39–40). It is among the young or among those in craft, personal service or independent professional employment (such as actors or designers), who are more likely to be available to, and motivated by, a resurgence of religious forms and ideas. (The corporate bureaucrat may remain a conventional denominational attender, but if he looks for new means of salvation, it is more likely to be acceptable if presented in rationalistic dress; thus, he may be in the market for TM or Scientology, but is much less likely to be attracted by Krishna Consciousness or the Jesus People. The explicitly religious is only likely to be acceptable as an 'added blessing', as in Neo-Pentecostalism.)

New religious movements, either generated locally, or imported
from culturally alien surroundings, compete with each other and
with other available leisure activities for the interest and loyalty
of the potential consumer groups:

> There is a profusion of styles to choose from and because the
> new movements have lost their local social base, they have much
> less significance for the social system in which they emerge.
> Like other leisure-time pursuits, they are a free choice which,
> providing that the law is not breached, are part of that con-
> sumption economy in which men can do as the modern phrase
> has it, 'their own thing'. (Wilson, 1976: 43-4)

Thus, for Wilson, the new religious movements in the West (in
contrast to those in Japan, for example, see Wilson, 1982) are, as
he puts it in a passage of characteristic elegance, a:

> confirmation of the process of secularisation. They indicate the
> extent to which religion has become inconsequential for modern
> society. The cults represent in the American phrase, 'the
> religion of your choice', the highly privatised preference that
> reduces religion to the significance of pushpin, poetry, or
> popcorns. They have no real consequence for other social
> institutions, for political power structures, for technological
> constraints and controls. They add nothing to any prospective
> reintegration of society, and contribute nothing towards the
> culture by which a society might live. (ibid.: 96)

These movements, Wilson avers, are 'irrelevant' to modern
western society. They reject the instrumental rationality and
large-scale impersonality upon which its operation is predicated.
They distrust the bureaucratic and the routine and offer
salvation by the application of exotic belief and practice (ibid.:
98). Thus, their essential thrust is contrary to prevailing 'social
order and received cultural values' (ibid.: 99). They are 'random
anti-cultural assertions . . . a congeries of options in a plural
society – a diverse set of options "out"' (ibid.: 110).
  Their very survival is in doubt, since their appeal is based
largely upon spontaneity, exotic novelty and access to ecstasy,
all characteristics readily undermined by institutionalisation.
They typically lack developed techniques and arrangements for
the socialisation of members' children. They offer a virtuoso
religion to those prepared to break with the conventional world,
thus limiting the extent to which they can affect, or recruit from,
the mass of the population. Their appeal to youth is in itself a
limitation since 'tomorrow's youth may make its generational
protest in different terms' (ibid.: 112).
  Wilson thus incisively demolishes the claim that the new religions
herald a significant reaction against the broad trend of secularisation, 'against which the cults are likely to be no more than
transient and volatile gestures of defiance' (ibid.: 112). Yet this

picture would seem better to represent those movements which did
primarily articulate a protest against the world. Elsewhere,
Wilson has argued that a movement such as Charismatic Renewal
also exemplifies the path of secularisation, constituting an
example of the very fragmentation of the Christian tradition.
Moreover, the Charismatic movement clearly involves an attempt
to recover a sense of immediacy, of affective impact, of experiental
content in a religious practice which has seen considerable
attenuation of such features in recent times. (For a fine study
of the way in which Catholic Pentecostalism re-sacralises the
world, reintroducing much of the magic and mystery lost within
the Catholic Church due to secularisation, particularly since
Vatican II, see McGuire, 1982. This study unfortunately came to
hand too late to be utilised effectively in this work, but would
have provided a rich and valuable source.)

But what of the world-affirming movements? Wilson does not
address these quite so explicitly, except to imply that they are
so much an element of the contemporary leisure consumer market,
that their potential for dramatically affecting the wider framework
of social relations is limited indeed. These movements have
embraced the individualism, the rationality, the bureaucracy, the
impersonality and the consumerism of the modern western world.
So too, they have embraced its secularity. Their residual commitment to occult forms and powers, and the naturalising and tech-
nologising of their approach to them, display little potential for
the re-sacralising of the world. Moreover, they remain largely a
feature of the private life of individuals. World-rejecting movements may dream of a vast restructuring of the public domain
from their location on the margins and in the interstices of
western industrial societies, while the world-affirming movements,
appealing more to a professional and managerial constituency
more centrally located in the modern world, provide resources for
the reconstruction of private life, experience and identity, and
make only the rarest assault upon prevailing public institutions
and practices.

The world-rejecting movement may remain defiantly religious in
its hostility to the status quo - indeed extreme rejection in
modern western society almost inevitably moves towards a religious
rhetoric as the antithesis of those features inveighed against -
yet it does so at the price of being isolated and numerically
insignificant. The world-affirming movement can gain widespread
support beyond a cadre of virtuosi, but only at the price of
commitment to the prevailing order, *including* its secularity. The
world-accommodating movement revives an explicitly religious
commitment, principally among a segment of those whose religious
institutions have gradually succumbed before the onslaught of
secularisation, and for them too, represents a private reassertion
rather than a public transformation. As Wilson so compellingly
puts it:

But will such new movements become a source of new values for

society as a whole? Not, certainly, if they appeal only to
sectional minorities nor if they remain so widely diverse in
orientation and structure; nor yet again if they fail to acquire
purchase on any facet of the institutional structure. They
persist in offering their solutions in what may be called the
evangelical mode, as if private virtue and personal discipline
could transform modern society. That vision might have been
plausible in Victorian England; it is scarcely so now. Making
men new appears to have little impact on the inexorable cost-
efficiency processes of modern economics and technology;
private virtue appears to be irrelevant to public performance
and to modern organization. The new religions may achieve
much for individuals in their personal lives, they may even
create new subcultures into which some men can permanently,
and others occasionally, retreat from the abrasiveness of the
impersonal society of the modern world. But as yet we have
little reason to suppose that they have any likelihood of transforming the structure of society and the alien experience that
it produces into the encompassing community of love, of which
- inside the new religions and out - men still so vividly dream.
(1979: 214-15)

The new religions are a product of secularisation, moving into
the gaps created by the retreat of traditional religious institutions, drawing the most sharply discontented into movements of
radical protest at the margins; or offering more immediate reassur-
ances to those who remain committed to the prevailing order,
either in some more enthusiastic variant upon existing practice,
or - for those who have cut themselves off from the market for
traditional faiths - in a more exotic or more persuasively modern
guise. Where traditional religion remains strong, as in Catholic
southern Europe, or in Ireland, the new religions have little
impact. But even where, as in the secularised world of Protestant
western Europe and North America, a market exists, it is only a
very small proportion of the population who are available for the
more clearly religious of the new movements, and even then often
for only very brief periods during the transition to adulthood.
For others, the new religious commodity is acceptable only as a
voluntary, private, part-time endeavour which may provide
resources to endure the secular world, but in the end provides
no challenge to, or interference with it. For most, of course, in
no matter what form they may manifest themselves, the new
religions are merely a matter of profound indifference.

5 The middle ground and the 'integrative hypothesis'

Although reference has been made to several actual new religious movements which it was felt best exemplified the analytical types, it should be remembered that, in fact, *all* the empirical cases lie somewhere within the conceptual space bounded by the characteristics of each type. That is, all actual new religious movements are likely to combine elements of each type to some extent. It is none the less possible to identify movements that exhibit the characteristics of one more sharply than another, and this has been done in the preceding chapters. It is *also* possible and useful to identify a range of movements, more clearly occupying the middle ground between the types, which possess particular characteristics in virtue of the orientations they combine, and some of which had a special role to play in the context of the collapse of the counter-culture. These latter movements include the Divine Light Mission, the followers of Meher Baba, and those of the Yogi Bhajan in the Healthy-Happy-Holy organisation, as well as large sections of the Jesus People. They combine in varying degrees elements of all three types, and more particularly elements of the conventional society and the counter-culture. Thus, while they may sometimes adopt a communal life-style, they may also encourage members to take, or to retain, 'respectable' jobs in conventional society. While their religious beliefs and practices may be regarded as unorthodox, these movements characteristically forbid or discourage sexual relations between unmarried members and the use of drugs. They often have a rather conservative political philosophy (cf. Gregg, 1973 on a Jesus People group for example).

They do not insist on such a sharp break between members and their families and former friends as is often the case with world-rejecting sects. The institutions of the wider society are not so uniformly condemned, and indeed some aspects of worldly society may be enthusiastically accepted by the sectarians. At the same time, however a new and deviant means of salvation is being offered by the movement which draws upon, and resonates, themes in the youth culture of the advanced societies. Followers of Yogi Bhajan in the Healthy-Happy-Holy Organisation (3HO for short) assume Punjabi names, wear white clothes and turbans, eat only vegetable foods, practise yoga, and the more committed live in communal ashrams. However, as a student of this movement observes, 3HO is not for those seeking an escape from worldly involvements; for marriage, responsible employment, and social service are normative for all its members (Tobey, 1976). Similarly,

members of the Divine Light Mission might at one time, if
sufficiently committed to its practices as a way of life, live
communally in ashrams, eating a vegetarian diet, giving up
tobacco and alcohol, and handing their income and their
possessions into the communal fund. However, 'ashram premies',
as such committed adherents were called, normally continued to
work in the outside world and they might marry. Many, perhaps
most, premies, however, were less committed and attended *satsang*
or inspirational talks at the ashram, but otherwise their lives
changed relatively little after having 'received knowledge' (i.e.
after having been taught the meditational technique) (Price, 1979,
Pilarzyk, 1978b).

Meher Baba was an Indian spiritual master, now deceased,
with a small American following until the mid-1960s when it grew
substantially among young people, including a large proportion of
former drug-users and 'hippies' (Robbins and Anthony, 1972).
Meher Baba proclaimed a message of universal love - of which he
was regarded by his followers as the personified embodiment -
and encouraged the abandonment of drug use. His philosophy of
inner detachment and advocacy of 'selfless service' provided the
basis for a return to conventional work roles of alienated young
people, and thus the potential for reassimilation into careers
abandoned in earlier years.

The Jesus People was the generic title for what was undoubtedly
the best-known movement of the middle ground. It consisted of a
wide range of groups, ministries and evangelistic endeavours
which emerged late in the 1960s. Although they differed considerably in terms of style, details of theology and practice, and pre-
cise mode of social organisation, they shared a commitment to a
fundamentalistic interpretation of the Bible. Their worship
focused on the person of Jesus, but characteristically also
involved a conception of the working of the Holy Spirit through
Pentecostal charismata. This traditional American evangelical
package was synthesised, however, with features of a counter-
cultural way of life. 'Street Christians', as they were sometimes
known, eschewed sex and drugs, but remained attached to hippy
garb, long hair, rock music, and a communal life-style (Ellwood,
1973; Balswick, 1974; Peterson and Mauss, 1973).

Movements of this type occupied in the late 1960s and early
1970s a curiously strategic position between conventional culture
and the counter-culture from which their early recruits were
often drawn. They provided a kind of 'half-way house' through
which former drop-outs, radicals and rebels could pass on their
journey back to conventional society. A number of observers
have commented on the *reintegrating* role of such movements as
the Jesus People, Meher Baba and the Divine Light Mission,
arguing that they functioned as a transitional stage between
counter-culture and final return to conventional society for
individuals who had become thoroughly alienated by the failure
and decay of hippie life, radical politics, drugs, and secular
communitarianism, providing an acceptable route toward rapproche-

ment with the 'respectable' world. Thomas Robbins and Dick
Anthony argue, regarding American followers of Meher Baba,
that their numbers increased substantially after the middle 1960s
and that, 'Most of our respondents had been involved in other
counter-culture expressive milieux prior to involvement with the
group . . . some degree of disillusionment with these milieux
generally preceded cultic involvement' (Robbins and Anthony,
1972: 128). They also argue that, 'Numerous Baba Lovers have
been led to give up illegal drug use . . . *and* either resume
educational career preparation or exchange casual and primarily
menial "odd job" patterns for long-term career involvements.
This change usually involves a concomitant upgrading of social
respectability' (ibid.: 135).

Mauss and Petersen (1974) argue this point strongly, claiming
from their observations that, 'It is difficult to avoid character-
izing the Jesus Freaks . . . as a movement of penitent young
prodigals.' They claim that conversion to the Jesus movement has
allowed stigmatised youth 'to return gradually to the "system"
with a minimum of "culture shock" by providing a kind of "asylum"
or haven from *both* the system and the counter-culture, in which
they could temporarily, at least, retain the *style* of the counter-
culture, while changing their *values and behaviour* in the direction of establishment requirements'. Adams and Fox (1972) argue
similarly that a more intense core of the Jesus People was composed of 'young adults (usually in their twenties) who have
opted out of the drug culture. Many are former peace movement
activists who have dropped out of society over the past four or
five years. For them, the Jesus Movement constitutes a ritual of
re-entry into the system.' (Probably the first to make this point
was James Nolan in a 1971 *Ramparts* article reprinted as Nolan,
1973).

Robbins, Anthony and Curtis more abstractly define the
'integrative hypothesis' as follows:

> that new youth culture religious movements have the con-
> sequences of reconciling and adapting alienated young persons
> to dominant social institutions, and in so doing, they perform
> latent pattern maintenance for the social system. (Robbins,
> Anthony and Curtis, 1975: 49)

They recognise, however, that those who have proposed this
hypothesis have not always been aware of the differences between
youth culture religious movements. They, therefore, distinguish
adaptive and *marginal* movements. Adaptive movements 'facilitate
the reassimilation of converts into conventional vocational and
educational routines' (ibid.: 56). They have in mind such movements as the Jesus People, Divine Light Mission and Meher Baba.
Marginal movements, by contrast, 'actually *remove* members from
conventional pursuits and lock them into social marginality'
(ibid.). They have in mind here such movements as Krishna
Consciousness, the Children of God, and the Unification Church.

However, they argue that even 'marginal' movements may still be 'integrative' in assisting members off drugs and redirecting them from political radicalism. This is not terribly convincing, since the evidence is that the movements do very little to assist young people to abandon drugs. I have found nothing to support this claim in my researches on the Children of God, and Judah (1974: 135) asserts of Krishna devotees that, 'Probably nearly all became disenchanted with drugs before their conversion.' Moreover, there is no evidence that members had been actively politically radical. Indeed, there is some evidence that they were *not* drawn from the more politically involved sections of the counter-culture. Judah found that, 'Many members of the counter-culture became social activists and participated in demonstrations to try to change conditions, but very few of those who later became devotees of Krishna had engaged in such activism' (Judah, 1974: 160).

There is also no reason whatever to believe that converts would have become politically radical had they not found a place for themselves in a 'marginal' movement when they did. James Beckford's investigations led him to conclude that members of the Unification Church were not potentially disruptive or seriously alienated before joining (Beckford, 1978). Hence, the allegedly 'integrative' character of such movements, which yet leads numbers of young people into the thoroughly deviant cognitive and interactive world of the Children of God or Krishna Consciousness, seem to amount to nothing more than a fiction of functionalist theorising.

However, even in the case of 'adaptive' movements, proponents of the integration thesis often overstress the active role of the movement and its beliefs and practices in producing the outcome of a more behaviourally and morally conforming member of society. The limited available evidence tends to show that those who joined the movements of the middle ground having some reintegrative effect were *well on their way back from the margins of society before* they had any contact with the religious movement. Michael McGee's study of twenty-two Meher Baba devotees led him to suggest that although possessing above average educational qualifications:

> Many of the persons in the cult . . . have had a very irregular educational history, a pattern characterised by idealistic and hopeful educational starts, speedy disillusionment, and a glum and angry dropping out. The next step is a dramatic and futile wandering which leads eventually to a partial recovery of faith in mankind, the system, or whatever they have lost faith in, and a return to college to repeat the cycle over again.
> (McGee, 1976: 56)

Converts to movements of this kind were often attracted to them because their beliefs, values and practices were supportive of steps *already taken* in the movement back to conventional social reality encouraging and approving changes in life-style, manners and mores, while at the same time also supporting counter-cultural values and beliefs, to which the returning prodigal still retained some commitment (McGee, 1976: 69).

However, while it is true that some movements of the middle ground played this reintegrating role without realising it, it is also true that in other cases the possibility of using youth cultural styles of music and dress, as part of a *conscious* strategy to win back errant youth from the counter-culture, *had* occurred to some religious activists, particularly among the more fundamentalist and evangelical of the christian denominations in America in the late 1960s. The founders of the Berkeley-based Jesus People group, the Christian World Liberation Front, had previously been active in the conventional evangelical organisation, Campus Crusade (Heinz, 1976a: 1976b). Organisations such as the Full Gospel Businessmen's Fellowship and conventional churches helped to establish and support Jesus People type groups with a ministry to youth, as a means of winning them back from drugs, idleness and sexual promiscuity (Enroth, Ericson and Peters, 1972; Pilarzyk and Jacobson, 1977: 143-4). It is no surprise that movements begun on such a dependent basis were not pronouncedly radical in their social and political views, unless - as in such cases as the Children of God - they escaped the control of representatives of the dominant society (Wallis, 1976a).

It should be stressed, however, that only a limited range of new religions can reasonably be presumed to have played a reintegrating role with the decline of the counter-culture, whether as an intended or as an unintended consequence of their activities. In figure 1 (page 6) this was represented by locating such movements close to the world-accommodating area of the conceptual space. The evidence available on other movements, e.g. The Process, suggests that those attracted in the late 1960s and early 1970s, even if they had any contact with the counter-culture before joining often *remained* socially highly *marginal* on leaving (Bainbridge, 1978).

In a more recent formulation of this argument, Robbins and Anthony (1978) advance what may be either a partial recognition that it was false in its earlier incarnations, or an attempt to rescue it by rendering it irrefutable:

> It is arguable that notwithstanding short run integrative and co-optive trends, the new religions constitute a long run disintegrative force or factor in American society . . . the very existence of the deviant religious movement may reflect significant disintegrative processes in the society which, more-over, may be more significant in the long run than the observed [sic!] integrative consequences associated with these movements and with their institutionalization. (1978: 8, emphasis omitted)

Robbins and Anthony provide no additional grounds for belief in - and I would, therefore, continue to doubt - even the short run integrative character of some of the movements in question. However, they do at least begin to recognise that some movements may have disintegrative consequences, even if they are only prepared to attribute them to the 'long run'. Thus, the addition does nothing to support the integrative hypothesis, and indeed, if anything, only serves to weaken it further, unless it is to be rendered irrefutable by allocating all evidence of disintegration to the category of 'long-run' consequences, while only such evidence as can be construed to indicate the integrative character of the movement is treated as a 'short-run' manifestation. But it is hard to believe that Robbins and Anthony would fall victim to such a logical flaw, and thus we can only assume they have seen something of the weakness of their case, but have not yet entirely freed themselves from the constraints of functionalist conceptualisation.

The essential characteristic of movements of the middle ground, of course, is the fact that they possess in substantial measure characteristics of two or more types. They may, therefore, display considerable ambiguity during their early years about what kind of movement they are, and hence what kinds of recruit to seek. Two examples of this appear to be The Process, and the Divine Light Mission. Both of these movements passed through periods in which they seemed precariously balanced between the communalism of world-rejection, focusing on the messianic and millennialistic aspects of their beliefs on the one hand; and the individualism of world-affirmation, focusing on the therapeutic/self-improvement/self-realisation elements of their beliefs on the other. In their formative years, both movements teetered uneasily sometimes in a more world-rejecting, and sometimes in a more world-affirming direction. Such divergent orientations straining towards different goals, methods and recruits, are likely to provide a major source of conflict and the basis of fission.

William Bainbridge's valuable history and ethnography of The Process (which he calls 'The Power') enables us to trace out this tension through its development. The movement began in London in 1963 as a psychotherapeutic cult, called Compulsions Analysis, and its belief system was originally based around ideas drawn largely from Alfred Adler and from Scientology. Its early clientele were principally drawn from members of the founder, Robert de Grimston's, network of friends and acquaintances. Virtually all were thoroughly middle class, engaged in or training for respectable professional occupations. Compulsions Analysis was a characteristically world-affirming movement except perhaps in the intensity of involvement which it encouraged, among those attracted to it. The gratifications of involvement were such that several abandoned their education or job to pursue its activities full time. The group's ideas began to take on an increasingly spiritual orientation, and to develop a more collectivistic character. The group's ethos rapidly took on a greater hostility to conventional middle-class London life, and its members began to isolate themselves from former friends and acquaintances, abandoning previous activities and aspirations. The subsequent exodus of the group from England, first to the Bahamas and later to the Yucatan peninsula of Mexico, thus largely formalised an early emergent world-rejecting trend. The movement now became The Process, later The Process - Church of The Final Judgement, acquiring in Mexico an elaborate millennial theology based on worship of Christ, Jehovah, Satan and Lucifer. In subsequent wanderings the movement grew to a high point of perhaps 250 full-time members, surviving economically primarily through street begging; and cultivating an 'outrageous' theatrical style in long cloaks, with Satanic insignia and a reputation as devil-worshippers. This theatricality, however, combined with allegations that Charles Manson had been influenced by Process thought provoked public hostility and opposition to the movement. This reaction conflicted with a growing desire among many of the movement's leaders to secure greater approbation from those formerly des-pised as the 'Grey Forces'.

During 1970 and 1971, The Process became more 'open' and conventional as a religious organisation. Lay followers were accepted who did not have to commit themselves *totally* to the movement. They could remain in ordinary jobs, donning Process uniform at weekends, and tithing one-tenth of their earnings. Entry into the church was made easier, with less prior training and probationary waiting. The movement became less mobile, establishing fixed Chapters. In common with other movements with world-rejecting features, The Process was erasing some of those which created the greatest hostility, and directing itself to a constituency (and to an audience) with more conventional expectations.

In many cases, conventionalisation has varied causes: the mobilisation of severe disapproval or social control measures threatening its survival; the disappearance of a constituency seeking quite such radical alternatives to the conventional world; a desire to stabilise or to ensure adequate income; or a desire for worldly status and respectability for the leaders. Bainbridge argues that apart from factors such as these, quite pragmatic and mundane considerations could be influential, such as the need to secure resident alien status, and possibly citizenship in the United States for the British nationals representing themselves as 'Ministers'. 'The more like a conventional religious organization the cult looked, the easier it was to achieve this. Immigration was one of a whole series of practical factors pushing The Power back toward conventionality' (Bainbridge, 1978: 113).

Late in 1973 and early in 1974, this led to a crisis in the move-ment between Robert de Grimston, its founder, who wished to retain the world-rejecting theology and style, and his wife and most other leaders who wished to abandon the publicly disapproved theology and to cultivate a less 'shocking' style, i.e. to continue in the direction of compromise initiated through the changes listed above and those later introduced, such as social work programmes, hospital visiting, etc. De Grimston's favouring of more liberal

sexual relations within the movement was a source of dissension,
but only as part of a broader set of:

> cultural contradictions which had been with The Power since
> the beginning. The cult had sought escape from the world; it
> had sought glory within the world. Both quests had failed, but
> the economic livelihood of the group was now tied to accommoda-
> tion with society. [De Grimston] represented the impractical
> but unrepentant cult desire to transcend the limitations of
> reality. He urged liberation while the Masters had come to
> demand control. (Bainbridge, 1978: 226)

De Grimston was ousted from leadership. The remaining adherents
formed The Foundation - Church of the Millennium, acknowledging
a single god, Jehovah, and presenting a more conventional style
of religious life. De Grimston briefly attempted to restore a
world-rejecting quadrotheistic Process, but without success.

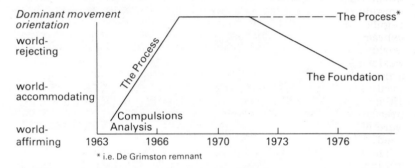

Figure 3   The development of The Process

Since Bainbridge's book was written, the movement has moved
even further in a world-accommodating direction, becoming The
Foundation Faith, and operating in Toronto where I last had
any contact with it in 1979, as The Christian Renewal Centre.
    Having begun as a psychotherapy the movement retained a
certain ambiguity - even at its most intensely world-rejecting
stage - concerning individual, this-worldly self-realisation and
the development of personal power (Bainbridge, 1978: 33). The
Process continued to practise, and members to engage in, various
types of therapy and self-development-orientated exercise throughout this stage (ibid.: 197-223). Bainbridge asserts that many
members possessed phantasies of superhuman personal prowess
(ibid.: 150). It might be said that the ambivalence regarding the
dominant society, or the precarious balance between *affirmation*
and *rejection* of that society, is captured neatly and symbolically
by the movement's worship of Jehovah *and* Lucifer, Christ *and*
Satan. The tension between these two orientations was ultimately
too great to be contained within the same movement, and most of

the following settled for compromise with the world.

The Divine Light Mission emerged on the basis of a meditational technique, but this limited basis of ideological elaboration was supplemented - at least until a massive, but unsuccessful, festival in Houston in 1973 called 'Millennium 73' - by millennialist expectations. The individualism of the meditational technique was balanced by the collective ideal of life in the communal ashrams of the Mission. Pilarzyk (1978a) notes, however, that in 1974, only some 1,200 of an estimated 50,000 American members or 'premies' lived in ashrams, devoting all their earnings to the movement and fully subordinating themselves to its prescriptions. Others lived a less thoroughly disciplined and ascetic life in 'premie houses', joint residences of a group of premies. In the ashram, premies lived in chastity, donating their income often derived from conventional jobs, and obedient to the detailed regulations of their lives by movement leaders. Up to 1973, the Mission was acquiring increasingly the characteristics of a world-rejecting movement (for example, a communal life-style; worship of Guru Maharaj Ji as an incarnation of God; strict regulation of the lives of members, at least those living in the ashram; etc.). Thereafter, it began rapidly to develop a greater world-affirming tendency. The Guru adopted a more conventionally western style of appearance and performance. In 1974, he married his American secretary and broke with his own Indian family and many of the Indian traditions of the Mission (Pilarzyk, 1978a: 37). Celibacy thus became less ideal a state and many premies left the ashram to marry. Subsequently many ashrams were disbanded and communalism was no longer actively encouraged.

The Divine Light Mission was always hinged in considerable ambiguity between rejecting the world of western capitalist society, and affirming it. The Guru clearly enjoyed many features of western life and happily embraced many of its values while the orientation of his Indian relatives and mahatmas was in a more characteristically Hindu world-rejecting direction. Ideologically, the movement had little on which to build except the virtues of an individualistic meditational technique, yet its Guru was presented as a divine saviour about to usher in the Millennium. This ideology provided little normative support for a communal life-style, which was anyway adopted by only a small fraction of adherents. Hence, despite the early drift towards world-rejection it was probably little short of inevitable that the two orientations would come into conflict.

The break with Guru Maharaj Ji's mother, the failure of the Houston festival and ensuing economic crisis, and hostile press reaction to the movement probably all combined to lead the Mission in an individualistic direction at this point (Downton, 1979). A more western style was, adopted, with 'Mahatmas' becoming 'Initiators', and a more rationalised and routinised set of procedures being introduced to prepare for 'taking knowledge' (Armstrong, 1978: 63) and becoming Initiators (Downton, 1979:

192). Guru Maharaj Ji came to be viewed, and presented, in a more secular manner. Administration of the Divine Light Mission became more bureaucratic. Encounter group methods were introduced to premies 'as a way of extending their own growth and augmenting their sense of community' (ibid.: 193).

Some observers, such as Stoner and Parke saw this as a calculated commercial reaction:

> Divine Light leaders seem to think their mission has more of a future if it concentrates on becoming a business which trains people in the techniques of meditation and discipline than it does if it continues as a religion, worshipping the contemporary incarnation of God. (1977: 41)

They claimed that the type of follower tended to change in consequence:

> Once Divine Light proselytized among druggies and dropouts promising a constant high without drugs. . . . But a contemporary . . . recruit is more likely to be a student, musician, artist, lawyer, or teacher – a well-educated man or woman who is, or is destined to become a solid member of the community. (ibid.)

These observations are confirmed by an internal position paper circulated within the movement in 1976 (a copy of which is available in the New Religious Movements collection at the Graduate Theological Union Library, Berkeley) which identified the image towards which Maharaj Ji was moving as 'humanitarian world leader'. It summarises appositely some of the problems to which its world-rejecting stance has led:

> Divine Light Mission must cease to separate itself from the society of which it is a part, and establish co-operative and friendly relationships with other kinds of social groups, i.e. civic, business and so forth. Our isolation from the mainstream of human experience over the past few years threatens to render us entirely ineffective in the field of human affairs.

At this stage, the tension between the individualism and communalism appeared to have been resolved in favour of individualism. The movement seemed set to become the purveyor of its meditational technique as a consumer commodity to businessmen and professionals rather than as a sacred life-style for ex-hippies. However, late in 1976, this trend was again reversed with an unanticipated 'charismatic revival'. Guru Maharaj Ji displaced the organisational leadership of the movement, encouraged a return to ashram life and a restoration of his own status as 'Lord' and 'Messiah' (Downton, 1979: 196-203). Eastern practices and ritual returned, but the pendulum in each of these areas did not swing as far back as their location in the early 1970s. Whatever the

ultimate outcome of these shifts, they clearly exemplify the
presence of a tension between world-rejection and world-
affirmation, communalism and individualism, and the concrete
implications of changing orientations.

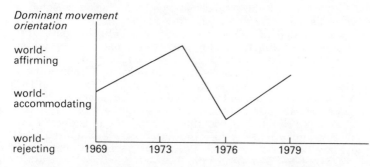

Figure 4 The development of the Divine Light Mission

Arthur Parsons's (1974) analysis of a Kundalini Yoga group
lead by a follower of Yogi Bhajan, founder of 3HO, suggests a
developmental path for this movement similar to that for the
Divine Light Mission prior to 1976 also. Attractive initially to
hippies and still, at the time of his observations, drawing mainly
upon the socially isolated, who found 'human warmth and
expressiveness . . . within the Yoga community' (1974: 228),
none the less, he observes that:

> The world of Karma was not refused; they actively desired to
> improve their mundane roles through the possession of God-
> consciousness. Hence they covertly qualified their world-
> rejection; they hoped to return to the world with a more
> dominating stature. . . . Ultimately the proof of Kundalini's
> authenticity was sought in the enhancement of mundane
> identities. (Parsons, 1974: 229)

Some groups manage to find ways of institutionalising to a
considerable degree the different orientations, so as to minimise
tensions between them. Nordquist's study of Ananda Co-operative
Village is suggestive here. Nordquist (1978: 32) indicates that,
in its early years, such tensions were quite clearly manifest; for
example around 1969, he says:

> There were many different ideas as to what Ananda should be.
> A whole set of dichotomies of spectrums [sic] existed. One
> . . . was 'free expression vs self-discipline', another was
> 'communal vs individualistic' ideas.

These tensions eventually led to a schism in which the more
individualist-oriented left the community. But Ananda retained

a high degree of openness to the world, and continued to provide
facilities and resources for persons whose attachment was far
from total. A differentiated arrangement subsequently evolved to
cope with the differing levels of commitment and world-rejection/
accommodation. The Friends of God, a monastic order, was formed
in 1971, to provide for those who had most thoroughly rejected
the world: 'this monastic order was formed for all the single
members who decided to follow the more strict religious path of
renunciation – forsaking family life and traditional worldly
obligations' (Nordquist, 1978: 35). Those unwilling to break with
the world so radically may live as householders in a family with
its own residence, with a job in the outside world from which they
can make the monthly payments required of each member or
family. However, although not making so complete a break with
the world as the Friends of God, the householder is expected to
commit himself and his family to a life entailing a substantial level
of ego and familial subordination. Nordquist quotes the community's
Membership Guidelines of 1976:

> The householder, as well as the monk or nun, should live his
> life in a spirit of renunciation. At Ananda, this means seeing
> service to the community as an important form of one's *dharma*
> (spiritual duty). It is essential to understand that Ananda is
> not a place for individual families to enjoy a country life
> centred on their own personal interests. The ideal for the
> family is the yogic household based on the spiritual ideals of
> selflessness and loving service to God, Guru, and the larger
> family. Being a householder at Ananda means constant striving
> to view service to the individual family within a context of
> service to the community – and this as a means of serving God.
> (Nordquist, 1978: 46)

However, for those with a more evidently world-accommodating
orientation, there is the 'Apprentice Program' which involves
courses in yoga, meditation, organic gardening, bee-keeping,
wood-working, etc., for visitors who come for a two-month
stay for which they pay $100 plus working for the community. So
far, Ananda seems successfully to have resolved the divergent
tensions between being a monastic order of world-renunciates
and a 'New Age' holiday camp.
    While a shift towards greater accommodation with the world may
be the norm, in the case of Catholic Pentecostalism we may have
a reverse pattern in that it has been argued that two types of
leadership exist within the movement, one of which is more open,
inclusive, democratic, and deferential to church authority (i.e.
more world-accommodating); and another which is authoritarian,
exclusivist and potentially schismatic from the church (Ford,
1976). This latter type favours the formation of communities
insulated from the secular society, and has encouraged followers
to move away from highly secularist centres, such as San

Francisco, to group together in more protected and mutually reinforcing communities of the like-minded (Lane, 1978).

6 Developments I
The precariousness of the market

Accommodation to the surrounding world is the outcome for most new religious movements in the long run if they survive. Denominationalisation is the best known form of such an accommodation to worldly values and practices, although it is by no means inevitable. The 'established' sect, e.g. Jehovah's Witnesses, the Hutterites, Exclusive Brethren, etc., is another form which survival without absorption may take.

Being some way along the path toward an easy, stable relationship with the world about it, the new religious movement of a world-accommodating type may be under less external pressure to change than, for example, one of a world-rejecting character. Demanding less intense and less all-embracing commitment than the latter, it is therefore less likely to be riven by internal feuds, especially those emerging on the death of a charismatic founder. Being less rigidly authoritarian, the movement's survival and success are not so intimately bound with a single leader, and the transmission of leadership is thus likely to prove problematic.

Historically, world-rejecting movements such as millennarian sects have tended to be born from the anxiety, despair and deprivation of the socially marginal. Thus, social changes which produce the alleviation or elimination of their particular sources of marginality are likely to eliminate at the same time the sources of their recruits, forcing them to rely increasingly upon their own offspring, or to modify their style and form, to secure converts elsewhere. Thus, while *new* world-rejecting movements are likely to emerge so long as social change continues to marginalise some group or other whose hopes and fears can be dressed in a religious form, they are likely to retain their original character only briefly, adapting under pressure from a hostile society, torn apart by the intensity of internal social relations, or fossilising under the erosion of their recruitment base drawn increasingly into the social sun as their circumstances have improved.

Those world-rejecting movements which emerged in the 1960s, however, were often born out of the specific historical conditions of the disintegration of the counter-culture, and depended upon the existence of a substantial constituency of young people sufficiently alienated from their society to be prepared to seek such drastic alternatives to it. The economic recession of the 1970s gradually eroded the bases for such a constituency just as the economic expansion of the early 1960s had generated it.

The recession of the 1970s created a more precarious job
market. Economic contraction was incompatible with a widespread
sense of social progress and experimentation. Fewer young people
were prepared to jeopardise their occupational future by embark-
ing upon any counter-cultural digression from the established
paths of entry into adult life. The hippie as a social type had
largely disappeared, and young people in general were more
concerned with ensuring their job prospects than with pursuing
social ideals. As the economic order of their society became more
precarious, fewer young people wished to abandon it, even
temporarily.

The disappearance of the constituency for many of the youthful
world-rejecting movements has been reflected in two ways. First,
there has been a tendency for them to stagnate numerically.
J. Stillson Judah, for example, commented in 1974 that, 'The
decline of hippiedom already seems to have slightly reduced the
number of Hare Krishna temples' (Judah, 1974: 183). Lofland
(1977), in his resumé of recent developments in the Unification
Church, suggests that its rate of recruitment has slowed
considerably in recent years. His opinion is supported by Welles
(1976) who opines that, 'the Unification Church has shown no
membership growth since 1974' in America. Even beyond the
youthful counter-cultural movements, Krause (1978: 77) observes
that, 'Like many of the cults and esoteric religions which began
attracting Americans in the late 1960s People's Temple had lost a
large part of its membership by 1978.' It is not clear in this case
that the drop in membership was a result of the disappearance of
a relevant constituency. It seems more likely that the increasing
totalitarianism of the movement was a major factor here. However,
in general it appears that, after considerable expansion in the
late 1960s and early 1970s, the world-rejecting movements have
more recently tended to remain static or even to decline. Second,
the disappearance of their constituency has produced pressure
upon these movements to adapt in the face of their changed circumstances. In order to locate a new constituency, the movements
have often felt a need to change their style and their methods of
proselytisation in a manner which would draw them closer to the
world-accommodating area of the conceptual space. Even initially
extreme world-rejecting movements, such as Krishna Consciousness
and the Children of God, have modified their public presentation
in ways which would gain them greater access to less marginal
sectors of society.

The Children of God were in their earliest years, from 1968-71,
even more radically world-rejecting than they were to become
subsequently. In the first period, virtually everyone outside their
movement was a servant of Satan. Thereafter, their attitude
softened somewhat. There were 'Other Sheep' outside the Children
of God; one could be an 'Associate' or a 'Friend' of the movement
without submitting entirely to its way of life. Even such slight
compromises with the world as these provoked some followers to
abandon the movement (Wallis, 1979a: chapter 4). Later, the

Children of God moved away from street proselytisation of young drop-outs, to witnessing in expensive bars, discos and hotels to middle-aged businessmen and other relatively comfortable social groups to be found in such milieux. Later they focused, too, on witnessing door-to-door in order to reach young married couples with children and the elderly, for whom they might also provide a regular 'Church of Love' in their homes, a Bible Study group, or a Sunday or vacation Bible club for the neighbourhood children. The Children of God acknowledged readily enough in interviews that one reason for this change in style was the disappearance of the 'drop-out' as a potential recruit, or at least 'drop-outs' of the calibre of those so prevalent in the late 1960s and early 1970s.

In a related fashion, the Unification Church has begun a 'Home Church' programme addressed to older people in a settled way of life, and laying little stress on dropping out of the world into the communal life. (See *The Advisor: Journal of the American Family Foundation*, 2, 2 April 1980: 2). The Unification Church has also begun to foster a dialogue with other churches, theologians, and even with those who might be hostile to its activities, as well as secular academics, through the many international conferences which it sponsors.

After its early phase as an embodiment of youth revolt, Krishna Consciousness has begun to develop a relationship with the immigrant Indian communities of the western societies where it is located, accommodating itself to that extent, as zealous and enthusiastic religious virtuosi, serving an ethnic and religious minority (Carey, unpublished). Devotees of the Krishna Consciousness movement now dress relatively conventionally when engaged in street solicitation, or selling copies of the movement's books to libraries and bookshops. They have begun to encourage the involvement in the movement of older people with family attachments, on a part-time basis while otherwise continuing a fairly conventional life-style. One can merely visit the Temple for an hour or two to participate in meditations, devotions, seminars or a meal. An article in a recent issue of the movement's magazine, *Back to Godhead*, (the exact date is unfortunately not available) points out that:

> To begin Krishna consciousness one does not have to suddenly leave home, renounce everything, and become a *brahmacārī* monk. Rather, while remaining at home, one can perform the recommended spiritual practices preferably with the other members of one's family, and in this way advance very quickly in Krishna consciousness. (Brahmananda Swami, 'How to begin devotional yoga')

E. Burke Rochford (1982: 406) argues that in the USA, 'By the mid-1970s, ISKCON was a declining social movement. Few recruits were being attracted, and Prabhupada's death in 1977, with the resulting politicisation of ISKCON [as his closest disciples jostled for power and their own legitimacy in turn was challenged by followers], resulted in an exodus of many long-time Krishna devotees.' As a result, centralised‹control weakened; many ISKCON communities relaxed the rigour of their practices and membership criteria, and became more susceptible to influences from outside. Rochford (1982: 406-7) suggests that relationships with non-devotees became more common, as did other influences from the surrounding environment, particularly in the Los Angeles community:

> Automobiles, televisions, furniture, newspapers, and weekly news magazines have become commonplace within the community. An attempt by the leadership to purge these objects, especially television, in 1980 was largely unsuccessful. A number of Los Angeles devotees held jobs outside the ISKCON community, and an increasing number are living on the outskirts of the community where they are less under the control of the leaders.

There has emerged a conscious strategy to recruit 'part-time devotees', and to cultivate members of the East Indian Community who contribute financially to the movement and participate in Sunday temple rituals.

Although no simple unilinear sequence can be claimed (particularly in the case of the Children of God: see Wallis, 1982c), it is widely recognised that such a pattern of initial zealous rejection of the world and later progressive accommodation to it is characteristic of many religious movements which later settle into thoroughly respectable denominations (Niebuhr, 1957; but see also Wilson, 1959).

With the gradual decline of the counter-culture too, the strategically placed movements of the middle ground which embodied sufficient world-rejecting features to be acceptable to counter-cultural refugees, but sufficient world-accommodating features to be a pathway home, have either largely disappeared, or transformed themselves in still more conventional directions. Most of the Jesus People groups have not survived, their followers having gradually found their way back to the more evangelical of the conventional denominations. Others have become still more world-accommodating, thereby making themselves increasingly attractive to recruits from 'respectable' social groups rather than the marginal. Mauss and Petersen (1974), for example, suggest that:

> the Jesus Movement in general (with small schismatic exceptions) is in the process of being routinized, with the symptoms of such routinization including a shrinkage of membership; a rapprochement with the conservative sector of organized Protestantism, particularly the pentecostal branch; the abandonment of street preaching in favor of less obtrusive kinds of proselyting (sic); the recruitment of a more 'normal' and less stigmatized youthful population.

This bears out the suggestion by Robbins, Anthony and Curtis (1975: 58) that 'There may . . . be a general tendency for youth culture religious movements to evolve in a more adaptive direction.'

The world-affirming movements, such as Scientology or Trans-cendental Meditation – and their more overtly secular competitors – born out of pervasive features of advanced capitalist societies seem, *as a type*, in no danger of an early demise. They are, however, the most highly *marketed* of the types. They tend to construe themselves in terms of a consumer commodity market, and are thus liable to its vicissitudes, and subject to fluctuations in consumer taste.

Transcendental Meditation for example, elided many features with which it began life in the West, that contrasted sharply with the surrounding culture, seeking to adapt in particular to broad cultural changes during the 1960s and 1970s. Eric Woodrum (1977) has identified three stages in the development of TM. The first period, which Woodrum calls the 'Spiritual-Mystical Period', extended from 1959 to 1965. This period was one in which, 'TM was interpreted as the most important component of a holistic program for spiritual evolution, nonattachment to the relative, material realm, eventual liberation from the cycle of rebirth, and attainment of nirvana' (Woodrum 1977: 39).

The second phase, extending from 1966 to 1969, Woodrum refers to as the 'Voguish, Self-Sufficiency Period'. During this period, TM expanded rapidly by identifying itself with aspects of the counter-culture. The movement began to differentiate itself organisationally to provide new vehicles for its changing image. In this phase,

> the traditional Hindu understanding of the goals and effects of TM were significantly modified. The goal of 'cosmic conscious-ness' was described in terms of bliss, energy, and peace without reference to the loss of the individual ego or the serious implications of nonattachment to the relative, material realm. (Woodrum, 1977: 40-1)

The third period Woodrum identifies as covering 1970 to the time of his study, and this he calls the 'Secularized, Popular Religious Phase'. In this period the movement emphasised 'the practical physiological, material and social benefits of TM for conventional persons with almost no other-worldly references' (Woodrum, 1977: 41).

Woodrum thus supports the view of Robert McCutchan, a former official of the movement reported earlier, that over time TM dropped most of its distinctively religious rhetoric and style (except for an inner core of followers), in order to emphasise the practical benefits to be gained from the technique, its utility in business and other bureaucratic endeavours such as the military, and the allegedly scientific basic of its theory and practice as displayed through the researches of those such as

Dr Keith Wallace (1970; 1971). However, since the late 1970s, the movement appears to have undergone something of a reversal, with the introduction of the 'Siddhis', a programme designed to enable the believer to mobilise occult powers (on which more below).

Susceptibility to fluctuations in the market may thus mean that particular world-affirming movements are relatively transient in character. Among the more clearly secular world-affirming movements, for example, it has been suggested that the marathon encounter group movement, and perhaps even the group move- ment as a whole, has entered a decline since the early 1970s (Weigel, 1977: 206). Weigel argues that the sources of this decline are to be found in 'fadism', sensationalism, exploitation by leaders and extremism, and also their failure to deliver the long- term personal changes sought. He fails to draw the implication that is suggested by his observation (Weigel, 1977: 211), that:

> at a number of college and university counseling centers across the country [USA] . . . student requests for encounter experiences have plummeted in the last couple of years. Students asking for group experiences now are much more likely to ask for specific types that focus on skill acquisition, such as communication skills, life planning and the like.

If the observation is reliable, it suggests that these students are interested in 'group experiences' not as a means of liberation from constraint as their predecessors were, but as a tool of self advancement in a harsher economic climate. Eva Hoffman (1977: 212) alludes to a change of this kind when she draws a parallel between such movements as *est* today and comparable movements of a decade ago:

> When, for a brief time, affluence seemed assured, easy to gain, and even boring, people could turn their attention toward such psychological luxuries as alternative life-styles or self- fulfilment. In a recession economy, the quest for emotional extras becomes too expensive. People need all of their energies to maintain what they have to stay even. No wonder that they respond to therapies that endorse materialistic incentives, arouse the will to act, and urge the virtues of unprotesting discipline. 'Let it all hang out' encounter groups told us. 'Get your act together - and toe the line', is the lesson of est.

Hoffman perhaps underestimates the degree to which some move- ments in this area are successfully able to combine elements of both philosophies (e.g. Scientology), and also the extent to which even in the 1960s some people were anxious to 'get ahead', but she points to a diversity of commodities available in the world-affirming range, between which market preference may shift (see also the three themes described in chapter two). Product diversification is thus a likely consequence.

Product diversification is evident in the innovation referred to in the Transcendental Meditation movement. In recent years, TM has begun to experience a considerable decline in the numbers of new persons seeking 'initiation'. It then introduced the 'Siddhi programme', featuring among other things, instruction in 'levitation' and other occult powers. The 'Siddhi course' cost $3,000 in 1980 and was said to endow those who took it with supernatural powers such as vision at a distance, invisibility, and the ability to pass through material barriers. These were examples of the results that could be secured through the 'contact with the Absolute' that this training allegedly produced, enabling the individual to actualise any desire, to turn any idea into reality. Diversification has been notable in Scientology which has generated a vast range of new courses and procedures. It has also been especially characteristic of the Human Potential Movement, as will be seen shortly.

The market for the products offered by the world-affirming movements, then, is likely to remain, although it will be susceptible to the fad and fashion characteristic of the leisure, consumer, non-durable market in general, and despite the fact that the organisations producing and purveying these commodities are able normally to command only the most transient brand-loyalty.

NEW RELIGIONS, SUPERNATURALISM AND THE STARK-BAINBRIDGE THEORY

A developmental feature common among movements of a world-affirming type has been a tendency for them to shift in a more supernaturalistic direction, becoming more explicitly religious over the course of time. The Church of Scientology developed from an earlier naturalistic system, a lay psychotherapy called Dianetics. In Dianetics, amateurs would carry out a simple set of techniques on each other, known as 'auditing', to eliminate the presumed deleterious effects of past emotional and physical traumas which continued, it was believed, to affect present intellectual and other performance. Scientology, introduced in 1952, directed itself to the recovery of the individual's spiritual abilities, possessed a theory of reincarnation, and was incorporated as a church shortly thereafter (Wallis, 1976b).

Various offshoots from Scientology underwent a similar transition. William Bainbridge (1978) has described how The Process developed an elaborate religious philosophy and ritual practice from its early naturalistic psychological origins in Scientology and Adlerianism. Charles Berner, a Scientology schismatic in the mid-1960s, first organised a primarily naturalistic training called Abilitism and gradually expanded its spiritual features until, by the early 1980s, he had become Acharya Yogeshwar Muni, devotee of Sanatana Dharma Shaivism and leader of a following of yogic renunciates and householder disciples. Another Scientology schismatic, Jack Horner, organised his own practice

of Dianology which later became transformed into the Church of
Eductivism.
But other movements, too, show evidence of such a progression.
Transcendental Meditation took great pains to obscure its
religious features during the 1960s and early 1970s, but then
developed a programme designed to release the individual's
occult powers, the 'Siddhis'. In the Human Potential Movement
a drift towards supernaturalism is evident in various forms.
The Human Potential Movement is a loose congeries of groups,
organisations and practitioners which share a commitment to
enabling people, by self-directed means, to realise a greater
amount of the potential that they possess by way of ability,
awareness, creativity, insight, empathy, emotional expressivity,
capacity for experience and exploration, and the like. Its basic
principle is that human beings are born perfect and are progressively warped and crippled by society, particularly as
mediated by the nuclear family (e.g. Liss, 1974: 27). It has its
origins in various psychoanalytic heresies, psychodrama, Gestalt
psychology, existentialism and phenomenology, and eastern
traditions of thought and practice transmitted via yoga,
Theosophy, Gurdjieff's 'Work', etc. (on some of these connections
see Rowan, 1976).
The Human Potential Movement flowered in the mid-1960s with
the spread of encounter groups, Gestalt Therapy, Primal Therapy,
Bioenergetics, and a hundred and one permutations and elabor-
ations upon these themes as well as the invention and application
of dozens of other ideas and practices (Wallis, forthcoming). In
recent years it has displayed a much greater spiritual concern.
For example, more overtly spiritual ideas and practices have been
developed, such as Psychosynthesis and other Transpersonal
Psychologies which take as their focus the evocation and therapeutic use of mystical and spiritual states and experiences. Many
practitioners within the Human Potential Movement have found
themselves drawn to address spiritual issues more explicitly in
their practice, and in the programmes of activities of Growth
Centres such as the Esalen Institute, they have loomed larger.
Many formerly entirely secular therapists and group leaders
have attached themselves to movements possessing a clear
spiritual philosophy such as Arica, which appears to draw heavily
on the theory and practice of Gurdjieff's 'Work', or have 'taken
orange' as sannyasins and disciples of Bhagwan Shree Rajneesh.
It is indicative of the same phenomenon that while secular Growth
Centres have found it hard to survive after the first enthusiastic
phase of the Human Potential Movement, the various centres of
the Bhagwan's devotees - which provide a wide choice of
activities derived from the Human Potential Movement - have
continued to thrive.
Rodney Stark and William S. Bainbridge believe that their
'theory of religion' discussed in chapter four can account for this
shift from naturalistic to supernaturalistic systems of belief. They
argue that the failure to appear of highly desired and scarce

rewards of a naturalistic kind leads to a willingness to accept
religious compensators instead (Stark, 1981; Stark and Bainbridge,
1980).

Bainbridge and Jackson (1981) argue that 'Siddhi training'
was Transcendental Meditation's response to failure signified by
a marked decline in initiations and new members. Stark (1981)
argues that Synanon's failure to attain a successful rate of
rehabilitation of drug addicts, of Compulsions Analysis to
produce 'wholly wonderful people' (1981: 170), and of Dianetics
to produce 'clears' with substantially increased IQs, resistance
to illness, freedom from psychological disability and the like,
led to their transformation into religions. But to support the
Stark-Bainbridge theory, the transition must have been made
because those involved saw that the movement had failed to
provide the rewards originally promised, and therefore were
attracted by the supernaturalistic compensators offered in substitution. What Stark and Bainbridge show is the following:

(i)   At time t, the movement promises a naturalistic reward X.
(ii) Some people, not necessarily members of the movement,
      think this reward has not appeared.
(iii) At time t+1, the movement promises supernaturalistic reward
      Y.

They therefore conclude that it is because the members of the
movement saw that it had failed to provide the naturalistic reward
that they accepted the supernaturalistic compensator. But this
claim is not supported by any evidence, largely because Stark
and Bainbridge eschew biographical data. An analysis of the
biographies of followers of Dianetics shows that many did in fact
believe Dianetics had failed to provide what it had promised, and
they therefore quit the movement for other things. Those who
remained through the transition to Scientology either believed
they had received substantial naturalistic rewards, or they had
been looking for something spiritual all along, and saw what
Dianetics could offer as a step towards that ultimate goal.
Similarly, interviews by the author with former members of The
Process showed that those who persisted through its various
transformations into a religion believed that it had in fact been
producing the goods, that the benefits produced opened up a new
range of goals to pursue *in addition* to the earlier goals, and
they therefore remained with it.

There is every reason to suppose that the case of TM, discussed by Bainbridge and Jackson (1981), is analogous, except
that TM always had a spiritual core which appealed to some of the
more religiously inclined followers. It is likely that it was those
already attracted by the spiritual promises of Cosmic Consciousness and the like, rather than those who experienced the movement as having failed to provide naturalistic rewards, who remained
attached when it developed more explicitly supernaturalistic
practices. The Synanon case discussed by Stark (1981) also

provides little support for the theory. He alleges that Synanon's
record of rehabilitation of drug-addicts was poor and this is
almost certainly correct (Ofshe 1980). Synanon was founded in
1958 by Charles E. ('Chuck') Dederich, an alcoholic who had
ceased drinking through Alcoholics Anonymous. After two years
in AA, Dederich tried to take control of his Santa Monica chapter,
but failing to do so, he set up in competition, directing his
organisation more towards heroin addicts, beginning to be seen
increasingly as a social problem. Unlike AA, however, Dederich
brought addicts into a 'total institution' type of environment where
in a context lacking privacy and in which self-revelation was
pursued intensively by such means as the Synanon Game - an
encounter group of varying size and duration - members would
enforce powerful controls upon each others' behaviour (see, for
example, Yablonsky, 1967). From the outset, then, Synanon
adopted a communal form of organisation, at first in Dederich's
own apartment. Those recruited to - or later referred by courts,
juvenile agencies, etc. to - Synanon were expected to go through
a three-stage process: first living and working within the
community; second, living in the community but going out into
the world to work; third, after two or three years, 'graduating'
into both living and working in the outside world. Originally
this therapeutic process was seen as taking from one to two and
a half years (Ofshe, 1980). The world was seen as possessing
many faults and flaws for the vulnerable, but addiction was seen
essentially as a *personal* failing which once resolved would permit
the individual to return to a 'normal' and 'worthwhile' conventional
life. Inevitably a proportion of those who did graduate returned
to heroin:

> How many of its graduates return to their former ways was a
> statistic Synanon, if it knew, never divulged. But the question
> evidently worried Dederich. He began brooding about it, and
> the more he brooded, the more convinced he became that the
> problem was not merely the dope and alcohol that were avail-
> able on the outside, but the outside itself. As the years
> passed, he railed with growing stridency at the 'unholiness'
> and 'evil' of the world beyond Synanon's walls. . . . Hence-
> forth, Synanon would be a permanent experience, an all-
> inclusive way of life from birth to death. (Anson, 1978: 34)

Ofshe (1980) suggests that the available evidence indicates a very
low rate of rehabilitation to a drug-free life outside the community.
Moreover he quotes Dederich in 1971 as saying that the idea of
'graduating' from Synanon had never been more than ' a sop to
social workers and professionals'. Even before the goal of
rehabilitation was formally abandoned, however, Synanon had
begun to view itself as offering a commodity of value not only to
drug addicts but to the non-addicted as well. At first (from 1966),
they were able to involve themselves in the Synanon Game at
various Game Clubs in major cities. From around late 1968, how-

ever, along with the abandonment of the idea of 'graduation'
came the decision to admit these non-addict enthusiasts to
Synanon as full live-in members ('life-stylers') (Ofshe, 1980;
Lang, 1978). These changes signalled an important shift in
orientation away from rehabilitation of damaged individuals into a
world, the values of which were accepted, to one which saw the
world as an evil, from which the community could only rescue
and preserve them, and by experiment create a superior world
within its own confines. Many 'life-stylers' gave up their
outside careers and became employees of Synanon (Olin, 1980).
The movement developed its own school system, and began intro-
ducing innovations in social organisation, such as separating
parents from children at six months of age (Ofshe, 1980).
Synanon henceforth appears to have seen itself increasingly as a
religious movement, and so described itself from around 1975.
    However, although its record of rehabilitation of addicts may
have been poor, the transition of Synanon to a religion can
scarcely be accounted for in terms of *failure* as suggested by
the Stark-Bainbridge theory. The evidence suggests that
although the *declaration* of Synanon as a religion did come after
a fall in resident population, it was during a year in which
numbers were once again rising (i.e. 1974-5). But also this was
not the first occasion on which numbers had fallen. There had
been another in 1969-70 (Ofshe, 1980: 112). Moreover, although
resident population had fallen, income was rising dramatically
(1974-5 gross income $5.6m, 1975-6 $8.7m). Further, there is
no evidence that Dederich regarded the non-rehabilitation of
addicts to the world as a failure, rather, since at least 1971,
Dederich was explicit that rehabilitation and return to the world
was not at all his intention for his followers (Ofshe, 1980: 111).
Equally, there is no evidence that he regarded the reduction in
population as a failure, rather all the evidence indicates that he
wished this to occur. Indeed, at the time of the declaration of
Synanon as a religion, Dederich was actively pursuing a policy
designed to bring down the population and increase standards of
living to produce a more luxurious way of life for fewer people.
(Ofshe, 1980: 122). Indeed, Ofshe argues (1980: 125) that it was
precisely the purpose of the various changes introduced by
Dederich to reduce numbers by eliminating 'those least willing to
be deployed by management'. Finally, although Dederich declared
Synanon a religion in 1974, the transition had, in fact, been a
gradual one. The Ouija board had been introduced into 'Dissipa-
tions' (a particular form of the Synanon Game) some years previously, for example. It is hard to see how any of this can
provide effective support for the Stark-Bainbridge theory.
    I would propose that a more successful explanation for this sort
of development among world-affirming salvational movements can
be found in terms of the distinctive character of the movements
concerned, rather than in terms of the inherent propensity of
people to substitute compensators for the failure to materialise
of naturalistic rewards. That is, the careers of these movements

exemplify the consequences of, or attempts to grapple with,
forms of precariousness to which new movements are particularly
susceptible.
    World-affirming movements are precarious precisely because of
their commitment to provide individuals with resources to achieve
the valued goals which they set for themselves in the world
around them. Born into the capitalistic environment of the western
world, world-affirming movements also affirm the virtues of
commitment to the market, and are therefore inevitably susceptible
to the logic of the market. Hence the variations in terms of
market forces described earlier in this chapter. But further
than this, they must organise themselves in terms of a *clientele*
of *consumers* who operate in a free market in which they retain
consumer sovereignty. Purchasing salvational goods and services
as they would purchase any other goods and services, the
consumer retains the prerogative of deciding what does or does
not articulate with his conception of the good or the true. The
seller may believe his commodity vastly superior, but authority
in such matters, must in the market situation, lie with the consumer. He may sample at will; buy something of what is offered
by one producer and move on to another, synthesising his
own selection of purchases to suit his own taste.
    Producers of salvational services in such a market therefore
have little control over their clients, and in the absence of any
successful strategic response to these circumstances, must
perforce pass the way of the Human Potential Movement. Since
its origins, this movement has seen a vast proliferation in ideas
and practices (see Wallis, forthcoming, from which the next few
paragraphs derive).
    The Human Potential, or Growth, Movement possesses a commit-
ment to whatever may enhance self-realisation, but specifies
little as to the constraints on how that might be achieved. Hence,
members of the movement adopt an exploratory approach to what
the movement makes available, sampling among the approaches
and facilities offered, but usually with no extensive commitment
to any single supplier.
    The market metaphor seems particularly apposite. The customer
is the final arbiter of whether he needs, or has benefited from,
a particular service, and there is, therefore, an incentive for
suppliers to pursue a policy of product differentiation to attract
custom. That is, the ability of clients to pick and choose at will
means that, to survive, practitioners need to be able to
accommodate quite diverse interests and backgrounds, and is thus
an incentive to secure new methods and to offer an eclectic range
in their practice. Moreover, there are few constraints on
synthesis and innovation since each member is the ultimate
repository of authority (his own 'experience' being what counts
most), and each possesses the right, therefore, to advance his
own amalgam of techniques and new ideas as an improvement upon
those which he has borrowed. Jerome Liss expresses this theme
in what he says of leadership in groups: '*Everyone is Leader.*

The Leader is leader only in so far as people let him act that
way and no one supersedes his functions. Anything the leader
does, anyone can do' (Liss, 1974: 133, emphasis in the original).
There are few readily exercisable controls over suppliers or
customers, since suppliers may operate quite independently of
each other within the same broad market. Customers cannot
effectively be controlled while they continue to view themselves
as the definitive authority on the virtues of the products they
consume. This point is made by Liss in the following quotations:

> To respect a person means to respect the individual's point,
> even and especially when it is at variance with one's own . . .
> 'What's mine is good for me, as I claim it to be. What's theirs
> is good for them, just as they claim it to be. Theirs would not
> be good for me, nor mine for them.' (1974: 85)

> Utlimately, no one can speak for anyone else, only for oneself,
> because experience is in essence private. (1974: 105)

Proliferation is thus an inevitable consequence of product
differentiation promoted by the priority of the client's own
experience. Equally, eclecticism is the inevitable consequence of
resting decisions as to whether or not to incorporate a new idea
or practice into one's corpus on the individual's judgment of fit
and compatibility with his experience. Commercialism and
professionalisation follow from similar effects of individualism and
a diffuse belief system.

Early activists in the Growth Movement hoped that it would
prove the basis for a way of life. Will Schutz, articulates this
view when he avers that: 'Encounter is a way of life, not just a
therapeutic technique. It concerns itself with relations among
people and offers an alternative to the present structure of
society' (1980: 179). However, it soon became apparent that
most people involved were not committing themselves to a total way
of life. They were only partially involved in this movement and
even more partially in any particular variant of it. Although some
early followers, often now leadership cadre, continued to view
the Growth Movement as a way of life, they found themselves
very largely on their own after the initial phase of enthusiasm.
The bulk of those participating in the movement wished to do so
only on a part-time basis. Being only one supplier among many
of a commodity or service not irreplaceably unique, groups and
Growth Centres had few resources to control members and could
only seek to maintain commitment and enrolments by following
customer demand (Clark, 1956). They began to abandon the notion
of the Growth Centre as a co-operative, mutually participatory
endeavour in pursuit of a way of life, and to organise themselves
on more business-like lines or go to the wall. (This appears to
embody a major transition at Esalen, as I understood it from
conversation with its founder, Michael Murphy, and to reflect
the experience of the early London Growth Centres.) Many failed

to negotiate that transition successfully, became financially non-
viable, and disappeared.

If the involvement of most people in the movement was only
part-time and viewed as purchasing a service rather than undertaking a way of life, then it makes good sense to believe that
those groups which explicitly organised themselves on commercial
lines at the fringes of the Human Potential Movement (Scientology,
est, Silva Mind Control, etc.) should - while there remained a
buoyant market for their particular form of the Growth
commodity - prosper and meet the need of much of the available
clientele. However, for those who preferred their services to be
available in less glossily packaged, or mass produced, form, there
remained the broad range of Human Potential therapists and group
leaders. The latter were often drawn from among those who, in
the movement's initial flourishing, had construed it as a major
life interest, throwing themselves whole-heartedly into running
groups, organising centres, administering conferences and
societies, only to find in a relatively short space of time that
the co-participatory way of life had not developed. They were
doing all the work, while a less committed body of persons con-
sumed the services thereby provided.

The breakdown of the co-participatory basis of mutual exploration among people engaged in the pursuit of a way of life meant
that those most actively engaged in the movement became a
distinctive group of individuals accorded a separate status,
rather than them merely being seen as slightly more experienced
versions of the average enthusiast. Providing a service rather
than engaging in a co-operative exploration, and increasingly
taking on individual clients from among the groups which they
led - those in need of more intensive therapeutic work than
could be provided in a group context - it was a natural and
obvious step for a more professional conception of the practitioner-
client relationship to emerge. This was more particularly so as,
after the movement's early enthusiastic phase, its composition
shifted away from the counter-cultural young, and an increasing
proportion of those involved were more conventional, middle-class
people often engaged in health care occupations, teaching,
counselling and social work. These people often sought techniques
and aids in their own work and, being used to more formalised
procedures of training, were an encouragement to their emergence
in the Human Potential Movement.

The rapprochement with the conventional world had the further
feature that the permeable boundary between the Growth Movement and the traditional therapies and counselling resulted on the
one hand in the introduction of ideas and practices from this more
conventional area of psychology and psychiatry. This was
particularly the case as some practitioners sought to make sense
of experience and practice deriving from *different* modes of
growth work. Eclecticism led to the need for a way of conceptualising and making sense of experiences which could not readily be
accommodated within the - often rudimentary - intellectual frame-

work of any particular element of the synthesis. Some turned to the more intellectualistic structures of psycho-analysis and the like.

The permeability of the boundary also meant that some at least of the practices involved in the Growth Movement were being carried back into conventional therapeutic and counselling practice. Group leaders were invited to provide trainings or groups in therapeutically respectable settings. The knowledge that there existed a market for Human Potential practices among a more respectable clientele and in more conventional institutions was also an incentive to practitioners to improve their collective image, regulating practice and ethics and seeking to weed out the more disreputable among their number. Developments of these kinds inevitably encouraged the adoption of a professional model of the relationship between practitioners and clients.

Commercialism and professionalism emerge from a situation where a market in practices has grown from the limited and partial involvement of the bulk of participants who - reserving to themselves the right to select those components they view as true or efficacious - endow suppliers with only a limited and competing role in the provision of desired services. The emergence of commercialism and professionalism as organisational principles are a direct consequence of the movement's precariousness, resulting from the location of authority with each member, that is, from its *epistemological individualism* (cf. Wallis, 1976b).

I have argued that the Stark-Bainbridge theory of religion does not, as they suppose, seem adequate to explain this phenomenon. It is undoubtedly true that many people came to the movement with very high expectations which could not be fully met by naturalistic methodologies, and many of those who became early leaders continued exploring both through the various emerging forms of Growth activity, and then beyond. In other cases, the success of the methods gave rise to new questions, awakened new interests, and therefore provoked further search again leading some into more spiritual, and therefore broader, approaches and ideas. I would argue, however, that a major factor involved in the shift for many of the early enthusiasts, and undoubtedly a significant factor in the flocking of group leaders into the movement of Bhagwan Shree Rajneesh, was that they remained committed to the notion of the Growth Movement as the basis for a way of life. The excitement of the early Growth Centres, and the composition of the early movement overwhelmingly among the counter-cultural young, gave substance to that aspiration. As the counter-culture receded, the hippies returned to the conventional world, and the Growth Movement was more clearly seen to consist of a small cadre of enthusiasts committing themselves almost full-time, and the bulk of participants involved only segmentally and transitorily. Those who could not adjust to the Growth Movement as a merely commercial or professional enterprise were often strongly attracted to a movement such as that of Bhagwan, which contained an extensive round of growth activities, within the

framework of a life of spiritual devotion and a community of the
like-minded.

Spirituality was thus for many a recourse in the face of the
undermining of the conception of the Growth Movement as a way
of life by the individualism and incipient instrumentalism that
early became widely prominent. For others, it was a response to
the success *or* failure of aspects of the enterprise which required
explanation and remedy at some deeper (or higher) level. For
others, spiritual conceptions provided a higher-order, conceptual
realm under which the diversity of effects from different modes
of practice could be subsumed in an integrated fashion.

However, some movements have faced the prospect of susceptibility to consumer demand, and sought to implement strategies
designed to overcome it. To achieve this end, *clients* must be
transformed into followers, undermining their authority to operate
in the market as free agents. *est*, for example, seeks to mobilise
its consumers as salesmen, proselytising friends and relatives as
to the benefits of the training, and thereby extending their
involvement beyond merely the purchase of a particular service.
But this strategy has only limited success. As long as the market
is buoyant, it produces new clients, but does little to retain the
commitment and investment of existing clients. In order to make
this further step, the market sovereignty of the consumer must
be undermined. Authority in such matters must be arrogated by
movement leaders, eliminating customer sovereignty, and thus
one major source of precariousness.

The most readily available method of arrogating authority is
through the proclamation of some spiritual revelation permitting
the transcendentalising of one's product, thereby giving it
greater breadth of relevance and the promise of vastly greater
efficacy, and providing the resources for demanding a higher
level of involvement, commitment and loyalty than hitherto. Such
is the logic of the transition which turned Dianetics into
Scientology.

This is not to say that all movements which make the transition
from naturalism to religion do so for these reasons, since one
cannot discount the likelihood of this occurring simply as a result
of a growing spiritual awareness emerging from the preoccupation
with fundamental issues of the self, being and meaning which
many such movements display. It is merely to argue that in
addition to such disinterested motives, a transition of this kind is
clearly seen by some leaders as a means of coping with the
particular forms of precariousness that their movements face, and
is thus an attractive strategy to pursue.

Shifts in market emphasis are a decisive problem for world-
affirming movements. Those that develop a self-conception
beyond merely providing some mundane resource for individuals,
and especially those that develop a world-transforming mission,
may experience difficulty coming to terms with adverse market
fluctuations. When *new* customers are less forthcoming, there is
a considerable incentive to seek to retain the loyalty of existing

customers, to activate further their involvement in the movement by developing an increasingly differentiated product and a hierarchy of sanctification. 'The' course becomes 'Basic' and 'Advanced'. 'Going clear' becomes merely the first step to O.T. (Operating Thetan). Transcendental Meditation, once the complete answer to the world's ills, is relegated to the status of prerequisite for training to achieve the powers of the Siddhis.

This effort to mobilise members, to retain their commitment rather than permitting them – having sampled this ware and come to their own judgment about it – to move on, is usually also accompanied by an effort not merely to encourage continued loyalty, but to *demand* it through the implementation of methods of social control. Transcendental Meditators are expected to employ the movement's rhetoric and conceptual vocabulary. Only those who clearly display their commitment and belief are permitted access to 'higher level' activity (interviews with former meditators). This transition is facilitated by a shift from offering a mundane or empirical product, to a more transcendentally based commodity or system of belief and practice. The movement shifts from cult towards sect, and begins to display greater inner cadre world-rejection. If it has judged the market well, the new, more differentiated and more transcendental commodity will not only secure the commitment of some worthwhile proportion of existing adherents, but also attract a new clientele, less transient than that which preceded it. If it has judged the market badly, differentiation, transcendentalisation, and sectarian control may simply drive away the remainder of the declining original clientele.

7   Developments II
The precariousness of charisma

The virtues of a new theory are best displayed not by its treatment of the same evidence as some other theory it seeks to
displace, but by its ability, having dealt with existing evidence,
to explain new evidence hitherto unconsidered. The notion that
major developments in new religious movements can be accounted
for in terms of particular problems of precariousness which they
face is not restricted to the case of world-affirming salvational
movements. As we saw at the beginning of chapter six, even
world-rejecting movements may face problems of market decline.
However, this focus on problems of precariousness can be
extended to enable us to understand common features of movements which exhibit a more world-rejecting pattern.

A number of world-rejecting movements display a curious
volatility and erraticness in their development, lurching with
little preparation or interlude from one innovation to another.
A notable example is that of Synanon (described in the previous
chapter) which developed over the course of time from being
predominantly world-affirming in character to a vigorous rejection of the conventional world. Ofshe (1980) describes four stages
in Synanon's development:

1. Voluntary Association, January-September 1958, during
   which members were principally alcoholics and the group
   was patterned on Alcoholics Anonymous.
2. Therapeutic Community, 1958-1968, in which rehabilitation
   of drug addicts was its avowed purpose.
3. Social Movement and Alternative Society, 1969-1975, in
   which the idea of return to the outside world ('graduation')
   was abandoned, and non-addicts were taken into residence.
4. Religion, 1975 on.

This last transition had clear mundane advantages, as is evident
from the letter advocating it, written by Synanon's lawyer, Dan
L. Garrett Jr. to Chuck Dederich in July 1974. The letter argues
that becoming a religion would reflect the emergent experience
of some members, and also that it would facilitate further rejection
of, and separation from, the world, and legitimate the communal
life-style and the high level of control. Garrett's letter suggests:

1. that declaring Synanon a religion 'might well have a
   unifying effect internally';
2. that there were already references in the literature to

103

Synanon as a religion;
3. that 'we could very probably achieve a near immunity from
   recurring attempts to license Synanon . . . State and
   Federal constitutional guarantees of freedom of religion
   would offer almost complete protection against . . .
   legislative or bureaucratic interference';
4. that there 'could be considerable advantages from a tax
   standpoint';
5. 'The last point which occurs to me is that we would eliminate
   a number of silly questions such as "when do they graduate?" and "why do they have to obey?" Nobody "graduates"
   from a religion. . . . Insofar as obedience is concerned,
   it is always crucial to the practice of one's religion that one
   obeys the tenets of the faith.'

(Quotations taken from Garrett to Dederich, 19 July 1974, copy
in New Religious Movements collection, Graduate Theological
Union, Berkeley.)

But, as Ofshe makes clear, these broad transitions were
accompanied, particularly in recent years, by a myriad of smaller
changes. White sugar and flour were abandoned, aerobics became
mandatory, as did handicrafts. Conventional time patterns were
replaced by the 'Cubic week' and the 'Cubic day' (Lang, 1978).
Male Synanites shaved their heads, and women adopted close-
cropped haircuts. All these changes were responses to suggestions
dropped into Synanon Games by Dederich, or broadcast to all
residents in one or another of his monologues transmitted to the
movement's various facilities by radio link (Olin, 1980).

Members became increasingly zealous in their devotion to
Dederich. When he stopped smoking, they stopped smoking; when
he argued that members should cease having children, most male
members had vasectomies and many pregnant women abortions
(Anson, 1978: 36; *Point Reyes Light*, 28 December 1978: 9). On
the death of Betty Dederich, his wife, he remarried and then
suggested that it would be a good idea for all married couples in
Synanon to part and take new partners. Two hundred and thirty
couples filed for divorce and were matched to new mates. Violence
began to appear as a feature of this hitherto non-violent movement. Outsiders seen as interfering with, or threatening, the
movement in any way were harassed and attacked; defectors were
assaulted, critics were subjected to threats of violence, and it is
alleged that some were victims of actual physical harm at the
hands of Synanon members, and at Dederich's instigation. A
specialist force of Synanon personnel were trained in combat and
weapon use. The movement had progressively shifted from an
attitude of dissatisfaction with what the wider society could offer
to its members (since it had led them to turn to drugs and had
not been able to get them off again), to an attitude of outright
rejection and hostility (*Point Reyes Light*, 28 December 1978: 9;
Anson, 1978; Ofshe, 1976; 1980).

These developments parallel transformations which took place

in the People's Temple, founded by the Reverend Jim Jones.
Jones's career began as a social radical seeking to demonstrate a
better way of life through his racially integrated church and its
social concerns, particularly for the welfare of poor black
Americans. His social and political preoccupations began to displace his religious message. He is reported to have thrown a
Bible to the floor in a sermon in 1961, complaining that 'Too many
people are looking at this instead of me' (*Newsweek*, 4 December
1978: 30). He began to warn against nuclear holocaust, moving
his following to Ukiah in Northern California where he told them
they might be safer, and from there to San Francisco. His services
began to include healing 'miracles' produced by the manipulation
of animal offal, and conversations with 'spirits', actually assistants
hidden from view. Rigorous social control was instituted with
children encouraged to inform on parents, and physical beatings
by way of punishment. Jones instituted sexual relationships with
numerous of his followers, male and female. In the face of
increasing investigation and adverse comment on his activities,
Jones relocated the movement to Guyana, leading to the cataclysm
in November 1978 (Doyle, 1979; Mills, 1979; Yee and Layton,
1981).

The parallels with a movement such as Manson's Family are not
merely a figment of anti-cult paranoia. Manson's group initially
differed little from the numerous vagabond tribes of communal,
drug-taking hippies, drifting around California and elsewhere in
the late sixties. One study which by chance touched upon the
Manson Family prior to their period of notoriety (Smith and Rose,
1970), treats them as merely an example of a type which had
emerged in the commune movement, the 'Group Marriage Commune'.
This study found Charlie Manson articulating a philosophy of
non-violence (although it did also suggest that he 'could
probably be diagnosed as an ambulatory schizophrenic' (ibid.:
116).

The group might never have received any significant attention
but for their growing readiness to secure what they wanted by
crime: direct theft and credit card forgery both being a frequent
recourse. Other innovations were Charlie's mystical conception
of himself as both God and Devil, and the aim of the group to
abandon attachments to material possessions and power over
others, as well as to overcome inhibitions concerning sex and
social conventions. The most important innovation, however,
appears to have been an apocalyptic vision of black revolt and
destruction of the whites: 'helter skelter'. This in turn promoted
a growing paranoia, and expectations of black attack. Manson,
too, began to demand greater displays of commitment from his
following, extending their attachment to him through sexuality,
and escalating their rejection of the surrounding world into
violence (Bugliosi, 1977).

But the erraticness and volatility of such movements may take
other forms than the emergence of violence or spurious miracles.
A particularly clear case is that of the Children of God. (On the

role and generation of charisma in this movement, see Wallis, 1982c, upon which the following paragraphs draw, and see also Wallis, 1982b.)

The Children of God is the name by which a movement effectively begun in 1968 by David Brandt Berg, an itinerant evangelist and his family, is best known. Initially under the name Teens for Christ (and in more recent times as the Family of Love), the movement began as part of the collapse of the counter-culture of the late 1960s which resulted in many young people – disappointed at the failure of their attempts to reform or reconstruct their world – becoming open to persuasion that only supernatural intervention could transform the world they rejected.

Berg's adolescent children sang and evangelised on the streets and beaches of Southern California coast towns around Huntington Beach near Los Angeles, gaining a small but enthusiastic following from among the disaffected young. Their message that materialistic, ungodly America was doomed to destruction by God; that the churches were hypocritical and the schools opposed to the revealed truth; that it was their parents who were the real rebels, against God, had great appeal to young people who had little affection for *the Great Society*.

In the movement's early period it displayed a style relatively common among Jesus People groups, albeit in slightly more radical form. Its members were required to 'forsake all' their possessions to the movement, to devote themselves full-time to it, to forbear from smoking and drinking alcohol (except for married couples who might take a little wine). They were enjoined to strict celibacy, and betrothal (marriage) was normally permitted only after some months of faithful discipleship.

The movement left Huntington Beach after the prosecution of some members for trespass in the course of their condemnation of local schools or churches. The members travelled across the United States for several months; witnessing and demonstrating in various cities before settling for a while in Texas and California. There, on property owned by a former employer of Berg, Fred Jordan, a radio and television evangelist, the Children of God saw themselves establishing a new nation on the model of the Children of Israel and of the kibbutz. Indeed, until Berg visited Israel, in 1970, and became severely disillusioned about the possibility of converting the Jews, his intention had been that he and his followers should move there *en masse* precisely for this purpose.

Instead, Berg encouraged his followers to go to Europe where the movement spread widely, gaining many new members. These developments were accompanied by changes in doctrine and practice. Berg was now receiving direct revelations from God, followed shortly by contact with various 'spirit helpers' such as Abrahim, the Pied Piper and Rasputin. He had taken a new young wife and progressively opened up to his following the antinomian trend of his thinking and life, encouraging greater sexual permissiveness among members and even the use of sex in the

attraction of converts and new members. This practice of 'Flirty
fishing' was enjoined upon all female followers.

Then in the late 1970s, a thorough purge of leadership ranks
took place virtually eliminating effective leadership between the
movement's prophet and his widely scattered followers, except
through his printed letters sent to all members, containing
exhortation, advice, visionary reports, prophetic utterances,
reflections on world events, and statements of policy. At this
stage a rapprochement appeared to be taking place between the
sect and society. Disciples were advised to return home from
foreign fields mainly to North America or Britain whence the
bulk of the early members had come. Berg recommended that they
obtain jobs to support themselves and their often numerous
offspring; that they begin to hold Bible study meetings or a
home church meeting for friends and neighbours, or even begin
to involve themselves in existing churches. Almost simultaneously,
however, he advocated that they all become mobile, living in
caravans or campers and rather than becoming settled, that they
prepare immediately for travel to a new mission field in South
America or in Russia.

Over the course of time the movement has changed substantially;
from being highly moralistic to antinomian; from being a large-
scale, self-sufficient community to widely scattered, highly mobile
family units and small groups; from Biblical fundamentalism to
a unique synthesis of Jesucentric Biblical literalism and exotic
interpretation and new revelation through the leader; from an
elaborate chain of command to impersonal organisation.

Of course, many movements in their early years, undergo
change as their organisations form, their doctrines crystallise and
adapt to circumstance, and their membership policies take shape.
The Children of God, however, have undergone *constant* change
during the past fourteen years, in structure, belief, practice,
leadership and administration, in economic basis, and in the
location of members.

How are such changes to be explained? I would argue that the
volatility of these movements is to be accounted for in terms of a
distinctive form of precariousness which they face. World-
rejecting movements inevitably possess authoritarian forms of
leadership. To make a distinct boundary between the movement
and the world, they must possess an authoritative location for
decisions as to what constitutes correct doctrine and practice, as
to who is and who is not a member. That is, world-rejecting
movements are almost inevitably sectarian. Their sharp break
with the world around them can only be legitimated by extraordinary authority. Thus, new world-rejecting movements are
characteristically founded by charismatic leaders.

The brief characterisations of charismatic authority sketched
by Max Weber are, by now, very well known, and therefore need
only the most summary presentation here. Weber applies the term
to leaders whose authority rests upon the recognition in him, by
his followers, of 'supernatural, superhuman, or at least specifically

exceptional powers or qualities . . . regarded as of divine origin
or as exemplary' (Weber, 1947: 358-9). This 'recognition' by the
following takes the form of 'complete personal devotion' to the
leader, who demands their obedience in virtue of his mission,
but who may be required periodically to offer miraculous signs or
proofs of his powers in order to maintain their commitment (Weber,
1947: 359; 1948: 246).

The direct object of charismatic authority and the immediate
administrative staff implementing his will is the *Gemeinde*, the
direct household living in 'an emotional form of communal relationship' (Weber, 1947: 360) with the leader (Theobald, 1980). The
members of this staff are not appointed on the basis of their
technical skill or training but rather, Weber argues, on the basis
of the charismatic qualification of those he summons (Weber,
1947: 360). I would suggest that the intensity of their devotion
is an equally important attribute (J. Wilson, 1973: 205 also makes
this point). Spheres of authority and competence are not clearly
delimited and the leader designates duties on an *ad hoc* basis
and intervenes in administration at will, as led by his revelations
(Weber, 1947: 360-1).

Charismatic authority is most sharply contrasted by Weber
with rational-legal authority; it rejects the rational and
methodical formulation of regulations and provision of income,
the constraints of rules and precedents (Weber, 1947: 360; 1948:
247). It involves a break with the mundane and the routine. As
John Wilson has argued, organisational skills are of less moment
for advancement in a charismatically led movement, than 'the
skills of personally relating to the leader. Flattery, emotional
display, ardor, devotion, and fealty are some of the attributes
which disciples must exhibit to gain and remain in favor' (J. Wilson,
1973: 206). Gerth (1940) also refers to 'the exuberant praise
and eulogy of the leader's actual or imputed virtues and qualities'
by the inner circle of followers competing for the leader's favour
and in constant fear of the loss of the leader's confidence, and
thus driven constantly 'to demonstrate their unswerving belief
in the leader's charisma'.

That Mo is not an *ideological* leader (J. Wilson, 1973) is clear from
the attitude that prevails toward his pronouncements. While some
members may wish to settle with the beliefs and policy of a
particular period, Mo has always insisted that whatever issues
from his mouth *now* is the truth as God has revealed it: 'If you
are going by last year's instructions, then you are way behind,
because we are getting new things all the time and ever changing'
(Moses David, 'Grace vs Law', 8 November 1977, para. 11). Hence
the commitment of his followers must be to him and his current
pronouncements, rather than to any particular body of doctrine.
Similarly, Jim Jones insisted that his followers look to him, not
the Bible, for direction, while Chuck Dederich could overthrow
seemingly established doctrine, such as the prohibition on violence
as 'just a position and we can always change our position', and
expected his followers to pick up and direct themselves in terms

of the latest suggestions and innovations in theory and practice
issuing from him over 'the wire', broadcast to all Synanon
facilities. The evidence would seem overwhelming that Moses David, Chuck
Dederich, Jim Jones and Charles Manson are correctly attributed
the status of charismatic leader. The attribution of charismatic
status makes more readily understandable something of the
erratic and arbitrary character of their leadership. John Wilson
has pointed out, for example, that having no need to justify his
decisions except by reference to 'a source of authority to which
he has sole access', produces the consequence of:

> a certain arbitrariness of decision making, due partly to the
> fact that no value is placed on rationality and none on precedent
> and partly to the fact that the leader is . . . exposed to highly
> selective information, as he relies on his favored disciples to
> channel opinions and reactions to him. (J. Wilson, 1973: 205)

However, a full appreciation of the degree of arbitrariness
displayed by charismatic leadership requires an understanding of
its relationship to its nemesis: institutionalisation.

INSTITUTIONALISATION OF CHARISMA

Weber argued that charismatic authority could only be maintained
in its pure form for a relatively brief period, that it could 'exist
only in the process of originating' (1947: 364). In the longer
term it tends to become transformed in a more rationalistic or
traditionalistic direction, giving way to a less spontaneous and
more predictable style of leadership and the emergence of a
stable institutional structure which constrains not only the
followers, but the leader as well.
The very effort to perpetuate the movement's mission and
spread it beyond the immediate band of disciples introduces the
need for mechanisms of coordination, supervision, and delegation.
It entails a degree of impersonality the larger the movement
becomes. Beyond this, however, the followers wish to ensure the
maintenance of the collectivity into which they have thrown themselves, and this demand encourages the growth of an institutionalised structure. The leaders and followers begin, particularly as
they grow older and rear families, to expect some predictability
and stability in the life and activity of the movement. Officials
establish rational procedures for operation, and also hope to preserve their hitherto ad hoc status and enjoy a commensurate
life-style and thus press for some tenure of office and the
regulation of office-holding in a non-arbitrary way. Hence, as
Weber puts it, 'the routinization of charisma also takes the form
of the appropriation of powers of control and of economic advantages by the followers or disciples, and of regulation of the
recruitment of these groups' (1947: 367). To pay for the 'perman-

ent routine structure' that thus emerges, some form of rational fiscal basis for the movement must be secured. The development of these mundane structures of legitimated regulations and rights among officials to hold offices to which they have been duly appointed, of dependence upon a routinised economic base and formalised procedures, constrain the leader and trammel his capacity for arbitrary behaviour and dramatic unilateral changes in doctrine or policy.

Charisma is thus inherently unstable and tends to become institutionalised. Charismatic leaders respond to this typical pattern of events in different ways. At least four can be identified: acquiescence, encouragement, displacement, and resistance.

(i) *Acquiescence*: A characteristic pattern is one in which institutionalisation proceeds and the charismatic leader, finding himself trammelled and constrained, acquiesces to the situation with more or less good grace. An example might be the Guru Maharaj Ji and the Divine Light Mission up to 1976, described in chapter five. Under the influence of his American administrative staff the movement underwent substantial rationalisation after 1973. Its 'style' became increasingly westernised ('Mahatmas' became 'Initiators', for example); its organisation more bureaucratic; imparting of its 'knowledge' more routine. From being a contemporary manifestation of God, Maharaj Ji came to be presented as merely a great humanitarian leader. He seems to have accepted these developments until 1976 when he reasserted his messianic status and demanded a new personal dedication and devotion. This reversal of attitude toward the onset of institutionalisation marked a change to the fourth pattern described below.

(ii) *Encouragement*: Another pattern displayed in some movements is one in which the charismatic leader embraces the possibilities involved in institutionalisation and actively directs that process in such a way as to control it and utilise institutionalised structures and procedures to buttress his authority rather than allowing it to constrain him. A well known example - best described by Bryan Wilson (1978) - is that of Mrs Mary Baker Eddy:

> Initially Christian Science was emphatically charismatic. Mrs Eddy herself supervised the process of bureaucratization, and some charismatic elements were retained. . . . Mrs Eddy built up a bureaucratic system which, while she lived, she could always alter or gainsay.

A similar case is that of L. Ron Hubbard and Scientology (Wallis, 1976b). Hubbard, like Mrs Eddy, began as a charismatic leader possessing a new revelation and a new means to secure salvation. Finding that there were difficulties in securing a monopoly of the means of revelation and unchallenged authority, he progressively developed a thoroughly routinised set of procedures and structures for controlling access to his knowledge and techniques,

and for constraining his followers and potential competitors.
He remained, however, the master of this apparatus, able to
prevent any inhibition of his powers, through absolute control
over appointments of senior officials, and through the possession
of a personally devoted and purely personally controlled elite
executive body, known as the 'Sea Org', with authority to
intervene in the regionally articulated institutional structure. As
these examples suggest, and I shall argue below, the pattern
wherein a charismatic leader encourages institutionalisation as
additional support for his personal authority, is likely to be
particularly characteristic of world-affirming movements.

   (iii) *Displacement*: A third case, also pointed out by Bryan
Wilson, is that in which institutionalisation proceeds without clear
recognition by the charismatic leader of what is occurring, until
too late for him effectively to reverse the situation despite a
strong antipathy toward it. Bryan Wilson has described how
George Jeffreys, founder of the Elim Pentecostal movement, aspired
through his revival campaigns to foster the cause of ecumenical
evangelism, but found himself in a short space of time the leader
of an emerging denomination. To facilitate his revival activities
an administrative apparatus developed, supervising the organisation of the movement, its property, appointment of ministers,
etc:

> Administration was refined and regularised until Elim had
> evolved a powerful central bureaucracy hidden behind its
> evangelist-leader, who appears, from his later statements,
> to have been wholly unaware of the process. (Wilson, 1978: 43)

His absolute authority was gradually undermined as day-to-day
control fell increasingly into the hands of the administrative
staff. Jeffreys himself assisted in vesting extensive powers in an
executive council which came increasingly to rely upon the leading bureaucratic official, the secretary-general. When finally, in
the 1930s, Jeffreys began to consider means by which Elim could
be reorganised more along lines he considered appropriate,
power had become so concentrated in the hands of the secretary-
general that, in the ensuing struggle for control, Jeffreys lost
and was ousted.

   Among the new religious movements, a case of this type is that
of Robert de Grimston, founder of The Process (Bainbridge, 1978)
also described in chapter five. De Grimston developed an elaborate theology for this movement based on worship of Christ,
Jehovah, Satan and Lucifer, and an outrageously theatrical style
of ritual and dress which secured for the movement a reputation
as Devil-worshippers. During the early 1970s, the movement began
to adopt more conventional patterns. It became less geographically
mobile, settling into fixed chapters, and pursuing greater
respectability through social welfare programmes. The emerging
routinisation and conventionalisation led to a crisis, late in 1973,
between De Grimston and his immediate entourage on the one

hand, and his estranged wife and most other leaders of the
movement on the other, who wished to abandon the publicly disapproved theology and to cultivate a less 'shocking' style, against
De Grimston's wish to maintain and even extend these. The
peripatetic prophet and teacher, having no means of access to
the following grouped in the local chapters, against the wishes
and influence of their immediate leaders, was ousted.

(iv) *Resistance*: There remains, however, a fourth pattern
which has not perhaps been explored to the same extent as the
other three. This is one in which the charismatic leader foresees
the threat of institutionalisation subverting his authority and
takes active and effective steps to forestall it. I would argue that
paradigmatic of this pattern is the case of Moses David and the
Children of God.

Mo's awareness of the process of institutionalisation is evident
from his writings. He criticised those among his leaders who
sought to build up powerful institutional structures and their own
base of power; recognised that, in order to maximise the mobilis-
ability of his following in their mission, he would have to overcome the tendency of his lieutenants to seek to stabilise the
membership for pragmatic reasons:

> The attitude of some leaders who don't want to let go of their
> flock is: 'we've got this big house and we have to pay rent,
> and we have to pay utilities and keep the home fires burning,
> so we can't let our people go!' (Moses David, 'Old Bottles',
> July 1973, para. 61).

In this same letter Mo also points to the tendency among these
'old bottle' leaders to seek to crystallise his revelations into a
fixed ideology, and to display some reluctance to face the
prospect of a constantly changing message: 'God is still pouring
out new wine, but some of our people have become old bottles
and can't take it' (para. 52). Mo recognised quite clearly that
such leaders were a challenge to his authority and a block to the
progress of the movement in terms of his latest revelations (see,
for example, his letter, 'The Childcare Revolution', 1 April 1975,
para. 34). Thus their dominion had to be curbed, their position
undermined, their power limited. Hence his attacks on leadership power and the 'tyranny' of officers; his attempts to demo-
cratise decision-making and give followers the right to challenge
leaders from his letters; and his urging of followers to break free
from leadership and head off to new missionary areas as he wished,
were all, in part or whole, designed to restrict the institution-
building and the authority of the administrative leadership.

At such times of liberation, *inspirational* leadership would come
to the fore, the more 'spiritual' rather than the pragmatic among
the leaders, the singers and pioneers, the prophets and zealots,
the more rootless and non-conformist. They would stir up a new
sense of enthusiasm to accompany the sense of liberation from
administrative bondage. Statistics for income, literature distribut-

ing and 'soul-winning' would go by the board, quotas would be neglected, 'systemite' (i.e. worldly) contacts would be affronted, normal procedures would be cast aside. The followers would feel themselves moved by a new spirit of freedom and commitment, released from the mundane drudgery of meeting their quota or seeking proper permission for action. By such means Mo recreated periodically the sense of 'emancipation from the routine' (Wilson, 1973: 203).

Harry Hiller has drawn attention to the fact that in social movements, 'Routinization may be resisted by perpetual environmental change and the shifting of goals' (1975: 344). Such a strategy not only brought down the institution-builders, the administratively inclined who sought to bridle the free reign of God's spirit through Mo, but it mobilised the following, freeing them from institutional controls, directing them away from mundane and routine considerations, ever more pressing as they produced children and grew older. Moreover it gave them the inspiration, the renewed sense of excitement and commitment needed to sacrifice their institutional security and comfort to head off once again in further missionary endeavour.

Similarly, Mo readily realised that in order to prevent ossification and compromise, the gradual drift into institutionalism and denominationalism, it was important to remove those whose commitment was declining, who found themselves too burdened to make still more changes, to live in constant unpredictability, to abandon beliefs once favoured but now overtaken by new revelations, who would seek to lead the movement into stability and regularity. Hence Mo's periodic directions to his followers to return home awhile, even if only for a visit, to give the faint-hearted a chance to purge themselves from the ranks.

However, there is a further reason for these reversals of policy, humbling of leadership, disruption of procedure and sending members home. Charisma exists solely in the recognition and devotion of the following. Once having become followers, however, commitment becomes overdetermined. A whole range of more mundane factors may keep the follower there, in spite of a loss of faith or decline in personal devotion to the leader. Such strategies then have the further role of providing the leader with reassurance of his followers' recognition of his charisma. Will they, despite having 'forsaken all' to the movement and having sought to serve their leader faithfully as an administrator for several years, accept a severe public reprimand, humiliation, being reduced to the ranks, *and still* continue to follow him? Will they, despite having four or five children, few resources and the onset of middle age, *still* be prepared to abandon all they have arduously established and head off to Latin America, or life in a caravan? Will they, despite having joined a movement which advocated sexual restraint and the sanctity of marriage, be willing to sleep with any other member and even with non-members when Mo determines this is God's will? Such changes have importance not solely for their content and direction, but as tests of the faith

of members in him. Hence those who do not obey, who lack
sufficient commitment to pursue the new policy wholeheartedly,
exhibit their lack of faith in him as God's prophet whose words
contain the truth and therefore should provide all the faith that
is necessary.

In this respect, Mo's strategy of seeking to maximise mobilis-
ability, to maximise the proportion of the movement who are
'deployable agents', would appear to resemble that of Chuck
Dederich in Synanon:

> placing an ever changing set of demands on the membership of
> a group has an effect beyond the obvious one of stimulating
> debate and making social life more interesting. It is a convenient
> way in which to test the power of management over members . . .
> provoke dissenters into revealing themselves and those who are
> at minimum unenthusiastic about being a deployable person into
> displaying enthusiasm no matter what they might privately
> think. (Ofshe, 1980: 123-4)

Dissenters, once identified can be pressured either into acceptance of the new party line, or into departure: 'The net effect of
such a management scheme will be to maximize the proportion of
the membership of an organisation that approximates the definition
of cadre at any point in time' (ibid.: 124).

But while those who disobeyed or were reluctant to implement
Mo's directives thereby displayed a lack of faith in him, those
who implemented the new freedoms too enthusiastically might also
be seen as challenging his authority. When Mo advocated
democracy, the problem arose of democracy coming to some other
decision than his own. When Mo advocated using his letters to
challenge the leaders, problems were created of members using
his past letters to challenge the validity of his own new departures.
When Mo freed the followers from quotas the problem arose of
those who would not 'litness' (i.e. distribute Mo's writings). When
all were liberated from the authority of institutional leaders,
problems arose of each doing his own thing or nothing at all.

Inevitably this caused ambiguities and contradictions, and
sudden changes in policy to recover the situation. Those who
left the movement would be referred to in honorable terms as
'graduates' one day, and 'dogs returned to their vomit' another.
Members would be asked to do what they had the faith for one
minute, and told they should have the faith for the entire message
the next. Complete obedience to the authority of local leaders
would be advocated and then sharply criticised.

Freedoms were in part a test of commitment and those who
accepted these freedoms but used them to do something other
than what Mo wished, who used them to secure any measure of
independence from him as well as from the institutional leaders,
had clearly failed the test. The freedoms provided an opportunity
to obey and stay close to Mo *unconditionally*, without institutional
constraint and regulation, thereby validating his charisma, his

role as the direct voice of God at this time.

Unfortunately, however, not everyone quite saw the point, or implemented it in the way Mo wished. As, on each occasion the institutional structure was torn down, as freedom was declared, and as inspirational leaders were elevated to replace the admini- strators, so the survival of the movement and the viability of its work would be threatened. Influential supporters would be 'blown away' by the licence, the dogmatic zealotry, or the hostility to the System. Income would suffer as members spent more time studying the Bible, personal witnessing, or involved in inspirational activities, than 'litnessing'. Reports would not be sent in. Administration would not be carried out. Extremist versions of points of doctrine or practice would prevail with the loss of potential converts. The institutionally inclined would find the movement becoming chaotic, falling apart and unproductive as changes were wrought, large numbers of disciples and families moved around or changed partners and their work was negated. Some would leave and thus membership numbers would fall. At such times, Mo would begin to curb the freedoms; threaten sanctions; demand discipline; reinstate former or appoint new administrators, less inspirationally inclined; and remove the inspirationalists from positions of control, sending them off to pioneer elsewhere.

While the liberations and de-institutionalisations create new enthusiasm and energy among those who remain committed - as well as bringing down administrative leaders who present a challenge to Mo's authority - they jeopardise the movement, and new constraints and tough administrative leaders are required to channel and control the energies which have been released, to restore some uniformity of practice and belief, and to re-establish the mundane procedures of printing, literature distribution and the like, essential to the movement's economy, and repair relations with influential systemites or social institutions.

It is a paradox of charisma that it essentially involves a break with constraint and regulation, and thus, potentially, also with constraint and regulation by the charismatic leader. Those who are freed may bite the hand which liberated them. Mo has seen the tension within the Christian tradition in his own movement between grace and works, love and law. He rejects the doctrine that works have any part to play in salvation. Similarly, he views himself as breaking with the law as regulator of the Christian life, in favour of love. It is a further paradox of charisma that law and regulation specify what may, and what must not, be done. Love, however, and liberty, have no finite limits nor concrete specification. Hence, the need to temper them, albeit reluctantly, with applications or restraints which channel and confine these subversively extensible concepts.

But as the new or reinstated old administrators begin to create order and stability once again, so, too, they begin to develop commitments to something other than Mo, to plans and structures of their own, to a particular fixed set of beliefs. They begin to

create attachments and loyalties to their own person in their
region, and mediate the words of the prophet to their followers.
They begin to make appointments of subordinate administrative
leaders on the basis of their qualifications and experience rather
than inspirational virtues, and to establish settled procedures.
As the life of the movement again settles into a routine, so, much
of the sense of adventure and excitement begins to attenuate.

Mo would, at such times, begin to sense a resurgence of legal-
ism rather than faith, a return to the bondage of law and
regulation rather than the freedom of grace:

> Apparently they were getting sucked in again to legalism and
> going back to old law-keeping in their self-righteous self-
> works trip.
>   See, there they are having a problem, a battle between
> legalism and grace. You see, when people don't want to obey
> the *grace* they always return to their *legalism* in self-defense.
> (Moses David, 'Grace vs Law', 8 November 1977, paras 26, 95)

The presence and activities of the institution builders once
again begin to slow the movement down in the prophet's eyes,
and to constitute a challenge to his absolute authority, and so a
new wave of de-institutionalisation, of movement and change,
begins. Hence, the degree of change within the movement is, in
part, directly attributable to Mo's successful efforts to prevent
the emergence of institutional structures and officials able to
inhibit the Spirit, and to restrict his charisma. But further
change is thereby *indirectly* encouraged by the removal of those
sources of inhibition on the implementation of what, to a non-
believer, would appear to be each new whim. In the early years
of the movement his family were able to persuade him to hold back
some of his pronouncements, to introduce changes with a certain
caution. Once their power was broken, little restraint remained
on his impulses and revelations, which were immediately implemented, regardless of how much they conflicted with prior
policies.

The process thus tends to be self-reinforcing. Removing institutional structures not only constitutes change, and eliminates the
constraints to further change, it also creates ambiguities and
conflicts of policy and practice which leave the member without
any clear guidelines to action. Only by constantly watching the
prophet, subordinating himself totally to the prophet's inspiration
of the moment, and being willing to humble himself for his
failure to follow that inspiration closely enough, can he remain
one of the favoured.

Thus the prophet's charisma is further heightened through the
fact that the only certainty left is himself, or as it is in the
Children of God, only Jesus is unchanging, but the only sure
interpretation of what Jesus is and wishes at any particular
moment, is that given by his prophet Mo. Since Mo was the only
person who definitively heard from God, only by looking to Mo,

seeking to do his will, could one be confident one was in the Will
of God. The arbitrariness of his statements entailed that one
should not even be committed to any particular thing he said, but
to Mo *regardless* of what he said! The precariousness of charisma
in the face of incipient dangers such as institutionalisation, or the
re-emergence of individualism, rather than charisma *tout court*,
is the explanation for the degree and frequency of change in these
movements. (For further observations on charisma in the case of
the Children of God, see Wallis, 1982b; 1982c.)

The parallels with the People's Temple and Synanon seem
extremely close. Johnson (1979: 322) argues in the context of
the People's Temple that, 'charismatic leaders are extremely
vulnerable to erosion of their outstanding claims and to consequent
loss of their influence. [They therefore] seek ways to reinforce
their power and to overcome its precariousness.' He construes
many of the changes and innovations in this movement as a
strategic response by Jones to this problem of precariousness.
Similarly, although he does not discuss Dederich as a charismatic
leader, Ofshe (1980: 125) argues that the many innovations in
Synanon:

> were selected because they served to purge from the organ-
> ization those least willing to be deployed by management -
> those least approximating the definition of cadre. . . . Many
> of the particular elements that appeared in the new version of
> the organization appeared because of their potential value as
> issues that would serve to force out those members who were
> a potential threat to the stability of the power structure. The
> inference would be that the substance of the *particular* issues
> (eg, vasectomies, abortions and re-coupling pairs of individuals)
> chosen as the subjects on which to carry out the coerced [sic]
> conversions to the new model of the organization were organ-
> izationally unimportant and were selected because they would
> work well as devices for purging from the organization those
> of lowest commitment.

Jim Jones required frequent tests of faith and commitment from
his core followers: signing false confessions, suffering public
humiliation, drinking unidentified fluids and then restraining
expressions of fear or hysteria on being told they were poisoned.

Manson constantly imposed tests of faith and commitment upon
his followers. New female recruits were expected to permit him
to initiate them sexually into the Family and thereafter to be
available for indiscriminate sexual coupling at Manson's direction.
They were required to obey his commands without question, to
move hither and yon entirely at his bidding, to act as targets
for displays of his knife-throwing skills, to cut off their hair
when he required it, to undertake acts of theft and forgery and,
in the end, to kill at his suggestion (Sanders, 1973; Bishop,
1972).

The precariousness of charismatic authority encourages leaders

of this type to pursue strategies which maximise the dependence
of their followers. One such strategy is the introduction of
radical departures in belief or practice, not simply from a desire
to implement the new practice or principle, but also as a test of,
and means of enhancing, members' commitment, and undermining
inhibitions upon it. The erraticness and volatility of the movement is an inevitable consequence.

Not all world-rejecting movements will display such a pattern.
It is the outcome of strategic decision-making. Some may institutionalise a form of authority less susceptible to the precariousness
of charisma. Those that do so must needs implement bureaucratic
practices or traditional structures that are entailed by institutionalisation. To that extent, the movement has fallen into a set
pattern and established a relationship with the world around it,
predicated upon the assumption that constant change is not
necessary. Thus, to that extent, the movement has compromised
with the world and adopted some features of the world-
accommodating type.

A movement that legitimates itself so strongly in terms of tradition as ISKCON will be particularly likely to institutionalise
in this way, as will movements which wish to abandon some of
their more overtly world-rejecting features and come to terms
with the world in which they live, such as the Unification Church.
Acquiescence to, or encouragement of, institutionalisation is
perhaps most likely among world-affirming movements. They, too,
may be founded by individuals possessed of charisma, albeit of
a more attenuated sort than is attributed to the prophets and
messiahs typical in world-rejecting movements. Ron Hubbard,
Werner Erhard, Harvey Jackins and the Maharishi are examples.
They are possessors of unique technical knowledge and insight,
rather than agents or embodiments of the divine. World-affirming
movements commit themselves strongly to the modern world and its
forms, of which bureaucracy is one of particular prominence,
especially among organisations promoting goods and services in
a free market. Resistance to institutionalisation, on the other
hand, is particularly likely among movements which define themselves in opposition to the modern world and its forms. So great
a break with the conventional world can only be justified by the
authority of someone perceived as truly extraordinary. Too little
charisma and the gap between movement and conventional world
cannot be legitimated, and thus the movement will tend to
accommodate. But, on the other hand, a highly charismatic leadership would be likely to seem out of place and ineffective in its
arbitrariness and personal demands in a movement requiring little
break with the world - the more attenuated and widely dispersed
form of charisma found in Neo-Pentecostalism is thus more
characteristic in world-accommodating movements.

8   Concluding theoretical observations

Motivations for joining a new religious movement may be quite
diverse and may, of course, not in any concrete sense, exist
prior to contact with the movement itself. Contact may lead to
the acquisition of a new vocabulary or conceptual apparatus
which leads in turn to the reformulation of a broad range of
attitudes and values. None the less it would seem to be the case
that social categories are differentially receptive to the salvational
commodity which is purveyed by movements of each type. Distinctive kinds of social circumstances and social experience appear
to provide stronger grounds or more frequent occasions for coming to view the world as essentially evil or worthless, for example,
and to conceive as viable, some radical alternative to it.

   We can begin from rather commonplace observations. It is widely
acknowledged that the typical appeal of world-rejecting new
religious movements historically has been to the deprived, the
under-privileged, the socially excluded, and the oppressed.
This broadly recognised relationship can be readily understood
in the light of a relatively uncontroversial assumption about
human beings. By and large those who are comfortable, accepted,
respectable and respected, have a sufficient stake in the status
quo, and are receiving rewards from it, to a degree which renders
it most unlikely they will be attracted by a world-view condemning
that social order as corrupt, and advocating a thoroughly transformed alternative.

   The recruitment base for world-rejecting movements thus
primarily centres on social groups *marginal* to, or suddenly
marginalised by, the social order in which they live. They reject
a world by which they have been, or by which they feel, rejected;
a world, the institutions and dominant values of which, derogate
and devalue the characteristics which they bear, or prevent
them from attaining accepted standards of life-circumstances, or a
sense of social worth. These circumstances seem particularly
evocative of world-rejection when they are the common fate of
some class, stratum, ethnic group or age category, some body of
persons sharing elements of a pre-existing shared identity.

   But the experience of social marginality is clearly not sufficient
alone. Other factors may intervene to inhibit the translation of
a sense of rejection by the world into rejection *of* the world.
Social groups are differentially receptive to new values, and
differentially inured to their plight. The elderly, for example,
though socially marginal and under-privileged in advanced
industrial societies tend, the People's Temple notwithstanding, to

119

have become habituated to the prevailing social order and to a body of routines for minimising its discomforts. They recognise, moreover, their own limited capacity for enduring the rigours of any pronounced breach with the conventional world upon which they are dependent.

Moreover, world-rejection is likely to have an appeal of any great magnitude only among those sectors of the marginal which have come decisively to accept that their values cannot be implemented within the prevailing social order. Members of stigmatised ethnic groups and the poor, though marginal to dominant social institutions, may cling to a belief that the world's rewards, which they also value, *are* available to them with sufficient luck or hard work. They are unlikely in such circumstances to favour the disappearance of that which they might yet hope to acquire. The counter-cultural white middle class might be willing to reject the material benefits of their social position, but they were not enthusiastically copied by working-class and black youth, who had yet to enjoy such rewards of capitalist society.

This then raises the issue of recruitment to the world-rejecting new religions of the 1960s. It might be queried whether, drawn as they were from the white middle classes, they are not a counter-example. I think it can be shown readily enough that they are not. Movements like Krishna Consciousness, the Children of God, and the Unification Church drew initially from former members of the white middle classes who had entered marginality, often voluntarily, by dropping out of college or career, becoming drug-users or political radicals. Along the way many were nudged *further* into marginality by arrest for drug-related, or political-protest-related offences, or by less formal expressions of harassment and hostility by social control agents in one form or another, or by adult disapproval and exclusion.

The principal following and impetus for the growth of a world-rejecting movement then seems to be an appropriate constituency of the socially marginal to which it can appeal as an embodiment of a set of ideals more consonant with the values they possess than those embodied or operationalised in dominant institutions. The disappearance of such a constituency, either because entry into it is blocked, or because members of it can be accommodated rapidly by the dominant society, will lead to the fossilisation and atrophy of the movement recruiting from it, unless that movement sufficiently transforms its beliefs and organisation to appeal to a new constituency.

Although such movements may recruit non-marginal individuals attracted by certain aspects of the movement's message or style of life, normally the rigours entailed by world-rejection, the hostility it generates, the self-abnegation it demands, will prove too high a price to pay for more than a few individuals who are not thoroughly alienated by the conventional social world. They are thus likely to be rather transient as members, and not to form part of a movement's inner core while it remains world-rejecting.

Rejection of the world entails certain consequences. Both as
an aspect of that rejection and of the reciprocal hostility which
it promotes, movements of this type will tend to draw together
into highly cohesive units segregated from the world. The purpose they seek to fulfil is one much broader than any particular
individual or group. Implementing God's plan, awakening the
world to its fate, spreading the message of salvation, etc., are
all enterprises which far outweigh any individual and his
interests (except, perhaps, the individual who embodies or
interprets God's will, the leader or prophet). The movement's
collectivism follows from this breadth of purpose and from the
self-imposed segregation from the world. Self-interest is likely
to detract from implicit obedience to the dictates entailed by the
Grand Plan. Self must be subordinated to leader and collectivity.
The imperatives of the Grand Plan imply the authoritarianism
of its designer or interpreter. The intimacy entailed by collective
isolation, combined with a sense of being a saved elite, and with
the hostility directed toward the movement typically generates
a high degree of inter-member emotional attachment.

World-affirming new religions find their source and constituency
not among the socially marginal but among the socially integrated.
They are characteristically members of the respected groups and
strata in society, affiliated with the major social institutions and
rewarded relatively well by them in terms of national average
income and the like. Such persons have benefited substantially
from the status quo. They identify with its heroes and are
thoroughly imbued with its values. But they are thereby caught
in the ambiguities and contradictions implied by these values.
Achievement is a principal focus of their value-commitments, but
yet achievement is a relative concept. As entrepreneurial-
producer capitalism gives way to corporate-consumer capitalism
the shift from deferred gratification, self-control and application
to instrumental goals, towards consumatory indulgence, self-
expression and enjoyment may be hard to manage for those who
are constrained to work in order to secure the resources to
enjoy what they are now encouraged to consume.

As Bryan Wilson has shown in *Magic and the Millennium* (1973),
the demand for salvation from present evil has been very widespread indeed. Although the nature of the evil from which salvation is sought has varied as between one social context and
another, two basic responses have predominated: the conviction
of the imminence of a major social upheaval and an ensuing
millennial period of peace, plenty and rightousness; and the
reassurance provided by a magical technique or formula for
eliminating present evil or implementing present desires. Such
responses do not entirely disappear in advanced societies, and
one of their major manifestations in recent decades has been in
the form of movements described here as world-rejecting or world-
affirming in form.

The world-rejecting movement maintains the tradition of
religious excoriation of the evils of the prevailing order, anticipat-

ing the millennial transformation in its own community of the saved. Such a community may - in the event of the non-materialisation of the social and cosmic revolution - readily enough become a heaven on earth, an introversionist elect, in but not of the corrupted world around it, if, that is, it does not accommodate or disintegrate first in the face of the world's hostility or its own disappointment when the cosmic change does not occur.

The world-affirming movement is a modern version of the almost ubiquitous phenomenon of magic; the invocation, or manipulation, of occult forces or powers for personal ends. The ends may have changed somewhat from physical health, fertility and freedom from witchcraft, to psychological well-being, enhanced self-confidence and freedom from socially engrained inhibitions, but the enterprise is essentially the same.

World-accommodating new religions find their support among those who are securely attached to the prevailing social order, although unhappy with the level of impersonality and instrumentalism which pervades it, even within the religious institutions to which they often retain a firm attachment. They represent but the latest manifestation of a recurrent desire to revive and enhance the experiential content of religious practice.

But whatever the antecedents of the analytical types, something can also be discerned of the role of the empirical cases which contain features of more than one type, the movements of the middle ground. It can be seen that while in some cases, such as the Jesus People, they were a vehicle by means of which the socially marginal were able to secure reintegration into the conventional world, others - for example, the early Process - provided vehicles for those who, although highly integrated into society, sought means of transcending or escaping the conventionality which this involved, of breaking free from the mundane and routine. However, self-discovery, if pursued by collective means may generate a degree of intimacy which offers more than the satisfactions of the surrounding society. Rather than enabling one to secure worldly rewards more easily, intense involvement may generate alternative rewards which seem superior.

Indeed, it is at first glance a paradox that even among the most clearly identifiable world-affirming movements the rewards of participation may become vastly more important than the ends such participation was originally intended to procure. The partial involvement of the follower may be transformed into total commitment among a central core who will tend to abandon other activities to devote themselves to it as practitioners or staff members. For them, social reality outside the movement may come to seem a pale and worthless reflection of the social reality of the movement. This elite of virtuosi practitioners in the world-affirming movement may thus come in some ways to resemble the members of the world-rejecting movements, subordinating their own goals and interests in the pursuit of movement aims, willing

to disregard legal and conventional bounds in the furtherance
of the Grand Plan of world transformation propounded by their
leader.

The world-rejecting movement draws a sharp boundary
between itself and the world, both organisationally and ideologically. The membership of the movement is clearly delimited
(you are either in or out), and the belief system is thoroughly
specified (the movement has the truth and the rest of the world
is in error). World-rejecting movements are thus characterised
by epistemological authoritarianism (Wallis, 1975, 1976b). What
constitutes truth and heresy is determined not by individual
choice and personal preference, but by authoritative definition.
Since the movement possesses the truth, it must be protected
from contamination. Thus, only fully committed believers can be
permitted the privilege of membership, and any who depart from
or doubt the truth must be excluded. Totalitarian control is thus
exercised over the movement as a whole.

The world-affirming movement, however, accepts the world in
which it lives and draws no sharp dividing line. One can be
associated with such a movement in varying degrees. There
exists a *hierarchy of sanctification*, with more 'truth' being
revealed at each level of involvement and commitment. Hence
those at the lower levels of involvement cannot be required fully
to commit themselves to the entire belief system as it is accepted
by inner-movement members. Indeed at the very lowest levels of
involvement, as was shown earlier, they are normally told that
no commitment to any belief is required at all. Thus without
creating a sharp boundary with the world and hence alienating
potential recruits from among the respectable and socially
integrated, totalitarian control can normally be exercised only
over the most committed followers. In short, totalitarianism is
a *typical* feature of world-rejecting movements, but a *variable*
property of world-affirming movements.

In his analysis of The Process and its formation, William
Bainbridge (1978) offers the useful concept of *social implosion* to
refer to the course by which a quasi-therapeutic practice turned
into a world-rejecting sect. He argues that as the movement began
to emerge, it spread slowly via the social network of its founder
Robert de Grimston. However the level of interaction and intimacy
greatly increased among the small central core as a result of their
enthusiasm for the activities provided, and thus their interaction
outside this group rapidly declined. Social implosion, then, was
the result of the network fracturing along the line between high
and low intensity interaction. With The Process, this was a
relatively, rapid occurrence. For many world-affirming movements, however, this sequence is not a particular event, but an
immanent feature of the movement. Some participants or members
are constantly being drawn into such a tight inner circle of fully
committed activists for whom life within the movement and its
organisation is infinitely more enlivening and worthwhile than
life outside. However, due to the structural and economic depen-

dence of the movement on a broad recruitment pattern, and its
ideological dependence on purveying practices or ideas that will
assist people in the world, this process occurs only at the level
of the individual rather than at the level of the movement. Social
implosion for the movement as a whole is probably only likely
while the movement is very young and small, or at the cost of
a mass following. The Process illustrates this pattern, while
Scientology illustrates the more immanent and individualistic
variant. Many world-affirming movements institutionalise an elite
corps, however, for adherents prepared to commit themselves
completely to its activities. The Church of Scientology, for
example, possesses the 'Sea Org' (Sea Organisation) - once based
aboard a fleet of ships, but now largely land-based - whose
members sign 'billion year contracts' of service in a military-style
corps entirely at the disposal of the movement's highest leadership. For elite cadre of this kind, the means - that is the
pleasures and actual rewards of involvement - have come to outweigh the ends - that is the personal purposes, for which
involvement was originally sought. Intimacy, community and
intra-movement elite status have gained a higher priority than
worldly achievement or self-realisation as originally envisaged.
For them as for the adherents of world-rejecting movements, the
self and personal identity will become subordinated to the will
and personality of the leader. Personal goals have been transformed into movement goals, and the client into a deployable
agent.

Social implosion is, of course, a rather natural result of the
vehemence with which the world-rejecting movement opposes the
surrounding society. So sharply at odds with the conventional
world are its values and life-styles, that members are required
to abandon most pre-existing ties on joining, and the response
of the wider world to the movement and its beliefs ensures that
many ties will be broken by conventional outsiders, whatever
the adherents may do. It may be, therefore, that a more appropriate visual image for the conceptual relationship between these
movements would be that of a cone, drawing out the apparent
paradox of movements ostensibly at opposed extremes being
contiguous in terms of this social effect. This contiguity
emphasises the point that the conditions under which world-
rejecting behaviour develops may be quite diverse. While a
sense of rejection by the prevailing social order may often be a
major factor in coming to reject the world, it would seem that the
experience of heightened and purposeful interaction with a
body of the like-minded, the gratifications of participation, even
in a movement ostensibly offering techniques for more effective
participation in the prevailing social order, may provide such
a damaging comparison with the nature of the social life the
individual previously lived as to constitute grounds for abandoning it without compunction.[3] Zald and Ash (1973: 85) draw a
distinction between inclusive and exclusive social movement
organisations which, while by no means coextensive, overlaps

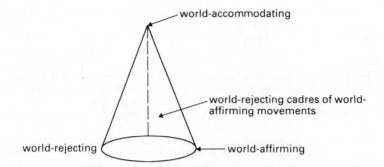

Figure 5 Visual representation of apparent contiguity paradox

with that drawn here between world-affirming and world-rejecting new religions:

> The 'inclusive' organization requires minimum levels of initial commitment – a pledge of general support without specific duties, a short indoctrination period or none at all. On the other hand the 'exclusive' organisation is likely to hold the new recruit in a long 'novitiate' period, to require the recruit to subject himself to organization discipline and orders and to draw from those having the heaviest initial commitment.
>
> Inclusive and exclusive MO's [movement organizations] differ not only in recruitment procedures or requirements but they also differ in the amount of participation required. The inclusive MO typically requires little activity from its members – they can belong to other organizations and groups unselfconsciously, and their behaviour is not as permeated by organization goals, policies, and tactics. On the other hand, the exclusive organization not only requires that a greater amount of energy and time be spent in movement affairs, but it more extensively permeates all sections of the members' life, including activities with non-members. A single MO may have attributes of both the inclusive and the exclusive organization, even the inclusive movement must have some central cadre.

They do not, however, suggest what underlies this distinction. In my view the crucial underlying factor is that of the perceived importance of the movement's product, its message, practice or way of life. A movement will be seen as of greater importance: (1) to the extent that it is salient for a broad range of the individual's concerns, or aspects of his life; *and* (2) to the extent that what it offers is seen to be unavailable elsewhere. That is, a movement is more likely to be exclusive if it is of wide *salvational scope*, or lays claim to a *broad salvational efficacy*, showing the path of truth, salvation or the good life, over a wide range of human preoccupations; and if it lays claim to *unique legitimacy* as the path to these ends.

World-rejecting movements regard themselves as possessed of a revealed truth entirely at variance with the wider society (and with other world-rejecting movements). They construe themselves as alone possessed of a truth relevant to every aspect of human existence, embracing the individual totally and the whole of society. Since there exists certainty as to their truth, there can be no compromising or temporising with other ideas. Members are expected to turn completely from alternative sources of belief, to embrace the truth unreservedly and to recognise that truth lies solely within the community of believers. It must therefore be defended against error and converts must display a high level of commitment and loyalty before complete acceptance, and work assiduously to spread such an important message to the world or assist in its being brought to fruition.

The world-affirming movement largely accepts the world and creates no great barriers between itself and a society which contains many admirable features. It may offer only a rather *specific* remedy, aid, or transcendence, salient only for some limited feature of conduct or life pattern - improved communications, reduced stress, contact with departed spirits, opportunity for temporary intimacy, etc. - at least at the lower levels of its hierarchy of commitment or sanctification, where the mass of followers are to be found. Or it may accept that other groups and movements are in a similar market, offering perhaps not quite such effective means, but equally, or nearly equally, legitimate ones to those which it purveys.

The world-affirming movement is characteristically (again, at least at its lower levels) offering a way to get more of what is already to be found in the world, while the world-rejecting movement conceives itself as possessing all the good there is within its own confines. But movement up the hierarchy of commitment in world-affirming movements accompanies a recognition that what was once seen only as a means to increasing self-confidence is, in fact, the means of saving mankind. Broader aspects of the individual's identity become implicated in an activity and set of ideas seen to have ever wider significance, stretching beyond the individual himself to society at large; the fate even of the world as a whole. The emergence of a world-rejecting ethos among inner cadre members of world-affirming movements is thus most likely when it develops a world transforming mission. This is particularly likely when, as in Scientology, the movement has found itself engaged in conflict with institutions and members of conventional society and is thereby encouraged to reject ever more of it. The world-transforming mission of Scientology is evident in its aspiration to 'clear the planet', to extend its activities to encompass the entire world. In Synanon, one of Dederich's remarks, widely displayed on wall hangings, is reported to be: 'Anything less than changing the world is Mickey Mouse to me' (Naranjo, 1979: 20). It appears also in the goal of *Kosenrufu* held by devoted followers of Soka

Gakkai (Nichiren Shoshu):

> the goal of Kosenrufu [is] the eventual construction of a
> 'third civilisation' or new world order – a world in which war
> is a ghost of the past and international peace and prosperity
> will flourish; a world in which each individual has within his
> grasp the opportunity to attain his highest potentiality or
> Buddha-like nature; a world in which creativity and self-
> actualisation become taken for granted; a world which, in
> short is shorn of all its present ills and constitutes the
> actual manifestation of that long-awaited heavenly city on
> earth. (Snow, 1976: 108-9)

In Japan this goal legitimated a considerable hostility to the
prevailing social order, highly aggressive proselytisation, and
physical attacks upon movement critics. In Japan subsequently,
and on transportation of the movement to America, this goal
has been subordinated to a policy of accommodating to the
world.

But clearly before exclusive features can be adopted, a
movement must develop a convincing conception of itself as
unique in terms of what it can provide. If the same commodity
is readily available elsewhere it is foolish to make your brand
more expensive. But the more a movement can credibly display
its product as unique, the greater the potential for developing
an exclusive stance and creating brand loyalty, thereby denying
the relevance of competition. These are strong incentives for
pursuing a policy of sectarianisation (Wallis, 1976b).

Thus, I suggest that the world-rejecting type of movement
is characteristically sectarian and exclusive in nature, preserv-
ing its purity through rigorous social control and excommunica-
tion. It proclaims a broad salvational message, claiming a
monopoly of access to the truth. The world-affirming type may
be inclusive, or it may maintain an inclusive stance at its lower
levels, and an exclusive inner cadre style. In the latter case,
a movement will typically have developed from being the
purveyor of a specific remedy or technique into a conception of
itself as the unique source of social transformation or individual
salvation. To the extent that a world-transforming mission and
inner cadre exclusivism develop in a world-affirming movement it
will display similarities to the world-rejecting movement in its
inner circles, and a more sectarian stance.

World-rejection and exclusiveness tend to be highly correlated.
Inclusiveness would entail the relaxation of standards of
membership, permitting concessions to consumer sovereignty
and thus a loss of central authority, and therefore very likely
of ideological purity and control. Such a position would render it
difficult to impose upon members any extensive set of self-
denying ordinances of the kind required to mark them off from
the world, and thereby to inhibit compromise with it. World-
rejection can only normally operate effectively where commitment

is high and social control viable, and thus the inducement is strong for world-rejecting movements rapidly to become sectarian, even if they do not start that way.

On the other hand, although it is possible to maintain a world-affirming orientation while being authoritarian and sectarian, it is difficult to do so for long. While such a movement proclaims itself open to the world ideologically, it is structurally closed to it, causing incompatibilities to arise in the minds of recruits between belief and structure. Members of Scientology sometimes experienced a tension between that movement's proclaimed aspiration to aid mankind, and its practices which displayed a high level of interest in protecting and advancing the movement regardless of the views expressed in the society around it. Some experienced a contradiction between its avowed aims of facilitating human freedom and its increasing exercise of constraint upon members. Some members of Re-evaluation Counseling experienced a discrepancy between commitment to the individual and his rights in a democratic society, and the centralised authority controlling movement operations.

The argument of the preceding chapters has been that each type of new religious movement has distinct social sources and constituencies. In part, the differences between these movements have been shown to lie in a difference of approach to the issue of exclusiveness and inclusiveness, which in turn derives from the diffuseness or specificity of the salvational resources offered, and the conception of its soteriological uniqueness which any movement can convey. It is to be expected that other factors will also correlate with these characteristics. An exclusive or world-rejecting movement is likely to have a different mode of conversion and recruitment from an inclusive or world-affirming movement for example, demanding a sharp break with a corrupt world and requiring some visible mark of commitment; conversion in the former movement will be relatively abrupt and sudden, a substantial leap having to be made in terms of changed behaviour, beliefs, or life-style. In the case of inclusive or world-affirming movements, recruitment is typically a more gradual process of socialisation into a new cognitive and social world. The recruit to movements of this type is unlikely to be able to specify any particular point in time when transformation of identity took place. However, world-affirming movements with an inner movement mission to change the world, and inner cadre exclusiveness, must develop an apparatus for transforming the goals and aims of persons who come seeking narrow, specific and concrete remedies, into a mission for the salvation of mankind, or at least for advancing in number and power its immediate vehicle, the movement itself. (For the case of Scientology, see Wallis, 1976b.)

Another area in which the two types of movement are likely to differ is in respect of recruitment practice (Snow, 1976; Snow, *et al.*, 1980). World-rejecting movements, being exclusive in character will tend to isolate members from former friends and kin.

Hence this will limit the extent to which pre-existing interpersonal networks can be mobilised for recruitment. They will
then be forced into public recruiting. World-affirming, inclusive
movements do not establish such barriers between the movement
and the world, nor encourage severance of former ties to an evil
world, and thus are more readily able to draw upon members' pre-
existing social networks.

But correlates can also be found at the level of leaders as
well as of the new recruit. The founders and leaders of a number
of new religious and quasi-religious movements display what may
often appear to be an intense paranoia concerning their safety,
fearing threat of seizure and incarceration by a hostile state, or
assassination by enemies of the movement. The background here
seems readily enough drawn. Belief that the movement possesses
the truth in a world of error is likely to provoke hostility from
the outside world where democratic tolerance displays a disapproval of the movement's dogmatism, or where the ideological
monopoly of the state conflicts with the ideological monopoly of
the movement. Such hostility will inevitably focus on the source
of the truth, and leaders will consequently fear that, as its
author or medium, they are most liable to attack. This leadership 'paranoia' is most likely in world-rejecting movements, for
example the Children of God, Unification Church, People's
Temple, and Synanon, but may also emerge in world-affirming
movements with an exclusive inner cadre ethos such as
Scientology.

> Even if they got rid of us all . . . what more could they do?
> Unless they get hold of me, they can't stop the Letters, so I'm
> the main one that has to watch my step and try not to get
> caught! I'm the one they are going to try the most to get ahold
> of! They figure if they cut off your head, that's it! (Moses
> David, 'Going underground', 14 December 1978)

Having to work in a world hostile to their message and
interests, exclusive movements will tend to camouflage their
activities in order to protect themselves, and thus to fall into
'heavenly deceit', or other forms of misrepresentation in order to
secure funds or recruits, or to defend the movement. Such practices have been observed in respect of the Unification Church,
the Children of God and the Church of Scientology, and the latter
even took its efforts at movement defence in a hostile environment to the extent of burglary and theft of documents from
government offices and private organisations. Allen Tate Wood
(1979: 136) reports of the Unification Church that:

> when we were working for ourselves we were sinning. When we
> were working for others, we could be sure that we were doing
> good. Even if we did things that seemed good to others, if we
> did these things out of our own vanity and egoism, then we
> were doing evil.

Hence, if they did things that seemed bad to others out of a concern for their good and the will of God, then they were behaving virtuously. Thus 'heavenly deception' could be legitimated.

The new religious movements of the post-war western world are multifarious in character and form. Human ingenuity has displayed itself at its most fertile in the elaboration of stories about the supernatural and about human possibility and destiny. Many and varied have been the structures of organisation and life-style erected upon these theological or metaphysical found-ations. It would be the utmost conceit to think that one might devise a simple conceptual scheme which could possibly reduce this diversity to total and all encompassing order without any ambiguity or blurring of categories. The point of a conceptual scheme is to identify some central features of the phenomena in question which seem particularly influential in its structure or behaviour. I have argued along lines similar to those employed by Bryan Wilson in his broader studies of religious sects, that a movement's orientation to the world is crucial in the under-standing of new religions. I have argued that three analytical types of orientation can be found within the new religions of the post-war West, and I have sought to demonstrate that these types have distinct social sources in the context of recent patterns of social change, and consequently different recruitment bases. I have further argued that in a wide variety of other ways, this broad analytical distinction is predictive of major attributes of, and divergences among, the new religions.

However, it is quite clear that such a simple typology cannot conceivably do all the analytical work that needs to be done in this field. It can only take us so far, at which time other schemes must be employed to push our understanding further. These will utilise conceptualisations which may sometimes overlap with those I have developed here, but which may sometimes cross-cut them to produce a more complex array of sub-types. For example, I have argued that empirically and theoretically, the world-rejecting movement will typically be found to be sectarian and exclusive in character. World-affirming movements are frequently cultic - or individualistic - and inclusive: but they may develop a world-rejecting, sectarian inner core on the strength of the conviction that, although designed initially to improve the members' benefits from the world, the movement is, in fact, vastly superior in what it can offer, thus closing off any desire to return to the world, and encouraging a world-transforming mission. Variations between movements in these respects, I have argued, have much to do with the salvational scope or breadth of efficacy of the beliefs and practices they offer, and with their success in con-vincing the relevant constituency of the uniqueness of their product.

The world-accommodating movement, about which I have had less to say because of its more limited empirical prominence and theoretical interest, is, of course, the most denominational of the forms discussed. The major example considered has been the Neo-Pentecostal movement which is inclusive, tolerant of substantial theological diversity, and normally views itself as an 'added blessing', a fulfilment of the potential of the churches rather than a complete replacement of them. It is the 'denominational' variant in another sense, however, namely that over the course of time there is a tendency for even those few ardently world-rejecting movements which manage to turn aside the many forces encouraging disintegration, to accommodate to the world in some measure unless, like the People's Temple, they abandon it altogether.

Appendix   Substance and method in studies of new religious movements

The study of new religious movements has been a contentious field, not simply because different observers have arrived at substantively different explanations for their character and effects, but because the evidence for these accounts has been arrived at by markedly different routes. The relationship between the two can be illustrated from a range of monographs and collections which have sought to illuminate these phenomena in recent years, and I have selected from among them almost at random.

These writings can be divided into two categories: *externalist* and *internalist*. The externalist account is essentially based on observation of the movement from outside, approaching the activity involved primarily in terms of a positivistic method which applies some standardised measuring device to each instance. The externalist thinks in terms of causal variables mechanically producing an effect upon susceptible minds. Persons are *caused* to perform in particular ways. Their thought and behaviour are seen as produced principally by processes other than rational evaluation. The internalist account on the other hand seeks an interpretive understanding of a movement through its own beliefs and a variably close acquaintance with the everyday life of the believers. It interprets behaviour as strategic responses to prevailing circumstances informed by particular – and perhaps even sometimes peculiar – beliefs, no matter how faulty the logic or how unsound or ignoble the premises upon which the actions are predicated.

These two approaches will be familiar enough to any sociologist. It would certainly be my view that those of the recent dozen or so books considered here which can be classified as predominantly externalistic in approach are inferior in character and achievement to those that adopt an internalist approach. This is not to say, however, that a close acquaintance with belief and practice, and an effort to understand a movement employing a little interpretive charity, are the royal road to success. Far from it; several of the internalist accounts are weak as intellectual products. Moreover, there is another dimension which has had considerable impact on the final form of the work, resting on the attitude of the observer to his object of study. Broadly, we may distinguish between those who are, and those who are not, hostile to the movement in question. These two dimensions then produce the classification shown in figure 6. While several of the books treated here show signs of more than one type, they will be discussed in the context of their dominant orientation.

Orientation to the movement

		Hostile	Non-hostile
Method	Externalist	1	2
	Internalist	3	4

Figure 6 A classification of empirical studies of new religious movements

HOSTILE EXTERNALIST ACCOUNTS

Three of the more recent books seem to be informed by an anti-pathy to one or more new religious movements to such an extent that even direct contact with the movement and its adherents has been too disagreeable a research technique to contemplate (Enroth, 1977; Horowitz, 1978; Conway and Siegelman, 1978). The volumes by Enroth and by Horowitz are clearly motivated by an ideological stance. Enroth is an evangelical Christian, Horowitz an anti-authoritarian socialist. Conway and Siegelman seem to be informed by no more ideological animus than a conviction that moderation is desirable in all things, and a sympathy for the beliefs and actions of those engaged in the 'anti-cult' crusade. Enroth not only did not undertake anything approaching participant observation in the groups on which he writes, but did not even meet some of the 'cult' defectors he interviewed by long distance tape recording. At such a distance from the subject matter, subtle and even some gross distinctions are blurred. It is thus no surprise at all for him to write: 'In a real sense the familiar expression, Once you've seen one, you've seen them all, is applicable to current cult groups. . . / The commonality of certain means to certain ends is so striking . . . that one is tempted to conclude that conspiratorial forces are at work' (Enroth, 1977: 12). Enroth's accounts of seven new religious movements are based primarily upon a single informant in each case. In his commentary following the presentation of the seven cases he employs Lifton's 'Thought Reform' model to explain the conversions, despite the entirely voluntary attachment of members and the socially deviant status of the ideology being transmitted, surely not insignificant differences from the situation prevailing in Chinese civilian prisons. Moreover, it fits very well with this approach that Enroth should employ Kanter's ideas about commitment in utopian communities. Kanter (1972) shows a correlation between various 'mechanisms' or features of utopian life, and levels of commitment, with the implication that the more such mechanisms are operating, the greater the level of commitment. Such an approach encourages a thoroughly mechanistic appreciation of how commitment arises, and entirely disregards the possibility of an alternative direction of causality, i.e. that greater prior commitment produced more of the alleged 'mechanisms'. Hence Kanter and Enroth can on a superficial reading be seen to have shown that regardless of individual will and idiosyncracy, commitment to a bizarre way of life can be generated almost mechanically by the right set of techniques. Such a conclusion is a most attractive one to those hostile to the new religions. It was formerly attractive in the guise of William Sargant's (1957) physiological psychology variant.

Horowitz's book is, if anything, a poorer example of the same genre. In this case, the investigator has scarcely been able to bring himself closer to the Unification Church - upon which he does not look at all favourably - than the extant newspaper and magazine reportage. The book is a composite of articles from popular magazines and sociological journals, extracts from the writings of Sun Myung Moon, trial documents and other unpublished sources, with a prologue and epilogue by Horowitz. The book makes a genuflection toward the notion of fair debate by including items of Moon's writings, although chosen by Horowitz for his own purposes, and a sympathetic contribution from Frederick Sontag's book on the church (on which, see below).

Horowitz's book is mainly occasioned by Moon's reactionary politics, involving support for a vicious military regime in Korea, and support for Nixon in America. His dislike of such a political stance justifies Horowitz's reprinting of the circumstantial evidence and massive speculation concerning the relationship between Moon's movement and the KCIA. The book may be a significant document in the history of the controversy regarding the Unification Church, but it does little to further our understanding of the movement.

Flo Conway and Jim Siegelman (1978) however have probably already cornered a large slice of the anti-cult book-buying market with their curious volume *Snapping*. The title refers to the expression they allegedly found to be used by many former 'cult' members: 'Something snapped inside me', to describe their conversion. The book is a composite of well-systematised cult prejudice dressed neatly, and perhaps to the uninitiated, 'scientifically', with a terminology drawn from information theory and the currently fashionable - although in this context quite vacuous - catastrophe theory.

Their methodology is epitomised by the statement that 'we found very few people who got out of the Unification Church or any other cult on their own' (1978: 36). In the course of several years' research on new religious movements I must have met dozens of people who left such movements 'on their own', so it is not much to the credit of Conway and Siegelman that they had so little success. It is not, however, surprising since the anti-cult movement seems in this case too to have been their principal source of informants.

The main drift of this volume lies in the attempt to support the notion that it was only as a result of something 'snapping' in their rational information-processing capacities that people join religious and non-religious cults. The information theory language in fact merely renders more contemporary the now hoary psychology of William Sargant. The attachment to some alternative view of the world - consequent upon 'snapping' - to that purveyed by Conway and Siegelman is labelled 'information disease', betraying a somewhat excessive, and by no means clearly merited, complacency, if not conceit, on the part of the authors concerning their own ability to process information.

'Snapping' and 'information disease' are, in sound Sargant fashion, held to be the result of: poor diet; prolonged lack of sleep; and of 'intense experiences that abuse an individual's natural capacities for thought and feeling' (Conway and Siegelman, 1978: 114). No suggestion here that anyone might come to believe notions wildly at variance with the great western capitalist consensus on the basis of any rational reflection on the ideas proffered, experience of their mental or emotional consequences, or gut attraction to new friends or life-style. Conway and Siegelman have not only not troubled themselves to look to the many thousands of healthy, voluntary and unaided, cult defectors (one could scarcely ask them to talk to the thousands of entirely rational and coherent members of new religious movements) but also they have not troubled to talk to, or read the reports of, the many impartial sociologists and anthropologists who have investigated the process of conversion and its consequences, and found it to be neither ineluctable nor mechanical, and certainly no more irrational than falling in love. (Perhaps we shall shortly be offered an account of falling in love that finds it to be a result of poor diet or prolonged lack of sleep.)

Work of this genre frequently adopts a 'brainwashing' perspective on recruitment to new religious movements, which seeks to understand the behaviour of members in terms devoid of any close appreciation of the realities of everyday life in such groups. It is often informed by clinical psychological or psychiatric judgments arrived at in circumstances of a kind quite alien to the subject under examination, for example in a clinic or mental hospital, while under duress or constraint, or as a result of action of the courts. (Bryan Wilson has advanced such arguments in comments in defence of the Exclusive Brethren, see Wilson, 1981.)

Alternatively, work of this type is constructed upon the basis of *hostile internalist* accounts of defectors or 'deprogrammees', 'rescued' from the movement concerned and anxious to justify in terms of psychological compulsion, and therefore deflect on to others, guilt for behaviour they are now unable to defend.

NON-HOSTILE EXTERNALIST ACCOUNTS

Less meretricious and intellectually impoverished than these are the accounts which do *not* define their orientation from the outset as inimical to that of the believers under investigation. An exemplar here is Nordquist (1978). Nordquist presents a history of the development of the Ananda Community in Nevada, a study of its world-view, and an analysis of its members' attitudes and background characteristics. Although Nordquist engaged in periods of observation in the community, he sought to persuade members to complete an extensive battery of questionnaire and psychological test schedules. Since the members of Ananda were primarily counter-cultural dropouts with a decidedly 'laid-back' approach to life, it is not altogether surprising that only twenty-eight out of a hundred or so completed the questionnaires and tests. In the event, moreover, lacking any meaningful comparative groups, Nordquist is able to do little more than report in table after table the results of this enterprise, results which often seem to lack any clear meaning.

Where Nordquist does seek to compare his results in the attitudinal tests with those obtained on earlier trials by the instruments' inventors, the results seem often trivial or incomprehensible. For example it is scarcely any surprise that the members of a community who have abandoned the urban industrial rat-race for spiritual development, craft work, a vegetarian diet, and an agrarian environment should display in one scale attitudes 'reflecting a concern with run-away technology, a polluted and defiled environment, depersonalization in work, and the suppression of spontaneity in bureaucratic organizations and they very strongly favour mysticism and a simple life in a natural environment' (Nordquist, 1978: 153). Had the scale not shown that, he would surely have thrown away the scale. In short, this is a rather mechanical study of a potentially interesting topic. The historical and ethnographic accounts are uninformed by any developed theoretical or analytical focus but a nebulous concern with the counter-culture, and fail to resonate as a closely empathic interpretation of this particular group of believers and their style of life. Attitudinal scales are a poor sustitute for either conceptual sharpness or interpretive insight.

This is a lesson unfortunately not learned by Richardson, Stewart and Simmonds (1979), from whom Nordquist evidently gained much inspiration. Their study of a Jesus People movement, which they call Christ Communal Organisation (CCO), promises a great deal. The three principals, supplemented at times by up to six others, spent periods of time over several years in locations of this movement, observing, interviewing, surveying and personality testing. They claim, credibly enough, that they have gathered vast quantities of data. Some of this provides the basis for interesting description of the origins and

development of the movement, features of daily life within it, and
background characteristics of members. But, unfortunately, most
of the data were gathered to 'test' various theories in a manner
little short of a parody of positivism in sociology. This involves
here profoundly laboured commentary on prior theoretical work
to arrive at a set of curious tests. For example, they take up
Berger's notion of alienation as involving a situation in which
people 'forget' that their social world is created by them.
Richardson *et al.* translate this into 'an "alienation scale" that
seemed to access [sic] the domain of substance addressed by
Berger' (Richardson, Stewart and Simmonds, 1979: 213). (The
volume's literary qualities also leave something to be desired.)
This alienation scale comprises the following questions:

1. Do you think that God has a hand in the nomination and
   election of our country's leaders?
2. Do you think that the leaders of our country are guided by
   God in making decisions?
3. Do you think it is a sin to break a law of the land?
4. Do you think that the United States generally is an
   instrument of God in the area of world politics? (1979:
   214)

Affirmative answers to these questions (95 per cent to q.1; 65
per cent to q.2; 91 per cent to q.3; 47 per cent to q.4), lead
Richardson, *et al.* to conclude that 'alienated people (were)
attracted to or formed by this group' (1979: 216). The assumption
here seems to be that the notion of a God who intervenes in
social and political affairs entails that those committed to such
a notion have forgotten that their social world is created by
them. But believing it sinful to break the law is scarcely
incompatible with the notion that the law is man-made. 'Render
unto Caesar' incorporates this well-known principle. Again,
it is perfectly coherent to believe that God 'has a hand' in
choosing a nation's leaders as in everything else *ultimately*,
while also believing that if you want to get good men elected
you have to campaign like the devil. Moreover, even if we
were to call these things indicators of alienation, how, without
any comparative evidence, do we know alienated people were
either attracted to, or formed by this group? They might have
been (i) more alienated before than they are now, but (ii)
less alienated then than everyone else. And surely it does
make a difference whether alienated people were attracted to or
formed by the group.

   Richardson *et al.* miss the chance to provide us with a close
interpretive account of the life of CCO and to generate new
theoretical insights from it because their preoccupation with
being scientists leads to the erection of massive barriers between
them and their subjects. These can henceforth only be viewed
through some standardised instrument related in the most
tenuous fashion to a body of thought, the abstractness and

generality of which scarcely lent itself to such particularistic
operationalisation in the first place, or through the categories
of endless models and typologies which are 'extended' and
'applied' with no apparent regard for whether anything is
thereby illuminated.

HOSTILE INTERNALIST ACCOUNTS

Normally of rather greater utility to the sociologist of religion,
because based on a closer acquaintance with the object of study,
are internalist accounts. A number of these have been produced
by sociologists, but others emanate from former members of the
movements in question. It is from among the latter that *hostile*
internalist accounts more frequently emerge; although a study
like that of the Manson Family presented in Bugliosi (1977) is
derived from such close scrutiny and careful reconstruction of
the life and beliefs of a particular movement as to attain a high
level of descriptive authenticity and thereby of utility for the
sociologist who would seek to derive from case studies a more
general analytical or theoretical framework. Apart from slight
differences in the reconstruction of the facts - inevitable in a
context where Bugliosi was seeking to prove the guilt of his
subjects of study - his account matches well those of Watson
(1978) and Atkins (1978). Interestingly, the two ex-member
accounts differ greatly in quality. Atkin's book provides little
new information or insight into Manson's gory group, while
Watson's book is a rich ethnographic document facilitating a
greater understanding of the dynamics of the Manson Family
and thus comparisons with similar totalitarian groups.
    But relatively few first-rate hostile internalist accounts are
available, for the simple reason that antipathy felt for the
movement is not conducive to viewing the thought and action of
its members as rationally considered and strategically motivated
in response to their circumstances. The tendency for the defector or the apostate is to dehumanise the movement's personnel,
to justify his own lapse from conventional behaviour by representing all recruited to this alien world-view as victims of some
routinely effective and ineluctable technology of mental control
by which they are, and he was, tightly gripped.
    Thus, the tendency is strong for defectors' tales [4] to drift
readily into hostile externalist accounts, despite the author's
close internal experience of the movement and his own recruitment to it. In the time between leaving the movement and writing
about it, the author has typically acquired a new, often very
divergent view of the world and a dramatically changed perception of the movement, dramatically changed in many cases through
the experience of 'deprogramming'.
    Such accounts as these, then, have a moral purpose and must
therefore be treated with reservations in some particulars. The
story we are being offered has been reconstructed, in part at

least, as a means of justifying past deviant behaviour or rehabili-
tating the formerly deviant author. This may lead to presentation
of certain features of the narrative, or relevant actors in it, in a
way that conforms to prevailing outsider stereotypes and thus
symbolises to significant others that the author is at last truly
seeing sense in these respects and is fully repentant of his
earlier misdeeds.

An example in this genre is Christopher Edwards' book *Crazy*
for God (Edwards, 1979). Edwards was for seven months a
member of the Unification Church in Berkeley during 1975-6,
from which he was kidnapped and 'deprogrammed' by Ted Patrick.
As the title vividly suggests, Edwards does not seek to display
the rational character of life in this particular religious movement.
His story stresses the infantile dependency which he believes to
be generated by the recruitment process; the repression of
criticism and progressive attenuation of critical evaluation; the
subordination of individual autonomy to authoritarian leadership;
the self-imposition of a rigorous and ascetic style of life; the
zealous commitment to arduous and demeaning methods of fund
raising; all in conformity to a set of beliefs which, on his account,
appear bizarre and even delusional. Only 'mind control', 'thought
reform', 'brainwashing' could explain such behaviour, Edwards
would have us conclude. Yet in what does this 'technology of
mind control' consist? It seems that Edwards can discover nothing
more pernicious than an intensive round of activity, constant
supervision and reinforcement by committed members, relatively
little sleep, reiterated proclamations of love and displays of
chaste affection by his companions, and appeals to his youthful
idealism and belief in God. His efforts to exhibit himself as the
victim of a cruel and mechanical subjection to a technology of
mind control are self-serving and unconvincing. His wounds, if
such they are, were self-inflicted. This is not to say that works
of this type cannot be utilised for sociological purposes, only
that they must be scrutinised and tested closely in the process.

But one cannot bring oneself too glibly to say the same of
Jeannie Mills, her family and friends in the People's Temple.
Mills (1979) does refer to herself and other members as 'brainwashed', but she resorts less readily than Edwards to the
cliches of 'mind control' and 'hypnosis'. Indeed after reading her
book one remains unclear as to her reasons for joining the Temple
and feels that in this respect she remained as hazy as we do.

Jeannie and Al married in 1968, bringing five children from
previous marriages with them, but lacking friends outside their
family. Al had been dedicated to the civil rights cause since the
time of Selma, and one can see why the People's Temple of 1969
in Ukiah, California should be attractive to him in its attempt at
racial integration; and Jeannie as a reluctantly lapsed Seventh-
day Adventist was perhaps in the market for a faith. They were
both attracted by the warmth and friendship that they found
there on their first and subsequent visits, and the apparent,
mutual concern felt by members. They were awed by Jim Jones's

confidence, by his 'divine revelations', by his miraculous healings, and by his apparent discovery of a means of saving his
followers in the event of the nuclear holocaust widely feared
around that time. Yet surely it is more than merely the fact that
European societies are less mobile than America, that people here
are less ready to pull up stakes on a whim, that makes it difficult for me to comprehend how these could be such compelling
reasons for selling a farm bought only the preceding year and
abandoning their jobs to move 120 miles with five children to
become a part of Jones's church after a mere few months'
acquaintance. It only took *that* long because of the need to sell
one home and buy another. Their *decision* to join had been made
after only two visits.

Such sudden conversions are not without precedent of course.
The early disciples of Jesus abandoned home, family and work
to follow their saviour and yet this is only to dignify such whims,
not to explain them.

It seems equally hard to render rational and reasonable their
remaining attached for years to a leader, so clearly in retrospect,
manipulative, mendacious, cruel, rapacious and paranoid but,
of course, that is part of the problem of being a defector recol-
lecting in tranquillity. With hindsight, Mills came to see Jones in
that light as did most of us, but in the *living* of it those attri-
butions were less obviously applicable, flickering briefly into
consciousness only to be brushed aside as disloyal, as needing
to be balanced by his great purpose and goals, as only possible
from ignorance of his full plan, or as based upon inadequate
data or comprehension. They could be rationalised away until
the stage when they could no longer be denied, and from then
silence was maintained from fear rather than self-doubt.

Hindsight does not entirely destroy the sense of lived experience, and it is in the areas of the manufacture of charisma and
the maintenance of attachment that Mills's account is most
valuable. Jones produced an aura of power through his healings,
prophecies, the striking down of the doubter or dissident, and
the raising of the dead. The healing of cancer was a clever
subterfuge in which assistants inserted chicken liver into the
sufferer's mouth under cover of a cloth, causing him or her to
gag and spit out this offal which seemed to come from their own
body. The prophecies and revelations were normally produced
by the activities of assistants who explored the contents of the
church member's house or garbage can while they were out, or
by telephoning someone from whom relevant information could be
obtained representing the inquiries as part of a social survey
or the like. The striking down of doubters and dissidents seems
to have been effected by the surreptitious administration of
poison, and raising the dead by calculating relatively closely
the duration of its effects. The powers manifested by Jones,
plus his avowed utopian aims and the sense of purpose with
which he endowed the lives of his followers, the welcoming
community around him, and his promises of greater things to

come, all provided grounds for excusing his bouts of temper
and cruelty, his growing preoccupation with sex, the increasing
frequency of his humiliation and punishment of members, the
rising demands for their personal and financial dependence. But
of course, beyond that, members like Jeannie and Al had entered
into numerous commitments. They had moved into the area, were
fostering numerous Temple children whom they loved and whose
future they cared about. They began working for the Temple,
becoming dependent upon it for income. They signed over their
property to be managed by the Temple, and wrote letters des-
cribing crimes and immoralities they had not committed in a
display of loyalty and faith in Jim. They began to fear the
possibility of public humiliation and physical punishment, that
the children they loved would be taken from them, that their
lives might be in danger. For fear of the doubts and concerns
being reported to Jones each member would stifle what could
be forced out of consciousness and keep to himself what could
not. Pluralistic ignorance heightened the sense that doubts were
a personal failing rather than a common condition. Even before
being isolated in Guyana, then, there were powerful forces to
maintain the attachment of members even to a leader who was, it
is now clear, for some years before the awful massacre a
dangerous paranoid.

But what is obvious now, clearly was not obvious then, and
for all the accuracy of the detail and wealth of human insight
that Mills provides it can hardly be otherwise than that her
account of those six years with Jones is coloured by the moral
purpose of making sense of an association which subsequently
became too incredible and horrendous to bear.

NON-HOSTILE INTERNALIST ACCOUNTS

However it is not merely hostile internalist accounts that can
be adapted to a prior normative position. Sontag's (1977) study
of the Unification Church clearly aims to fulfil quite the opposite
purpose. Out of apparently almost unlimited access to persons
and documents, including a nine-hour interview with Moon himself, emerges an analytically quite trivial work designed, it
might seem, to achieve no other end than to improve the public
relations of the Unification Church. Sontag seems cautiously to
have confined his questions and his probing to topics approved
by the church's leaders and information sources controlled by
them. He makes no effort to compare information gained by such
means with information from other sources, such as defectors,
nor to explore other pressing questions about Moon and his
movement beyond whether or not it may be divinely inspired
(and it is no surprise when he answers that question affirmatively).

Equally weak, but for quite different reasons, is Damrell's
(1977) study of a Vedanta church. Damrell engaged in participant
observation in the Church Universal, an organisational form of

Vedanta in a Californian city. Damrell appears to be engaged
in an exercise in existential phenomenology. This seems to mean
that the book is almost entirely about Damrell's subjective
experience of engagement in the Church Universal. He eschews
a structural or interactional account on the ground that his
approach is somehow purer and more valid. The problem for
the reader, however, is to discern any sociological relevance in
Damrell's experiential narrative. Are we to assume that his
experiences somehow exhibit features typical for members of the
church? Damrell provides no reason for believing that this is so.
Moreover, even if it were, there seems little virtue in presenting
the experience of members of a group unless this leads to the
uncovering of some relationship between the experience and more
general properties of social relations. But there is little of
intrinsic interest in Damrell's idiosyncratic experiences in a
movement which appears otherwise sociologically rather dull from
his account.

Even a hostile internalist account, such as that of Watson
(1978), is of more use in this regard, since in an untutored and
unselfconscious way, Watson tells us biographical details of
members of the Manson group as well as its structural characteristics, and relates these to the group's development or to the
experiences of participants. Understanding an alien or deviant
world-view as a participant is only the *first* step in doing
sociology.

A somewhat better example within the same genre as the book
by Damrell, is Downton's (1979) study of the Divine Light
Mission. Downton's book is based on intermittent observations
and lengthy interviews with eighteen premies in Boulder,
Colorado. His efforts to determine the validity of his findings
from such a small sample of informants by gathering additional
questionnaire data are not terribly convincing, since they draw
upon only a further twenty-three followers of the Mission. Four
of the interviews are presented in edited version for the first
quarter of the book and others are reported as illustrative
material, to support the limited range of analytical and theoretical
points Downton then makes through the rest of the book. The
analysis is of a fairly low order and Downton does not, I think,
offer any significant theoretical advance on the basis of this
study. Moreover his account of the Mission organisationally is
rather thin. The nature of the movement's structure can be
gleaned and some elements of its developmental history are
presented, but there is little effort to utilise this information to
any theoretical end. Indeed, theoretically Downton's ideas are
rather dated - Starbuck and Salzman on conversion, for example
- and he has no great familiarity with the literature on sectarianism or new religious movements which might have focused his
theoretical thinking to more purpose. But the subject matter of
the book is of considerable intrinsic interest to those working in
these fields and the information he has gathered is extremely
useful on a movement concerning which little reliable information

is yet available. While Downton's conceptualisation of the
phenomena under investigation is not a major contribution,
his approach is basically sympathetic to his subjects and the
resultant materials are thus not forced into a form suitable to
a set of prior antipathetic assumptions.

By far the best of the studies considered here, however, is
Bainbridge's major work on The Process, which he calls 'The
Power' in his book *Satan's Power* (Bainbridge, 1978). Bainbridge
cultivated an acquaintance with this movement over several
years, participating in its activities, befriending its members
and leaders, studying its writings. The book is a sympathetic
work but loses nothing of its objectivity or analytical clarity
for that. Bainbridge evokes a sense of the tangibility and
personality of the people involved. He conveys an understanding of the people and their style of organisation without constantly dusting off someone else's model or typology, or in
laboured and pedestrian fashion operationalising some set of
contrived and inconsequential 'hypotheses'. Bainbridge almost
errs too much the other way. He is rather cavalier about referring
to any comparable studies or relevant analytical or theoretical
ideas, and is sometimes less than explicit about the analytical
implications of his descriptive material.

Bainbridge does not entirely eschew the task of producing
theoretical formulations, however, and it is the combination of
first-rate ethnography with some important and suggestive ideas
concerning the formation of groups of this kind that make it far
the most valuable of these studies.

CONCLUSION

The lessons to be gathered are evident enough. New religious
movements must be carefully understood before they are
explained. The consequence of observing a new religious sect
at a distance or largely through the reports of hostile defectors
whose justifications for their former behaviour have become
thoroughly systematised in a rhetoric of 'mental kidnapping',
'hypnosis', or 'brainwashing', is to render the activity of the
movement mechanical and sinister; to dehumanise the behaviour
of its adherents; and to de-rationalise the beliefs - torn from
context - to which they display such commitment. Understanding
such movements is often likely to involve (but yet need not
entail) having some sympathy with them. Explanation and
analysis of any enduringly worthwhile kind are likely to emerge
from close and direct observation, particularly when this is
subjected to frequent comparative reference, rather than from
the mechanical application of standardised 'instruments'. The
latter style of exercise is likely to appear most fatuous when it
fails even in its *own* terms, by glossing over or ignoring the
need for adequate control groups subjected to the same standardised measures. Understanding even such alien groups as these

must begin from a position of interpretive charity in conceding the reasoned, if not always 'reasonable', behaviour of those involved, and in exploring that behaviour as the willed and motivated acts of the persons concerned. Explanations which begin from the premise that the bizarre and deviant behaviour which abounds in this field is a purely reactive response to mechanical compulsions, social or psychological, is likely to secure so little purchase upon the phenomena as to be of scant lasting value.[5]

Notes

1 References to conventional books and articles are given by the 'Harvard' system of author, date of publication and page, with full details given in the bibliography. Where a reference is to a movement publication with no author, or to ephemeral writings, details are given in the text. This reference is to a 'Mo Letter', the printed, occasional writing of Moses David (David Berg), leader of the Children of God.

2 This discussion of the Stark-Bainbridge theory was developed in association with Steve Bruce, and draws freely upon Wallis and Bruce (1983).

3 Dr Tom Robbins, in a characteristically acute commentary on an earlier version of this work, observed that a problem with my typology was that it conflated two quite different kinds of variable. On the one hand *ideological conceptualisations* of '*the world*', and on the other, *behavioural consequences of conversion*. Dr Robbins pointed out, for example, that students of the Black Muslims have argued that despite its ideological hostility to the world of white-dominated modern American society, the norms and values into which the movement socialised members were precisely those norms and values likely to enhance their propensity to succeed in and to be acceptable to that society. This is a significant point, which applies not only to world-rejecting movements, but also to world-affirming movements. For example, as shown above, while individuals may join such movements as Scientology in order to improve their circumstances in the world, absorption into the inner cadre may lead to behaviour distinctly hostile to the surrounding society. I would argue that in the present treatment the first case is handled in the discussion of the 'middle ground and the integrative hypothesis'. In so far as the behavioural consequences of movement membership are supportive of the prevailing society, to that degree the movement has moved away from the ideal-typical position of world-rejection, toward world-accommodation. The second case, of world-rejecting inner cadres in world-affirming movements is, of course, discussed above.

4 One of the best accounts by a former member of one of the new religious movements is Robert Kaufman's (1972) amusing, poignant and marvellously insightful account of his experience of Scientology.

5 An earlier version of this appendix appeared as Wallis (1980). I wish to offer a belated acknowledgment to Brooks Alexander and the Spiritual Counterfeits Project in Berkeley for generous access to SCP archives.

Bibliography

Adams, Robert L. and Robert J. Fox (1972), 'Mainlining Jesus: the new trip', 'Society' 9, 4: 50-6.

Alfred, H. Randall (1976), 'The Church of Satan', in Charles Glock and Robert Bellah (eds), 'The New Religious Consciousness', University of California Press Berkeley: 180-202.

Anson, Robert Sam (1978), 'The Synanon horrors', 'New Times', 27 November: 28-50.

Anthony, Dick and Thomas Robbins (1981), 'Culture crisis and contemporary religion', in Thomas Robbins and Dick Anthony (eds), 'In Gods We Trust', Transaction Books, New Brunswick.

Anthony, Dick and Thomas Robbins (1982a), 'Spiritual innovation and the crisis of American civil religion', 'Daedalus', 111, 1: 215-34.

Anthony, Dick and Thomas Robbins (1982b), 'Contemporary religious ferment and moral ambiguity', in Eileen Barker (ed.), 'New Religious Movements: A Perspective for Understanding Society', Edwin Mellen Press, New York.

Armstrong, Paul F. (1978), 'Taking Knowledge: A Sociological Approach to the Study of Meditation and the Divine Light Mission', PhD Dissertation Essex University, Colchester.

Atkins, Susan (with Bob Slosser) (1978), 'Child of Satan, Child of God', Hodder and Stoughton, London.

Babbie, Earl (1978), 'Unseating the horseman: world hunger', 'Downtown Magazine' (Honolulu), November.

Babbie, Earl and Donald Stone (1977), 'An evaluation of the est experience by a national sample of graduates', 'Bioscience Communication', 3: 123-40.

Back, Kurt W. (1972), 'Beyond Words: The Story of Sensitivity Training and the Encounter Movement', Russell Sage Foundation, New York.

Bainbridge, William S. (1978), 'Satan's Power: A Deviant Psychotherapy Cult', University of California Press, Berkeley.

Bainbridge, William S. and Daniel H. Jackson (1981), 'The rise and decline of Transcendental Meditation', in Bryan R. Wilson (ed.), 'The Social Impact of New Religious Movements', Rose of Sharon Press, New York: 135-58.

Bainbridge, William S. and Rodney Stark (1979), 'Cult formation: three compatible models', 'Sociological Analysis', 40, 4: 283-97.

Balswick, Jack (1974), 'The Jesus People movement: a generational interpretation', 'Journal of Social Issues', 30, 3: 23-42.

Barker, Eileen (1981), 'Who'd be a Moonie?', in Bryan R. Wilson (ed.), 'The Social Impact of New Religious Movements', Rose of Sharon Press, New York: 59-96.

Beckford, James A. (1978), 'Cults and cures', 'Japanese Journal of Religious Studies', 5, 4: 225-57.

Bellah, Robert N. (1967), 'Civil religion in America', 'Daedalus', 96, 1, 1967: 1-21.

Bellah, Robert N. (1969), 'Religious evolution', in Roland Robertson (ed.), 'Sociology of Religion', Penguin, Harmondsworth: 262-92.

Bellah, Robert N. (1970), 'Beyond Belief', Harper and Row, New York.

Bellah, Robert N. (1975), 'The Broken Covenant', Seabury, New York.

Bellah, Robert N. (1976), 'The new religious consciousness and the crisis of modernity', in Charles Glock and Robert Bellah (eds), 'The New Religious Consciousness', University of California Press, Berkeley: 333-52.

Berger, Peter (1965), 'Towards a sociological analysis of psychoanalysis',

'Social Research' 32, 1: 26-41.
Berger, Peter L. and Brigitte Berger (1976) 'Sociology: A Biographical Approach', Penguin, Harmondsworth. ⸜
Berger, Peter L., Brigitte Berger and Hansfried Kellner (1974), 'The Homeless Mind', Penguin, Harmondsworth.
Bird, Frederick (1979), 'The pursuit of innocence: new religious movements and moral accountability', 'Sociological Analysis' 40, 4: 335-46.
Birnbaum, N. (1955), 'Monarchs and sociologists: a reply to Professor Shils and Mr Young','Sociological Review', 3: 5-23.
Bishop, George (1972), 'Witness to Evil', Nash Publishing, Los Angeles.
Bradfield, Cecil D. (1975), 'An Investigation of Neo-Pentecostalism', PhD Dissertation, American University.
Brierley, P. (1978), 'UK Protestant Missions Handbook, Vol. 2: Home', Evangelical Alliance Bible Society, London.
Bromley, David G. and Anson D. Shupe (1979), 'Moonies' in America', Sage Publications, Beverly Hills.
Bry, Adelaide (1976), 'est: 60 Hours That Transform Your Life', Harper and Row, New York.
Bryant, M. Darroll and Susan Hodges (1978), 'Exploring Unification Theology', Rose of Sharon Press, New York.
Bugliosi, Vincent (with Curt Gentry) (1977), 'Helter Skelter: The Manson Murders', Penguin, Harmondsworth.
Campbell, Colin (1978), 'The secret religion of the educated classes', 'Sociological Analysis' 39, 2: 146-56.
Carey, Sean (unpublished), 'Preaching and conversion: ISKCON and the Asian community in Great Britain'.
Clark, Burton (1956), 'Organizational adaptation and precarious values', 'American Sociological Review' 21: 327-36.
Conway, Flo and Jim Siegelman (1978), 'Snapping: America's Epidemic of Sudden Personality Change', J.B. Lippincott, Philadelphia.
Currie, R., A. Gilbert and L. Horsley (1977), 'Churches and Churchgoers: Patterns of Church Growth and Decline in the British Isles Since 1700', Oxford University Press, London.
Damrell, Joseph (1977), 'Seeking Spiritual Meaning: The World of Vedanta', Sage Publications, Beverly Hills.
Daner, Francine Jeanne (1976), 'The American Children of Krsna: A Study of the Hare Krsna Movement', Holt, Rinehart and Winston, New York.
Dannenberg, Linda (1975), 'Tuning in to Mind Control', 'Family Circle', August: 16, 20, 21, 66.
Dator, James Allen (1969), 'Soka Gakkai: Builders of the Third Civilisation', University of Washington Press, Seattle, Wa.
Downton, James (1979), 'Sacred Journeys: The Conversion of Young Americans to Divine Light Mission', Columbia University Press New York.
Doyle, Paul Johnson (1979), 'Dilemmas of charismatic leadership: the case of the People's Temple', 'Sociological Analysis', 40, 4: 315-23.
Durkheim, Emile (1952), 'Suicide', Routledge & Kegan Paul, London.
Edwards, Christopher (1979), 'Crazy for God: The Nightmare of Cult Life', Prentice-Hall, Englewood Cliffs, NJ.
Ellwood, Robert S. (1973), 'One Way: The Jesus Movement and its Meaning', Prentice-Hall, Englewood Cliffs, NJ.
Ellwood, Robert S. (1974), 'The Eagle and the Rising Sun: Americans and the New Religions of Japan', Westminster Press, Philadelphia, Pa.
Enroth, Ronald (1977), 'Youth, Brainwashing and the Extremist Cults', Zondervan, Grand Rapids, Mich.
Enroth, Ronald, Edward Ericson and C.B. Peters (1972), 'The Jesus People', Erdmans, Grand Rapids, Mich.
Erhard, Werner (1973), 'If God had meant man to fly He would have given him wings', (no publisher given).
Fenwick, Sheridan (1977), 'Getting It: The Psychology of est', Penguin, New York.
Fichter, Joseph H. (1975), 'The Catholic Cult of the Paraclete', Sheed and Ward, New York.

Ford, J. Massyngberde (1976), 'Which Way for Catholic Pentecostals?', Harper, New York.

Forem, Jack (1973), 'Transcendental Meditation: Maharishi Mahesh Yogi and the Science of Creative Intelligence', Dutton, New York.

Foss, D. and Larkin, R. (1976), 'From "The Gates of Eden" to "Day of the Locust" an analysis of the dissident youth movement of the 1960s and its heirs in the 1970s - the post-movement groups', 'Theory and Society', 3: 45-64.

Gerth, Hans (1940), 'The Nazi Party: its leadership and composition', 'American Journal of Sociology', 44, 4: 517-41.

Greeley, Andrew (1972), 'Unsecular Man: The Persistence of Religion', Shocken Books, New York.

Gregg, Roy _Gene_(1973), 'Getting it on with Jesus: a Study of Adult Socialization', PhD Dissertation, University of Southern California.

Hammond, Judith Anne (1975), 'A Sociological Study of the Characteristics and Attitudes of Southern Charismatic Catholics', PhD Dissertation, Florida State University.

Hashimoto, Hideo and William McPherson (1976), 'Rise and decline of Sokagakkai in Japan and the United States', 'Review of Religious Research', 17, 2: 83-92.

Heinz, Donald (1976a), 'The Christian World Liberation Front', in Charles Glock and Robert Bellah (eds), 'The New Religious Consciousness', University of California Press, Berkeley: 143-61.

Heinz, Donald (1976b), 'Jesus in Berkeley', PhD Dissertation, Graduate Theological Union, Berkeley.

Hiller, Harry (1975) 'A reconceptualization of the dynamics of social movement development', 'Pacific Sociological Review', 17, 3: 342-59.

Hoffman, Eva (1977), 'Est: the magic of brutality', 'Dissent' 24, 2: 209-12.

Holtzapple, Vicki Rea (1977), 'Soka Gakkai in Midwestern America: A Case Study of a Transpositional Movement', PhD Dissertation, Washington University, St Louis, Missouri.

Horowitz, Irving Louis (ed.) (1978), 'Science, Sin and Scholarship: The Politics of Reverend Moon and the Unification Church', MIT Press, Cambridge, Mass.

Howard, John L. (1974), 'The Cutting Edge: Social Movements and Social Change in America', Lippincott, Philadelphia.

Jackins, Harvey (1978), 'The Human Side of Human Beings: The Theory of Re-evaluation Counseling', Rational Island Publishers, Seattle.

John-Roger (1976), 'The Christ Within', Baraka Press, New York.

Johnson, Doyle Paul (1979), 'Dilemmas of charismatic leadership: the case of the People's Temple', 'Sociological Analysis', 40, 4: 315-23.

Johnson, Gregory (1976), 'The Hare Krishna in San Francisco', in Charles Glock and Robert Bellah (eds), 'The New Religious Consciousness', University of California Press, Berkeley: 31-51.

Judah, J. Stillson (1974), 'Hare Krishna and the Counterculture', Wiley, New York.

Kanter, Rosabeth Moss (1972), 'Commitment and Community: Communes and Utopias in Sociological Perspective', Harvard University Press, Cambridge, Mass.

Kaufman, Robert (1972), 'Inside Scientology: How I Joined Scientology and Became Superhuman', Olympia Press, New York.

Keen, Sam (1973), 'Arica', 'Psychology Today' 7, 2 (July).

Kerns, Phil (with Doug Wead) (1979), 'People's Temple, People's Tomb', Logos International, Plainfield, NJ.

Krause, Charles (1978), 'Guyana Massacre', Washington Post Books, Washington, DC.

Lane, Ralph (1978), 'The Catholic Charismatic Renewal Movement in the United States: a reconsideration', 'Social Compass', 25, 1: 23-35.

Lang, Anthony (1978), 'Synanon Foundation: The People Business', Wayside Press, Cottonwood, Arizona.

Lasch, Christopher (1976), 'The narcissistic society', 'New York Review of Books', 30 September: 5-12.

Layard, Richard and John King (1969), 'Expansion since Robbins', in David Martin (ed.) 'Anarchy and Culture', Routledge & Kegan Paul, London.

Le Moult, John (1978), 'Deprogramming members of religious sects', 'Fordham Law Review', 46, 4: 599-640.

Liss, Jerome (1974), 'Free to Feel', Wildwood, House, London.

Lofland, John (1966), 'Doomsday Cult', Prentice-Hall, Englewood Cliffs, New Jersey.

Lofland, John (1977), 'The boom and bust of a millenarian movement: doomsday cult revisited', in his 'Doomsday Cult' (enlarged edition). Irvington Publishers, New York: 279-350.

Luckmann, Thomas and Peter Berger (1964), 'Social mobility and personal identity', 'European Journal of Sociology', 5: 331-43.

Lukes, Steven (1969), 'Durkheim's "Individualism and the intellectuals"', 'Political Studies' 17 1: 14-30

Mahesh Yogi, Maharishi (1962), 'The Divine Plan: Enjoy Your Own Inner Divine Nature', SRM Foundation, Los Angeles.

Mahesh Yogi, Maharishi (1977), 'Celebrating invincibility to every nation', (pamphlet) MERU Press, Geneva, 21 October.

Marin, Peter (1975), 'The new narcissism: the trouble with the Human Potential Movement', 'Harpers', 25, 1505: 45-56.

Martin, James M. (1977), 'Actualizations: Beyond est', San Francisco Book Co., San Francisco.

Martin, Rachel (1979), (as told to Bonnie Palmer Young), 'Escape', Accent Books, Denver, Colorado.

Mauss, Armand L. and Donald Petersen (1974), 'Les "Jesus Freaks" et le retour à la respectabilité', 'Social Compass', 21, 3: 283-301.

McCutchan, Robert (1977), 'The social and the celestial: Mary Douglas and Transcendental Meditation', 'The Princeton Journal of the Arts and Sciences', 1, 2: 130-63.

McGee, Michael (1976), 'Meher Baba - the sociology of religious conversion', 'The Graduate Journal' 9, 1-2: 43-71.

McGuire, Meredith (1975), 'Toward a sociological interpretation of the Catholic Pentecostal Movement', 'Review of Religious Research', 16, 2: 94-104.

McGuire, Meredith B. (1982), 'Pentecostal Catholics: Power, Charisma, and Order in a Religious Movement', Temple University Press, Philadelphia.

Mills, Jeannie (1979), 'Six Years With God: Life Inside Rev. Jim Jones' People's Temple', A. and W. Publishers, New York.

Moody, Edward (1974), 'Magical therapy: an anthropological investigation of contemporary Satanism', in Irving I. Zaretsky and Mark P. Leone (eds), 'Religious Movements in Contemporary America', Princeton University Press, Princeton, NJ: 355-82.

Naranjo, Betty Ann (1979), 'Biobehavioral Belonging: The Reorganisation of Behavior and the Reconstruction of Social Reality During Rites of Passage At Synanon', PhD Dissertation, University of California, Irvine.

Niebuhr, H. Richard (1957), 'The Social Sources of Denominationalism', Meridian, New York, (originally published 1929).

Nolan, James (1973), 'The Jesus freaks', in Jack Needleman, A.K. Biersman and James A. Gould (eds). 'Religion for a New Generation', Macmillan, New York: 35-43.

Nordquist, Ted (1978), 'Ananda Cooperative Village', Religionshistoriska Institutionen, Uppsala University, Uppsala, Sweden.

Ofshe, Richard (1976), 'Synanon: the people business', in C. Glock and Robert Bellah (eds). 'The New Religious Consciousness', University of California Press, Berkeley: 116-37.

Ofshe, Richard (1980), 'The social development of the Synanon cult: the managerial strategy of organizational transformation', 'Sociological Analysis', 41, 2: 109-27.

Oh, John Kie-chang (1973), 'The Nichiren Shoshu of America', 'Review of Religious Research', 14, 3: 169-77.

Olin, William, F. (1980), 'Escape From Utopia: My Ten Years in Synanon', Unity Press, Santa Cruz.

Parsons, Arthur S. (1974), 'Yoga in a western setting', 'Soundings',

57, 2: 222-35.
Patrick, Ted (1976), (with Tom Dulack), 'Let Our Children Go!', Dalton, New York.
Peterson, Donald W. and Armand L. Mauss (1973), 'The cross and the commune: an interpretation of the Jesus People', in Charles Y. Glock (ed.), 'Religion in Sociological Perspective', Wadsworth, Belmont, Ca.
Pilarzyk, Thomas (1978a), 'Conversion and alternation processes in the youth culture', 'Pacific Sociological Review', 21, 4: 379-405.
Pilarzyk, Thomas (1978b), 'The origin, development, and decline of a youth culture religion: an application of sectarianization theory', 'Review of Religious Research', 20, 1: 23-43.
Pilarzyk, Thomas and Cardell M. Jacobson (1977), 'Christians in the youth culture: the life history of an urban commune', 'Wisconsin Sociologist', 14, Fall: 136-51.
Price, Maeve (1979), 'The Divine Light Mission as a social organization', 'Sociological Review', 27, 2: 279-96.
Quebedeaux, Richard (1976), 'The New Charismatics', Doubleday, Garden City, NY.
Reis, John P. (1975), '"God is Not Dead, He Has Simply Changed His Clothes . . .": A Study of the International Society for Krsna Consciousness', PhD Dissertation, University of Wisconsin, Madison.
Richardson, James T., Mary W. Stewart and Roberta B. Simmonds (1979), 'Organized Miracles: A Study of a Contemporary, Youth, Communal, Fundamentalist Organization', Transaction Books, New Brunswick.
Robbins, Jhan, and David Fisher (1972), 'Tranquility Without Pills', Peter H. Wyden, New York.
Robbins, Thomas and Dick Anthony (1972), 'Getting straight with Meher Baba: a study of drug rehabilitation, mysticism and post-adolescent role-conflict', 'Journal for the Scientific Study of Religion', 11, 2: 122-40.
Robbins, Thomas and Dick Anthony (1978), 'New religious movements and the social system', 'Annual Review of the Social Sciences of Religion', 2: 1-28.
Robbins, Thomas, Dick Anthony and Thomas Curtis (1975), 'Youth culture religious movements: evaluating the integrative hypothesis', 'Sociological Quarterly', 16, 1: 48-64.
Robbins, Thomas, Dick Anthony, Thomas Curtis and Madalyn Doucas (1976), 'The last civil religion: the Unification Church of Reverend Sun Myung Moon', 'Sociological Analysis', 37, 2: 111-25.
Robbins, Thomas, Dick Anthony and James Richardson (1978), 'Theory and research on today's "new religions"', 'Sociological Analysis', 39, 2: 95-122.
Rochford, E. Burke (1982), 'Recruitment strategies, ideology and organization in the Hare Krishna Movement', 'Social Problems', 29, 4: 399-410.
Rowan, John (1976), 'Ordinary Ecstasy: Humanistic Psychology in Action', Routledge & Kegan Paul, London.
Rubin, Jerry (1976), 'Growing (Up) at Thirty-Seven', Evans, New York.
Ryan, Alan (1970), 'The Philosophy of the Social Sciences', Macmillan, London.
Sage, Wayne (1976), 'The war on cults', 'Human Behavior', 5, 10: 40-9.
Sanders, Ed (1973), 'The Family: The Whole Charles Manson Horrorshow', Panther Books, St Albans.
Sargant, William (1957), 'Battle for the Mind', Heinemann, London.
Schneider, Louis and Sanford M. Dornbusch (1958), 'Popular Religion: Inspirational Books in America', University of Chicago Press.
Schur, Edwin (1976), 'The Awareness Trap: Self-Absorption Instead of Social Change', McGraw Hill, New York.
Schutz, Will (1980), 'Encounter therapy', in Richie Herink (ed.), 'The Psychotherapy Handbook', New American Library, New York.
Scott, Gini Graham (1980), 'Cult and Countercult: a Study of a Spiritual Growth Group and a Witchcraft Order', Greenwood Press, Westport, Connecticut.
Scott, R.D. (1978), 'Transcendental Misconceptions', Beta Books, San Diego.
Shils, E. and M. Young (1953), 'The meaning of the Coronation', 'Sociological Review', 1: 63-81.

Shupe, Anson D. and David E. Bromley (1981), 'Apostates and atrocity stories: some parameters in the dynamics of deprogramming', in Bryan R. Wilson (ed.), 'The Social Impact of New Religious Movements', Rose of Sharon Press, New York.

Shupe, Anson D., Roger Spielmann and Sam Stigall (1977), 'Deprogramming: the new exorcism', 'American Behavioral Scientist', 20, 6: 941-56.

Silva, Jose and Philip Miele (1977), 'The Silva Mind Control Method', Pocket Books, New York.

Smith, David E. and Alan J. Rose (1970), 'The group marriage commune: a case study', 'Journal of Psychedelic Drugs' 3, 1: 115-19.

Snow, David Alan (1976), 'The Nichiren Shoshu Buddhist Movement in America: A Sociological Examination of its Value Orientation, Recruitment Efforts and Spread', PhD Dissertation, University of California, Los Angeles.

Snow, David A., Louis A. Zurcher and Sheldon Ekland-Olson (1980), 'Social networks and social movements: a microstructural approach to differential recruitment', 'American Sociological Review', 45, 5: 787-801.

Sontag, Frederick (1977), 'Sun Myung Moon and the Unification Church', Abingdon, Nashville.

Spiritual Counterfeits Project (1976), 'Who is this man and what does he want?', SCP, Berkeley.

Stark, Rodney (1981), 'Must all religions be supernatural?', in Bryan R. Wilson (ed.), 'The Social Impact of New Religious Movements', Rose of Sharon Press, New York.

Stark, Rodney (1983), 'Europe's receptivity to religious movements', in R. Stark (ed.), 'Religious Movements: Genesis, Exodus and Numbers', Rose of Sharon Press, New York.

Stark, Rodney and William S. Bainbridge (1980), 'Toward a theory of religion: religious commitment', 'Journal for the Scientific Study of Religion', 19, 2: 114-28.

Stone, Donald (1976), 'The Human Potential Movement', in Charles Glock and Robert Bellah (eds), 'The New Religious Consciousness', University of California Press, Berkeley: 93-115.

Stoner, Carroll and Jo Anne Parke (1977), 'All God's Children: The Cult Experience - Salvation or Slavery', Chilton, Radnor, Pa.

Taylor, David (1977), 'Thought reform and the Unification Church', paper presented to the Annual Meeting of the Society for the Scientific Study of Religion, Chicago, 28-30 October.

Taylor, David (1982), 'Becoming new people: the recruitment of young Americans into the Unification Church', in Roy Wallis (ed.), 'Millennialism and Charisma', The Queen's University of Belfast, Belfast, N. Ireland.

Theobald, Robin (1980), 'The role of charisma in the development of social movements: Ellen White and the emergence of Seventh-Day Adventism', 'Archives de Sciences Sociales des Religions' 49, 1: 83-100.

Thielmann, Bonnie (with Dean Merrill) (1979), 'The Broken God', David C. Cook, Elgin, Illinois.

Tipton, Steven M. (1979), 'New religious movements and the problem of a modern ethic', 'Sociological Inquiry' 49, 2-3: 286-312.

Tipton, Steven, M. (1982a), 'The moral logic of alternative religions', 'Daedalus', 111, 1: 185-213.

Tipton, Steven, M. (1982b), 'Getting Saved From the Sixties', University of California Press, Berkeley.

Tobey, Alan (1976), 'The summer solstice of the Healthy-Happy-Holy Organization', in Charles Glock and Robert Bellah (eds), 'The New Religious Consciousness', University of California Press, Berkeley: 5-30.

Underwood, Barbara and Betty Underwood (1979), 'Hostage to Heaven', Clarkson, N. Potter, New York.

Wallace, Robert Keith (1970), 'The Physiological Effects of Transcendental Meditation, A Proposed Fourth Major State of Consciousness', PhD Dissertation, University of California, Los Angeles.

Wallace, Robert Keith (1971), 'A wakeful hypometabolic physiologic state', 'American Journal of Physiology' 221, 3: 795-9.

Wallis, Roy (1974), 'The Aetherius Society: a case study in the formation of a mystagogic congregation', 'Sociological Review', 22, 1: 27-44, reprinted in Roy Wallis)ed.), 'Sectarianism: Analyses of Religious and Non-Religious Sects', Peter Owen, London, 1975.

Wallis, Roy (1975), 'Scientology: therapeutic cult to religious sect', 'Sociology', 9: 89-100).

Wallis, Roy (1976a), 'Observations on the Children of God', 'Sociological Review', 24, 4: 807-28.

Wallis, Roy (1976b), 'The Road to Total Freedom: A Sociological Analysis of Scientology', Heinemann, London.

Wallis, Roy (1977), 'Salvation from salvation', (title omitted from original), 'The Zetetic', 1, 2: 67-71.

Wallis, Roy (1978), 'The Rebirth of the Gods?', Inaugural Lecture, The Queen's University of Belfast, N. Ireland.

Wallis, Roy (1979a), 'Salvation and Protest: Studies of Social and Religious Movements', Frances Pinter, London, St Martin's Press, New York.

Wallis, Roy (1979b), 'Varieties of psychosalvation', 'New Society' 50, 897-898: 649-51.

Wallis, Roy (1980), 'What's new on the new religions', 'The Zetetic Scholar', 6: 155-69.

Wallis, Roy (1982a), 'The New Religions as Social Indicators', in Eileen Barker (ed.), 'New Religious Movements: A Perspective for Understanding Society', Edward Mellon Press, New York, pp. 216-31.

Wallis, Roy (1982b), 'The Social Construction of Charisma', 'Social Compass', Vol. 29, No. I, pp. 25-39.

Wallis, Roy (1982c), 'Charisma, commitment and control in a new religious movement', in Roy Wallis (ed.) 'Millennialism and Charisma', The Queen's University of Belfast, Belfast, N. Ireland.

Wallis, Roy (forthcoming), 'The dynamics of change in the Human Potential Movement', in Rod Stark (ed.), 'New Religious Movements: Genesis, Exodus and Numbers', Rose of Sharon Press, New York.

Wallis, Roy and Steve Bruce (1983), 'The Stark-Bainbridge theory of religion: a critique and counter proposals', 'Sociological Analysis'.

Watson, Tex (1978), 'Will You Die For Me?', Revell, Old Tappan, NJ.

Weber, Max (1947), 'The Theory of Social and Economic Organization', Free Press, New York.

Weber, Max (1948), 'The sociology of charismatic authority', in H. Gerth and C. Wright Mills (eds), 'From Max Weber: Essays in Sociology', Routledge & Kegan Paul, London.

Weigel, Richard E. (1977), 'The marathon encounter: requiem for a social movement', 'Small Group Behavior', 8, 2: 201-22.

Weldon, John (nd.), 'The frightening world of est', (pamphlet), 'Spiritual Counterfeits Project', Berkeley.

Welles, C. (1976), 'The eclipse of Sun Myung Moon', 'New York Magazine', 27 September: 33-8.

Wells, Jonathan (1978), 'Inside the Moon Movement', 'Yale Daily News', 31 October.

Westley, Frances (1978), '"The cult of man": Durkheim's predictions and new religious movements', 'Sociological Analysis', 39, 2: 135-45.

White, James W. (1970), 'The Sokagakkai and Mass Society', Stanford University Press, Stanford.

Whitworth, John McKelvie (1975), 'Communitarian groups and the world', in Roy Wallis (ed.), 'Sectarianism: Analyses of Religious and Non-Religious Sects', Peter Owen, London: 117-37.

Wilson, Bryan, R. (1959), 'An analysis of sect development', 'American Sociological Review', 24: 3-15.

Wilson, Bryan (1969), 'Religion in Secular Society: A Sociological Comment', Penguin, Harmondsworth.

Wilson, Bryan R. (1970a), 'Youth Culture and the Universities', Faber, London.

Wilson, Bryan (1970b), 'Religious Sects', Weidenfeld and Nicolson, London.

Wilson, Bryan R. (1973), 'Magic and the Millennium', Heinemann Educational Books, London.

Wilson, Bryan (1975), 'The Noble Savage: The Primitive Origins of Charisma', University of California, Berkeley.

Wilson, Bryan (1976), 'Contemporary Transformations of Religion', Oxford University Press, London.

Wilson, Bryan (1978), 'Sects and Society: A Sociological Study of Three Religious Groups in Britain', Greenwood Press, Connecticut. (Originally published by Heinemann Educational Books, London, 1961).

Wilson, Bryan R. (1979), 'The new religions: some preliminary considerations', 'Japanese Journal of Religious Studies', 6, 1-2: 193-216, reprinted in Eileen Barker (ed.), 'New Religious Movements: A Perspective for Understanding Society', Edwin Mellen Press, New York, 1982: 16-31.

Wilson, Bryan (1981), "The Brethren": a current sociological appraisal' (reprint) of a submission to the court, no publisher given).

Wilson, Bryan (1982), 'Religion in Sociological Perspective', Oxford University Press.

Wilson, John (1973), 'Introduction to Social Movements', Basic Books, New York.

Wilson, John F. (1979), 'Public Religion in American Culture', Temple University Press, Philadelphia.

Wolfe, Tom (1977), 'The me decade and the third great awakening', in his 'Mauve Gloves and Madmen, Clutter and Vine', Bantam, London, 1977: 111-47.

Wood, Allen Tate (with Jack Vitek) (1979), 'Moonstruck: A Memoir of My Life in a Cult', William Morrow, New York.

Woodrum, Eric (1977), 'The development of the Transcendental Meditation Movement', 'The Zetetic' 1, 2: 38-48.

Wuthnow, Robert (1978), 'Experimentation in American Religion', University of California Press, Berkeley.

Yablonsky, Lewis (1967), 'Synanon: The Tunnel Back', Penguin, Harmondsworth.

Yee, Min S. and Thomas N. Layton (1981), 'In My Father's House: The Story of the Layton Family and the Reverend Jim Jones', Holt, Rinehart and Winston, New York.

Yinger, J. Milton (1970), 'The Scientific Study of Religion', Macmillan, London.

Young, Jock (1971), 'The Drug Takers', McGibbon and Kee, London.

Zald, Mayer and Roberta Ash (1973), 'Social movement organisations: growth, decay and change', in Robert R. Evans (ed.), 'Social Movements: A Reader and Source Book', Rand McNally, Chicago, originally published in 'Social Forces' 44, 1965-66: 327-41.

Zamora, William (1976), 'Blood Family', Kensington Publishing, New York.

Index

Routledge Social Science Series

Routledge & Kegan Paul
London, Boston, Melbourne and Henley

39 Store Street, London WC1E 7DD
9 Park Street, Boston, Mass 02108
296 Beaconsfield Parade, Middle Park,
Melbourne, 3206 Australia
Broadway House, Newtown Road,
Henley-on-Thames, Oxon RG9 1EN

Contents

*Authors wishing to submit manuscripts for any series
in this catalogue should send them to the Social Science Editor,
Routledge & Kegan Paul plc, 39 Store Street,
London WC1E 7DD.*
● *Books so marked are available in paperback also.*
○ *Books so marked are available in paperback only.*
*All books are in metric Demy 8vo format (216 × 138mm approx.)
unless otherwise stated.*

International Library of Sociology
General Editor John Rex

GENERAL SOCIOLOGY

Alexander, J. Theoretical Logic in Sociology.
　Volume 1: Positivism, Presuppositions and Current Controversies. *234 pp.*
　Volume 2: The Antinomies of Classical Thought: *Marx and Durkheim.*
　Volume 3: The Classical Attempt at Theoretical Synthesis: *Max Weber.*
　Volume 4: The Modern Reconstruction of Classical Thought: *Talcott Parsons.*
Barnsley, J. H. The Social Reality of Ethics. *464 pp.*
Brown, Robert. Explanation in Social Science. *208 pp.*
● Rules and Laws in Sociology. *192 pp.*
Bruford, W. H. Chekhov and His Russia. *A Sociological Study. 244 pp.*
Burton, F. and **Carlen, P.** Official Discourse. *On Discourse Analysis, Government Publications, Ideology. 160 pp.*
Cain, Maureen E. Society and the Policeman's Role. *326 pp.*
● **Fletcher, Colin.** Beneath the Surface. *An Account of Three Styles of Sociological Research. 221 pp.*
Gibson, Quentin. The Logic of Social Enquiry. *240 pp.*
Glassner, B. Essential Interactionism. *208 pp.*
Glucksmann, M. Structuralist Analysis in Contemporary Social Thought. *212 pp.*
Gurvitch, Georges. Sociology of Law. *Foreword by Roscoe Pound. 264 pp.*
Hinkle, R. Founding Theory of American Sociology 1881–1913. *376 pp.*
Homans, George C. Sentiments and Activities. *336 pp.*
Johnson, Harry M. Sociology: *A Systematic Introduction. Foreword by Robert K. Merton. 710 pp.*
● **Keat, Russell** and **Urry, John.** Social Theory as Science. *Second Edition. 278 pp.*
Mannheim, Karl. Essays on Sociology and Social Psychology. *Edited by Paul Keckskemeti. With Editorial Note by Adolph Lowe. 344 pp.*
Martindale, Don. The Nature and Types of Sociological Theory. *292 pp.*
● **Maus, Heinz.** A Short History of Sociology. *234 pp.*
Merquior, J. G. Rousseau and Weber. *A Study in the Theory of Legitimacy. 240 pp.*
Myrdal, Gunnar. Value in Social Theory: *A Collection of Essays on Methodology. Edited by Paul Streeten. 332 pp.*
Ogburn, William F. and **Nimkoff, Meyer F.** A Handbook of Sociology. *Preface by Karl Mannheim. 656 pp. 46 figures. 35 tables.*
Parsons, Talcott and **Smelser, Neil J.** Economy and Society: *A Study in the Integration of Economic and Social Theory. 362 pp.*
Payne, G., Dingwall, R., Payne, J. and **Carter, M.** Sociology and Social Research. *336 pp.*
Podgórecki, A. Practical Social Sciences. *144 pp.*
Podgórecki, A. and **Łos, M.** Multidimensional Sociology. *268 pp.*
Raffel, S. Matters of Fact. *A Sociological Inquiry. 152 pp.*
● **Rex, John.** Key Problems of Sociological Theory. *220 pp.*
　Sociology and the Demystification of the Modern World. *282 pp.*
● **Rex, John.** (Ed.) Approaches to Sociology. *Contributions by Peter Abell, Frank Bechhofer, Basil Bernstein, Ronald Fletcher, David Frisby, Miriam Glucksmann, Peter Lassman, Herminio Martins, John Rex, Roland Robertson, John Westergaard and Jock Young. 302 pp.*
Rigby, A. Alternative Realities. *352 pp.*
Roche, M. Phenomenology, Language and the Social Sciences. *374 pp.*
Sahay, A. Sociological Analysis. *220 pp.*
Strasser, Hermann. The Normative Structure of Sociology. *Conservative and Emancipatory Themes in Social Thought. 286 pp.*

Strong, P. Ceremonial Order of the Clinic. *267 pp.*
Urry, J. Reference Groups and the Theory of Revolution. *244 pp.*
Weinberg, E. Development of Sociology in the Soviet Union. *173 pp.*

FOREIGN CLASSICS OF SOCIOLOGY

● **Gerth, H. H.** and **Mills, C. Wright.** From Max Weber: *Essays in Sociology.* *502 pp.*
● **Tönnies, Ferdinand.** Community and Association (*Gemeinschaft und Gesellschaft*). *Translated and Supplemented by Charles P. Loomis. Foreword by Pitirim A. Sorokin. 334 pp.*

SOCIAL STRUCTURE

Andreski, Stanislav. Military Organization and Society. *Foreword by Professor A. R. Radcliffe-Brown. 226 pp. 1 folder.*
Bozzoli, B. The Political Nature of a Ruling Class. *Capital and Ideology in South Africa 1890–1939. 396 pp.*
Bauman, Z. Memories of Class. *The Prehistory and After life of Class. 240 pp.*
Broom, L., Lancaster Jones, F., McDonnell, P. and **Williams, T.** The Inheritance of Inequality. *208 pp.*
Carlton, Eric. Ideology and Social Order. *Foreword by Professor Philip Abrahams. 326 pp.*
Clegg, S. and **Dunkerley, D.** Organization, Class and Control. *614 pp.*
Coontz, Sydney H. Population Theories and the Economic Interpretation. *202 pp.*
Coser, Lewis. The Functions of Social Conflict. *204 pp.*
Crook, I. and **D.** The First Years of the Yangyi Commune. *304 pp., illustrated.*
Dickie-Clark, H. F. Marginal Situation: *A Sociological Study of a Coloured Group. 240 pp. 11 tables.*
Fidler, J. The British Business Elite. *Its Attitudes to Class, Status and Power. 332 pp.*
Giner, S. and **Archer, M. S.** (Eds) Contemporary Europe: *Social Structures and Cultural Patterns. 336 pp.*
● **Glaser, Barney** and **Strauss, Anselm L.** Status Passage: *A Formal Theory. 212 pp.*
Glass, D. V. (Ed.) Social Mobility in Britain. *Contributions by J. Berent, T. Bottomore, R. C. Chambers, J. Floud, D. V. Glass, J. R. Hall, H. T. Himmelweit, R. K. Kelsall, F. M. Martin, C. A. Moser, R. Mukherjee and W. Ziegel. 420 pp.*
Kelsall, R. K. Higher Civil Servants in Britain: *From 1870 to the Present Day. 268 pp. 31 tables.*
● **Lawton, Denis.** Social Class, Language and Education. *192 pp.*
McLeish, John. The Theory of Social Change. *Four Views Considered. 128 pp.*
● **Marsh, David C.** The Changing Social Structure of England and Wales, 1871–1961. *Revised edition. 288 pp.*
Menzies, Ken. Talcott Parsons and the Social Image of Man. *206 pp.*
● **Mouzelis, Nicos.** Organization and Bureaucracy. *An Analysis of Modern Theories. 240 pp.*
● **Ossowski, Stanislaw.** Class Structure in the Social Consciousness. *210 pp.*
● **Podgórecki, Adam.** Law and Society. *302 pp.*
Ratcliffe, P. Racism and Reaction. *A Profile of Handsworth. 388 pp.*
Renner, Karl. Institutions of Private Law and Their Social Functions. *Edited, with an Introduction and Notes, by O. Kahn-Freud. Translated by Agnes Schwarzschild. 316 pp.*
Rex, J. and **Tomlinson, S.** Colonial Immigrants in a British City. *A Class Analysis. 368 pp.*
Smooha, S. Israel. *Pluralism and Conflict. 472 pp.*
Strasser, H. and **Randall, S. C.** An Introduction to Theories of Social Change. *300 pp.*

Wesolowski, W. Class, Strata and Power. *Trans. and with Introduction by G. Kolankiewicz. 160 pp.*

Zureik, E. Palestinians in Israel. *A Study in Internal Colonialism. 264 pp.*

SOCIOLOGY AND POLITICS

Acton, T. A. Gypsy Politics and Social Change. *316 pp.*

Burton, F. Politics of Legitimacy. *Struggles in a Belfast Community. 250 pp.*

Crook, I. and D. Revolution in a Chinese Village. *Ten Mile Inn. 216 pp., illustrated.*

de Silva, S. B. D. The Political Economy of Underdevelopment. *640 pp.*

Etzioni-Halevy, E. Political Manipulation and Administrative Power. *A Comparative Study. 228 pp.*

Fielding, N. The National Front. *260 pp.*

● Hechter, Michael. Internal Colonialism. *The Celtic Fringe in British National Development, 1536–1966. 380 pp.*

Levy, N. The Foundations of the South African Cheap Labour System. *367 pp.*

Kornhauser, William. The Politics of Mass Society. *272 pp. 20 tables.*

● Korpi, W. The Working Class in Welfare Capitalism. *Work, Unions and Politics in Sweden. 472 pp.*

Kroes, R. Soldiers and Students. *A Study of Right- and Left-wing Students. 174 pp.*

Martin, Roderick. Sociology of Power. *214 pp.*

Merquior, J. G. Rousseau and Weber. *A Study in the Theory of Legitimacy. 286 pp.*

Myrdal, Gunnar. The Political Element in the Development of Economic Theory. *Translated from the German by Paul Streeten. 282 pp.*

Preston, P. W. Theories of Development. *296 pp.*

Varma, B. N. The Sociology and Politics of Development. *A Theoretical Study. 236 pp.*

Wong, S.-L. Sociology and Socialism in Contemporary China. *160 pp.*

Wootton, Graham. Workers, Unions and the State. *188 pp.*

CRIMINOLOGY

Ancel, Marc. Social Defence: *A Modern Approach to Criminal Problems. Foreword by Leon Radzinowicz. 240 pp.*

Athens, L. Violent Criminal Acts and Actors. *104 pp.*

Cain, Maureen E. Society and the Policeman's Role. *326 pp.*

Cloward, Richard A. and Ohlin, Lloyd E. Delinquency and Opportunity: *A Theory of Delinquent Gangs. 248 pp.*

Downes, David M. The Delinquent Solution. *A Study in Subcultural Theory. 296 pp.*

Friedlander, Kate. The Psycho-Analytical Approach to Juvenile Delinquency: *Theory, Case Studies, Treatment. 320 pp.*

Gleuck, Sheldon and Eleanor. Family Environment and Delinquency. *With the statistical assistance of Rose W. Kneznek. 340 pp.*

Lopez-Rey, Manuel. Crime. *An Analytical Appraisal. 288 pp.*

Mannheim, Hermann. Comparative Criminology: *A Text Book. Two volumes. 442 pp. and 380 pp.*

Morris, Terence. The Criminal Area: *A Study in Social Ecology. Foreword by Hermann Mannheim. 232 pp. 25 tables. 4 maps.*

Rock, Paul. Making People Pay. *338 pp.*

● Taylor, Ian, Walton, Paul and Young, Jock. The New Criminology. *For a Social Theory of Deviance. 325 pp.*

● Taylor, Ian, Walton, Paul and Young, Jock. (Eds) Critical Criminology. *268 pp.*

SOCIAL PSYCHOLOGY

Bagley, Christopher. The Social Psychology of the Epileptic Child. *320 pp.*
Brittan, Arthur. Meanings and Situations. *224 pp.*
Carroll, J. Break-Out from the Crystal Palace. *200 pp.*
● **Fleming, C. M.** Adolescence: Its Social Psychology. *With an Introduction to recent findings from the fields of Anthropology, Physiology, Medicine, Psychometrics and Sociometry. 288 pp.*
● The Social Psychology of Education: *An Introduction and Guide to Its Study. 136 pp.*
Linton, Ralph. The Cultural Background of Personality. *132 pp.*
● **Mayo, Elton.** The Social Problems of an Industrial Civilization. *With an Appendix on the Political Problem. 180 pp.*
Ottaway, A. K. C. Learning Through Group Experience. *176 pp.*
Plummer, Ken. Sexual Stigma. *An Interactionist Account. 254 pp.*
● **Rose, Arnold M.** (Ed.) Human Behaviour and Social Processes: *an Interactionist Approach. Contributions by Arnold M. Rose, Ralph H. Turner, Anselm Strauss, Everett C. Hughes, E. Franklin Frazier, Howard S. Becker et al. 696 pp.*
Smelser, Neil J. Theory of Collective Behaviour. *448 pp.*
Stephenson, Geoffrey M. The Development of Conscience. *128 pp.*
Young, Kimball. Handbook of Social Psychology. *658 pp. 16 figures. 10 tables.*

SOCIOLOGY OF THE FAMILY

Bell, Colin R. Middle Class Families: *Social and Geographical Mobility. 224 pp.*
Burton, Lindy. Vulnerable Children. *272 pp.*
Gavron, Hannah. The Captive Wife: *Conflicts of Household Mothers. 190 pp.*
George, Victor and **Wilding, Paul.** Motherless Families. *248 pp.*
Klein, Josephine. Samples from English Cultures.
 1. Three Preliminary Studies and Aspects of Adult Life in England. *447 pp.*
 2. Child-Rearing Practices and Index. *247 pp.*
Klein, Viola. The Feminine Character. *History of an Ideology. 244 pp.*
McWhinnie, Alexina M. Adopted Children. *How They Grow Up. 304 pp.*
● **Morgan, D. H. J.** Social Theory and the Family. *188 pp.*
● **Myrdal, Alva** and **Klein, Viola.** Women's Two Roles: *Home and Work. 238 pp. 27 tables.*
Parsons, Talcott and **Bales, Robert F.** Family: Socialization and Interaction Process. *In collaboration with James Olds, Morris Zelditch and Philip E. Slater. 456 pp. 50 figures and tables.*

SOCIAL SERVICES

Bastide, Roger. The Sociology of Mental Disorder. *Translated from the French by Jean McNeil. 260 pp.*
Carlebach, Julius. Caring for Children in Trouble. *266 pp.*
George, Victor. Foster Care. *Theory and Practice. 234 pp.*
 Social Security: *Beveridge and After. 258 pp.*
George, V. and **Wilding, P.** Motherless Families. *248 pp.*
● **Goetschius, George W.** Working with Community Groups. *256 pp.*
Goetschius, George W. and **Tash, Joan.** Working with Unattached Youth. *416 pp.*
Heywood, Jean S. Children in Care. *The Development of the Service for the Deprived Child. Third revised edition. 284 pp.*
King, Roy D., Ranes, Norma V. and **Tizard, Jack.** Patterns of Residential Care. *356 pp.*
Leigh, John. Young People and Leisure. *256 pp.*
● **Mays, John.** (Ed.) Penelope Hall's Social Services of England and Wales. *368 pp.*

Morris Mary. Voluntary Work and the Welfare State. *300 pp.*
Nokes. P. L. The Professional Task in Welfare Practice. *152 pp.*
Timms, Noel. Psychiatric Social Work in Great Britain (1939–1962). *280 pp.*
● Social Casework: *Principles and Practice. 256 pp.*

SOCIOLOGY OF EDUCATION

Banks, Olive. Parity and Prestige in English Secondary Education: a Study in Educational Sociology. *272 pp.*
● **Blyth, W. A. L.** English Primary Education. *A Sociological Description.*
2. Background. *168 pp.*
Collier, K. G. The Social Purposes of Education: *Personal and Social Values in Education. 268 pp.*
Evans, K. M. Sociometry and Education. *158 pp.*
● **Ford, Julienne.** Social Class and the Comprehensive School. *192 pp.*
Foster, P. J. Education and Social Change in Ghana. *336 pp. 3 maps.*
Fraser, W. R. Education and Society in Modern France. *150 pp.*
Grace, Gerald R. Role Conflict and the Teacher. *150 pp.*
Hans, Nicholas. New Trends in Education in the Eighteenth Century. *278 pp. 19 tables.*
● Comparative Education: *A Study of Educational Factors and Traditions. 360 pp.*
● **Hargreaves, David.** Interpersonal Relations and Education. *432 pp.*
● Social Relations in a Secondary School. *240 pp.*
School Organization and Pupil Involvement. *A Study of Secondary Schools.*
● **Mannheim, Karl** and **Stewart, W. A. C.** An Introduction to the Sociology of Education. *206 pp.*
● **Musgrove, F.** Youth and the Social Order. *176 pp.*
● **Ottaway, A. K. C.** Education and Society: An Introduction to the Sociology of Education. *With an Introduction by W. O. Lester Smith. 212 pp.*
Peers, Robert. Adult Education: *A Comparative Study. Revised edition. 398 pp.*
Stratta, Erica. The Education of Borstal Boys. *A Study of their Educational Experiences prior to, and during, Borstal Training. 256 pp.*
● **Taylor, P. H., Reid, W. A.** and **Holley, B. J.** The English Sixth Form. *A Case Study in Curriculum Research. 198 pp.*

SOCIOLOGY OF CULTURE

● **Eppel, E. M.** and **M.** Adolescents and Morality: *A Study of some Moral Values and Dilemmas of Working Adolescents in the Context of a changing Climate of Opinion. Foreword by W. J. H. Sprott. 268 pp. 39 tables.*
● **Fromm, Erich.** The Fear of Freedom. *286 pp.*
● The Sane Society. *400 pp.*
Johnson, L. The Cultural Critics. *From Matthew Arnold to Raymond Williams. 233 pp.*
Mannheim, Karl. Essays on the Sociology of Culture. *Edited by Ernst Mannheim in co-operation with Paul Kecskemeti. Editorial Note by Adolph Lowe. 280 pp.*
Structures of Thinking. *Edited by David Kettler, Volker Meja and Nico Stehr. 304 pp.*
Merquior, J. G. The Veil and the Mask. *Essays on Culture and Ideology. Foreword by Ernest Gellner. 140 pp.*
Zijderfeld, A. C. On Clichés. *The Supersedure of Meaning by Function in Modernity. 150 pp.*
Reality in a Looking Glass. *Rationality through an Analysis of Traditional Folly. 208 pp.*

SOCIOLOGY OF RELIGION

Argyle, Michael and **Beit-Hallahmi, Benjamin.** The Social Psychology of Religion. *256 pp.*

Glasner, Peter E. The Sociology of Secularisation. *A Critique of a Concept. 146 pp.*

Hall, J. R. The Ways Out. *Utopian Communal Groups in an Age of Babylon. 280 pp.*

Ranson, S., Hinings, B. and **Bryman, A.** Clergy, Ministers and Priests. *216 pp.*

Stark, Werner. The Sociology of Religion. *A Study of Christendom.*
Volume II. *Sectarian Religion. 368 pp.*
Volume III. *The Universal Church. 464 pp.*
Volume IV. *Types of Religious Man. 352 pp.*
Volume V. *Types of Religious Culture. 464 pp.*

Turner, B. S. Weber and Islam. *216 pp.*

Watt, W. Montgomery. Islam and the Integration of Society. 230 pp.

Pomian-Srzednicki, M. Religious Change in Contemporary Poland. *Sociology and Secularization. 280 pp.*

SOCIOLOGY OF ART AND LITERATURE

Jarvie, Ian C. Towards a Sociology of the Cinema. *A Comparative Essay on the Structure and Functioning of a Major Entertainment Industry. 405 pp.*

Rust, Frances S. Dance in Society. *An Analysis of the Relationships between the Social Dance and Society in England from the Middle Ages to the Present Day. 256 pp. 8 pp. of plates.*

Schücking, L. L. The Sociology of Literary Taste. *112 pp.*

Wolff, Janet. Hermeneutic Philosophy and the Sociology of Art. *150 pp.*

SOCIOLOGY OF KNOWLEDGE

Diesing, P. Patterns of Discovery in the Social Sciences. *262 pp.*

● **Douglas, J. D.** (Ed.) Understanding Everyday Life. *270 pp.*

● **Hamilton, P.** Knowledge and Social Structure. *174 pp.*

Jarvie, I. C. Concepts and Society. *232 pp.*

Mannheim, Karl. Essays on the Sociology of Knowledge. *Edited by Paul Kecskemeti. Editorial Note by Adolph Lowe. 353 pp.*

Remmling, Gunter W. The Sociology of Karl Mannheim. *With a Bibliographical Guide to the Sociology of Knowledge, Ideological Analysis, and Social Planning. 255 pp.*

Remmling, Gunter W. (Ed.) Towards the Sociology of Knowledge. *Origin and Development of a Sociological Thought Style. 463 pp.*

Scheler, M. Problems of a Sociology of Knowledge. *Trans. by M. S. Frings. Edited and with an Introduction by K. Stikkers. 232 pp.*

URBAN SOCIOLOGY

Aldridge, M. The British New Towns. *A Programme Without a Policy. 232 pp.*

Ashworth, William. The Genesis of Modern British Town Planning: *A Study in Economic and Social History of the Nineteenth and Twentieth Centuries. 288 pp.*

Brittan, A. The Privatised World. *196 pp.*

Cullingworth, J. B. Housing Needs and Planning Policy: *a Restatement of the Problems of Housing Need and 'Overspill' in England and Wales. 232 pp. 44 tables. 8 maps.*

Dickinson, Robert E. City and Region: *A Geographical Interpretation. 608 pp. 125 figures.*
The West European City: *A Geographical Interpretation. 600 pp. 129 maps. 29 plates.*

Humphreys, Alexander J. New Dubliners: *Urbanization and the Irish Family.*
Foreword by George C. Homans. 304 pp.

Jackson, Brian. Working Class Community: *Some General Notions raised by a
Series of Studies in Northern England. 192 pp.*

● **Mann, P. H.** An Approach to Urban Sociology. *240 pp.*

Mellor, J. R. Urban Sociology in an Urbanized Society. *326 pp.*

Morris, R. N. and **Mogey, J.** The Sociology of Housing. *Studies at Berinsfield.
232 pp. 4 pp. plates.*

Mullan, R. Stevenage Ltd. *438 pp.*

Rex, J. and **Tomlinson, S.** Colonial Immigrants in a British City. *A Class
Analysis. 368 pp.*

Rosser, C. and **Harris, C.** The Family and Social Change. *A Study of Family
and Kinship in a South Wales Town. 352 pp. 8 maps.*

● **Stacey, Margaret, Batsone, Eric, Bell, Colin** and **Thurcott, Anne.** Power,
Persistence and Change. *A Second Study of Banbury. 196 pp.*

RURAL SOCIOLOGY

● **Mayer, Adrian C.** Peasants in the Pacific. *A Study of Fiji Indian Rural Society.
248 pp. 20 plates.*

Williams, W. M. The Sociology of an English Village: *Gosforth. 272 pp.
12 figures. 13 tables.*

SOCIOLOGY OF INDUSTRY AND DISTRIBUTION

Dunkerley, David. The Foreman. *Aspects of Task and Structure. 192 pp.*

Eldridge, J. E. T. *Industrial Disputes. Essays in the Sociology of Industrial
Relations. 288 pp.*

Hollowell, Peter G. The Lorry Driver. *272 pp.*

● **Oxaal, I., Barnett, T.** and **Booth, D.** (Eds) Beyond the Sociology of
Development. *Economy and Society in Latin America and Africa. 295 pp.*

Smelser, Neil J. Social Change in the Industrial Revolution: *An Application of
Theory to the Lancashire Cotton Industry, 1770–1840. 468 pp. 12 figures.
14 tables.*

Watson, T. J. The Personnel Managers. *A Study in the Sociology of Work and
Employment, 262 pp.*

ANTHROPOLOGY

Brandel-Syrier, Mia. Reeftown Elite. *A Study of Social Mobility in a Modern
African Community on the Reef. 376 pp.*

Dickie-Clark, H. F. The Marginal Situation. *A Sociological Study of a Coloured
Group. 236 pp.*

Dube, S. C. Indian Village. *Foreword by Morris Edward Opler. 276 pp.
4 plates.*

India's Changing Villages: *Human Factors in Community Development.
260 pp. 8 plates. 1 map.*

Fei, H.-T. Peasant Life in China. *A Field Study of Country Life in the Yangtze
Valley. With a foreword by Bronislaw Malinowski. 328 pp. 16 pp. plates.*

Firth, Raymond. Malay Fishermen. *Their Peasant Economy. 420 pp. 17 pp.
plates.*

Gulliver, P. H. Social Control in an African Society: a Study of the Arusha,
Agricultural Masai of Northern Tanganykia. *320 pp. 8 plates. 10 figures.*
Family Herds. *288 pp.*

Jarvie, Ian C. The Revolution in Anthropology. *268 pp.*

Little, Kenneth L. Mende of Sierra Leone. *308 pp. and folder.*
Negroes in Britain. *With a New Introduction and Contemporary Study by
Leonard Bloom. 320 pp.*

Tambs-Lyche, H. London Patidars. *168 pp.*
Madan, G. R. Western Sociologists on Indian Society. *Marx, Spencer, Weber, Durkheim, Pareto. 384 pp.*
Mayer, A. C. Peasants in the Pacific. *A Study of Fiji Indian Rural Society. 248 pp.*
Meer, Fatima. Race and Suicide in South Africa. *325 pp.*
Smith, Raymond T. The Negro Family in British Guiana: *Family Structure and Social Status in the Villages. With a Foreword by Meyer Fortes. 314 pp. 8 plates. 1 figure. 4 maps.*

SOCIOLOGY AND PHILOSOPHY

● **Adriaansens, H.** Talcott Parsons and the Conceptual Dilemma. *200 pp.*
Barnsley, John H. The Social Reality of Ethics. *A Comparative Analysis of Moral Codes. 448 pp.*
Diesing, Paul. Patterns of Discovery in the Social Sciences. *362 pp.*
● **Douglas, Jack D.** (Ed.) Understanding Everyday Life. *Toward the Reconstruction of Sociological Knowledge. Contributions by Alan F. Blum, Aaron W. Cicourel, Norman K. Denzin, Jack D. Douglas, John Heeren, Peter McHugh, Peter K. Manning, Melvin Power, Matthew Speier, Roy Turner, D. Lawrence Wieder, Thomas P. Wilson and Don H. Zimmerman. 370 pp.*
Gorman, Robert A. The Dual Vision. *Alfred Schutz and the Myth of Phenomenological Social Science. 240 pp.*
Jarvie, Ian C. Concepts and Society. *216 pp.*
Kilminster, R. Praxis and Method. *A Sociological Dialogue with Lukács, Gramsci and the Early Frankfurt School. 334 pp.*
Outhwaite, W. Concept Formation in Social Science. *255 pp.*
● **Pelz, Werner.** The Scope of Understanding in Sociology. *Towards a More Radical Reorientation in the Social Humanistic Sciences. 283 pp.*
Roche, Maurice, Phenomenology, Language and the Social Sciences. *371 pp.*
Sahay, Arun. Sociological Analysis. *212 pp.*
● **Slater, P.** Origin and Significance of the Frankfurt School. *A Marxist Perspective. 185 pp.*
Spurling, L. Phenomenology and the Social World. *The Philosophy of Merleau-Ponty and its Relation to the Social Sciences. 222 pp.*
Wilson, H. T. The American Ideology. *Science, Technology and Organization as Modes of Rationality. 368 pp.*

International Library of Anthropology
General Editor Adam Kuper

● **Ahmed, A. S.** Millennium and Charisma Among Pathans. *A Critical Essay in Social Anthropology. 192 pp.*
Pukhtun Economy and Society. *Traditional Structure and Economic Development. 422 pp.*
Barth, F. Selected Essays. *Volume 1. 256 pp.* Selected Essays. *Volume II. 200 pp.*
Brown, Paula. The Chimbu. *A Study of Change in the New Guinea Highlands. 151 pp.*
Duller, H. J. Development Technology. *192 pp.*
Foner, N. Jamaica Farewell. *200 pp.*
Gudeman, Stephen. Relationships, Residence and the Individual. *A Rural Panamanian Community. 288 pp. 11 plates, 5 figures, 2 maps, 10 tables.*
The Demise of a Rural Economy. *From Subsistence to Capitalism in a Latin American Village. 160 pp.*

Hamnett, Ian. Chieftainship and Legitimacy. *An Anthropological Study of Executive Law in Lesotho. 163 pp.*
Hanson, F. Allan. Meaning in Culture. *127 pp.*
Hazan, H. The Limbo People. *A Study of the Constitution of the Time Universe Among the Aged. 208 pp.*
Humphreys, S. C. Anthropology and the Greeks. *288 pp.*
Karp, I. Fields of Change Among the Iteso of Kenya. *140 pp.*
Kuper, A. Wives for Cattle. *Bridewealth in Southern Africa. 224 pp.*
Lloyd, P. C. Power and Independence. *Urban Africans' Perception of Social Inequality. 264 pp.*
Malinowski, B. and **de la Fuente, J.** Malinowski in Mexico. *The Economics of a Mexican Market System. Edited and Introduced by Susan Drucker-Brown. About 240 pp.*
Parry, J. P. Caste and Kinship in Kangra. *352 pp. Illustrated.*
Pettigrew, Joyce. Robber Noblemen. *A Study of the Political System of the Sikh Jats. 284 pp.*
Street, Brian V. The Savage in Literature. *Representations of 'Primitive' Society in English Fiction, 1858–1920. 207 pp.*
Van Den Berghe, Pierre L. Power and Privilege at an African University. *278 pp.*

International Library of Phenomenology and Moral Sciences
General Editor John O'Neill

Adorno, T. W. Aesthetic Theory. Translated by C. Lenhardt.
Apel, K.-O. Towards a Transformation of Philosophy. *308 pp.*
Bologh, R. W. Dialectical Phenomenology. *Marx's Method. 287 pp.*
Fekete, J. The Critical Twilight. *Explorations in the Ideology of Anglo-American Literary Theory from Eliot to McLuhan. 300 pp.*
Green, B. S. Knowing the Poor. *A Case Study in Textual Reality Construction. 200 pp.*
McHoul, A. W. How Texts Talk. *Essays on Reading and Ethnomethodology. 163 pp.*
Medina, A. Reflection, Time and the Novel. *Towards a Communicative Theory of Literature. 143 pp.*
O'Neill, J. Essaying Montaigne. *A Study of the Renaissance Institution of Writing and Reading. 244 pp.*
Schutz. A. Life Forms and Meaning Structure. *Translated, Introduced and Annotated by Helmut Wagner. 207 pp.*

International Library of Social Policy
General Editor Kathleen Jones

Bayley, M. Mental Handicap and Community Care. *426 pp.*
Bottoms, A. E. and **McClean, J. D.** Defendants in the Criminal Process. *284 pp.*
Bradshaw, J. The Family Fund. *An Initiative in Social Policy. 248 pp.*
Butler, J. R. Family Doctors and Public Policy. *208 pp.*
Davies, Martin. Prisoners of Society. *Attitudes and Aftercare. 204 pp.*
Gittus, Elizabeth. Flats, Families and the Under-Fives. *285 pp.*
Holman, Robert. Trading in Children. *A Study of Private Fostering. 355 pp.*
Jeffs, A. Young People and the Youth Service. *160 pp.*
Jones, Howard and **Cornes, Paul.** Open Prisons. *288 pp.*
Jones, Kathleen. History of the Mental Health Service. *428 pp.*

Jones, Kathleen with Brown, John, Cunningham, W. J., Roberts, Julian and
Williams, Peter. Opening the Door. *A Study of New Policies for the
Mentally Handicapped. 278 pp.*

Karn, Valerie. Retiring to the Seaside. *400 pp. 2 maps. Numerous tables.*

King, R. D. and Elliot, K. W. Albany: Birth of a Prison—End of an Era.
294 pp.

Thomas, J. E. The English Prison Officer since 1850. *258 pp.*

Walton, R. G. Women in Social Work. *303 pp.*

● Woodward, J. To Do the Sick No Harm. *A Study of the British Voluntary
Hospital System to 1875. 234 pp.*

International Library of Welfare and Philosophy
General Editors   Noel Timms and David Watson

○ Campbell, J. The Left and Rights. *A Conceptual Analysis of the Idea of
Socialist Rights. About 296 pp.*

● McDermott, F. E. (Ed.) Self-Determination in Social Work. *A Collection of
Essays on Self-determination and Related Concepts by Philosophers and
Social Work Theorists. Contributors: F. P. Biestek, S. Bernstein, A. Keith-
Lucas, D. Sayer, H. H. Perelman, C. Whittington, R. F. Stalley, F. E.
McDermott, I. Berlin, H. J. McCloskey, H. L. A. Hart, J. Wilson, A. I.
Melden, S. I. Benn. 254 pp.*

● Plant, Raymond. Community and Ideology. *104 pp.*

● Plant, Raymond, Lesser, Harry and Taylor-Gooby, Peter. Political Philosophy
and Social Welfare. *Essays on the Normative Basis of Welfare Provision.
276 pp.*

Ragg, N. M. People Not Cases. *A Philosophical Approach to Social Work.
168 pp.*

Timms, Noel (Ed.) Social Welfare. *Why and How? 316 pp. 7 figures.*

● Timms, Noel and Watson, David (Eds) Talking About Welfare. *Readings in
Philosophy and Social Policy. Contributors: T. H. Marshall, R. B. Brandt,
G. H. von Wright, K. Nielsen, M. Cranston, R. M. Titmuss, R. S. Downie,
E. Telfer, D. Donnison, J. Benson, P. Leonard. A. Keith-Lucas, D. Walsh,
I. T. Ramsey. 230 pp.*

● Philosophy in Social Work. *250 pp.*

● Weale, A. Equality and Social Policy. *164 pp.*

Library of Social Work
General Editor   Noel Timms

● Baldock, Peter. Community Work and Social Work. *140 pp.*

○ Beedell, Christopher. Residential Life with Children. *210 pp. Crown 8vo.*

● Berry, Juliet. Daily Experience in Residential Life. *A Study of Children and
their Care-givers. 202 pp.*

○ Social Work with Children. *190 pp. Crown 8vo.*

● Brearley, C. Paul. Residential Work with the Elderly. *116 pp.*

● Social Work, Ageing and Society. *126 pp.*

● Cheetham, Juliet. Social Work with Immigrants. *240 pp. Crown 8vo.*

● Cross, Crispin P. (Ed.) Interviewing and Communication in Social Work.
*Contributions by C. P. Cross, D. Laurenson, B. Strutt, S. Raven. 192 pp.
Crown 8vo.*

● Curnock, Kathleen and Hardiker, Pauline. Towards Practice Theory. *Skills and
Methods in Social Assessments. 208 pp.*

● Davies, Bernard. The Use of Groups in Social Work Practice. *158 pp.*

Davies, Bleddyn and Knapp, M. Old People's Homes and the Production of
Welfare. *264 pp.*

12

● **Davies, Martin.** Support Systems in Social Work. *144 pp.*
Ellis, June. (Ed.) West African Families in Britain. *A Meeting of Two Cultures. Contributions by Pat Stapleton, Vivien Biggs. 150 pp. 1 map.*
○ **Ford, J.** Human Behaviour. *Towards a Practical Understanding. About 160 pp.*
● **Hart, John.** Social Work and Sexual Conduct. *230 pp.*
Heraud, Brian. Training for Uncertainty. *A Sociological Approach to Social Work Education. 138 pp.*
Holder, D. and **Wardle, M.** Teamwork and the Development of a Unitary Approach. *212 pp.*
● **Hutten, Joan M.** Short-Term Contracts in Social Work. *Contributions by Stella M. Hall, Elsie Osborne, Mannie Sher, Eva Sternberg, Elizabeth Tuters. 134 pp.*
Jackson, Michael P. and **Valencia, B. Michael.** Financial Aid Through Social Work. *140 pp.*
● **Jones, Howard.** The Residential Community. *A Setting for Social Work. 150 pp.*
● (Ed.) Towards a New Social Work. *Contributions by Howard Jones, D. A. Fowler, J. R. Cypher, R. G. Walton, Geoffrey Mungham, Philip Priestley, Ian Shaw, M. Bartley, R. Deacon, Irwin Epstein, Geoffrey Pearson. 184 pp.*
Jones, Ray and **Pritchard, Colin.** (Eds) Social Work With Adolescents. *Contributions by Ray Jones, Colin Pritchard, Jack Dunham, Florence Rossetti, Andrew Kerslake, John Burns, William Gregory, Graham Templeman, Kenneth E. Reid, Audrey Taylor.*
○ **Jordon, William.** The Social Worker in Family Situations. *160 pp. Crown 8vo.*
● **Laycock, A. L.** Adolescents and Social Work. *128 pp. Crown 8vo.*
● **Lees, Ray.** Politics and Social Work. *128 pp. Crown 8vo.*
● Research Strategies for Social Welfare. *112 pp. Tables.*
○ **McCullough, M. K.** and **Ely, Peter J.** Social Work with Groups. *127 pp. Crown 8vo.*
● **Moffett, Jonathan.** Concepts in Casework Treatment. *128 pp. Crown 8vo.*
Parsloe, Phyllida. Juvenile Justice in Britain and the United States. *The Balance of Needs and Rights. 336 pp.*
● **Plant, Raymond.** Social and Moral Theory in Casework. *112 pp. Crown 8vo.*
Priestley, Philip, Fears, Denise and **Fuller, Roger.** Justice for Juveniles. *The 1969 Children and Young Persons Act: A Case for Reform? 128 pp.*
● **Pritchard, Colin** and **Taylor, Richard.** Social Work: Reform or Revolution? *170 pp.*
○ **Pugh, Elisabeth.** Social Work in Child Care. *128 pp. Crown 8vo.*
● **Robinson, Margaret.** Schools and Social Work. *282 pp.*
○ **Ruddock, Ralph.** Roles and Relationships. *128 pp. Crown 8vo.*
● **Sainsbury, Eric.** Social Diagnosis in Casework. *118 pp. Crown 8vo.*
● **Sainsbury, Eric, Phillips, David** and **Nixon, Stephen.** Social Work in Focus. *Clients' and Social Workers' Perceptions in Long-Term Social Work. 220 pp.*
● Social Work with Families. *Perceptions of Social Casework among Clients of a Family Service. 188pp.*
Seed, Philip. The Expansion of Social Work in Britain. *128 pp. Crown 8vo.*
● **Shaw, John.** The Self in Social Work. *124 pp.*
Smale, Gerald G. Prophecy, Behaviour and Change. *An Examination of Self-fulfilling Prophecies in Helping Relationships. 116 pp. Crown 8vo.*
Smith, Gilbert. Social Need. *Policy, Practice and Research. 155 pp.*
● Social Work and the Sociology of Organisations. *124 pp. Revised edition.*
● **Sutton, Carole.** Psychology for Social Workers and Counsellors. *An Introduction. 248 pp.*
● **Timms, Noel.** Language of Social Casework. *122 pp. Crown 8vo.*

● Recording in Social Work. *124 pp. Crown 8vo.*
● **Todd, F. Joan.** Social Work with the Mentally Subnormal. *96 pp. Crown 8vo.*
● **Walrond-Skinner, Sue.** Family Therapy. *The Treatment of Natural Systems.*
   172 pp.
● **Warham, Joyce.** An Introduction to Administration for Social Workers.
   Revised edition. 112 pp.
● An Open Case. *The Organisational Context of Social Work. 172 pp.*
○ **Wittenberg, Isca Salzberger.** Psycho-Analytic Insight and Relationships.
   A Kleinian Approach. 196 pp. Crown 8vo.

Primary Socialization, Language and Education
General Editor Basil Bernstein

Adlam, Diana S., *with the assistance of Geoffrey Turner and Lesley Lineker.*
   Code in Context. *272 pp.*
Bernstein, Basil. Class, Codes and Control. *3 volumes.*
● 1. *Theoretical Studies Towards a Sociology of Language. 254 pp.*
   2. *Applied Studies Towards a Sociology of Language. 377 pp.*
● 3. *Towards a Theory of Educational Transmission. 167 pp.*
Brandis, Walter and **Henderson, Dorothy.** Social Class, Language and
   Communication. *288 pp.*
Cook-Gumperz, Jenny. Social Control and Socialization. *A Study of Class
   Differences in the Language of Maternal Control. 290 pp.*
● **Gahagan, D. M.** and **G. A.** Talk Reform. *Exploration in Language for Infant
   School Children. 160 pp.*
Hawkins, P. R. Social Class, the Nominal Group and Verbal Strategies. *About
   220 pp.*
Robinson, W. P. and **Rakstraw, Susan D. A.** A Question of Answers.
   2 volumes. 192 pp. and 180 pp.
Turner, Geoffrey J. and **Mohan, Bernard A.** A Linguistic Description and
   Computer Programme for Children's Speech. *208 pp.*

Reports of the Institute of Community Studies

Baker, J. The Neighbourhood Advice Centre. *A Community Project in
   Camden. 320 pp.*
● **Cartwright, Ann.** Patients and their Doctors. *A Study of General Practice.
   304 pp.*
Dench, Geoff. Maltese in London. *A Case-study in the Erosion of Ethnic
   Consciousness. 302 pp.*
Jackson, Brian and **Marsden, Dennis.** Education and the Working Class: *Some
   General Themes Raised by a Study of 88 Working-class Children in a
   Northern Industrial City. 268 pp. 2 folders.*
Madge, C. and **Willmott, P.** Inner City Poverty in Paris and London. *144 pp.*
Marris, Peter. The Experience of Higher Education. *232 pp. 27 tables.*
● Loss and Change. *192 pp.*
Marris, Peter and **Rein, Martin.** Dilemmas of Social Reform. *Poverty and
   Community Action in the United States. 256 pp.*
Marris, Peter and **Somerset, Anthony.** African Businessmen. *A Study of
   Entrepreneurship and Development in Kenya. 256 pp.*
Mills, Richard. Young Outsiders: *a Study in Alternative Communities. 216 pp.*
Runciman, W. G. Relative Deprivation and Social Justice. *A Study of Attitudes
   to Social Inequality in Twentieth-Century England. 352 pp.*

Willmott, Peter. Adolescent Boys in East London. *230 pp.*
Willmott, Peter and **Young, Michael.** Family and Class in a London Suburb. *202 pp. 47 tables.*
Young, Michael and **McGeeney, Patrick.** Learning Begins at Home. *A Study of a Junior School and its Parents. 128 pp.*
Young, Michael and **Willmott, Peter.** Family and Kinship in East London. *Foreword by Richard M. Titmuss. 252 pp. 39 tables.*
The Symmetrical Family. *410 pp.*

Reports of the Institute for Social Studies in Medical Care

Cartwright, Ann, Hockey, Lisbeth and **Anderson, John J.** Life Before Death. *310 pp.*
Dunnell, Karen and **Cartwright, Ann.** Medicine Takers, Prescribers and Hoarders. *190 pp.*
Farrell, C. My Mother Said. . . *A Study of the Way Young People Learned About Sex and Birth Control. 288 pp.*

Medicine, Illness and Society
General Editor W. M. Williams

Hall, David J. Social Relations & Innovation. *Changing the State of Play in Hospitals. 232 pp.*
Hall, David J. and **Stacey M.** (Eds) Beyond Separation. *234 pp.*
Robinson, David. The Process of Becoming Ill. *142 pp.*
Stacey, Margaret *et al.* Hospitals, Children and Their Families. *The Report of a Pilot Study. 202 pp.*
Stimson, G. V. and **Webb, B.** Going to See the Doctor. *The Consultation Process in General Practice. 155 pp.*

Monographs in Social Theory
General Editor Arthur Brittan

● **Barnes, B.** Scientific Knowledge and Sociological Theory. *192 pp.*
Bauman, Zygmunt. Culture as Praxis. *204 pp.*
● **Dixon, Keith.** Sociological Theory. *Pretence and Possibility. 142 pp.*
The Sociology of Belief. *Fallacy and Foundation. 144 pp.*
Goff, T. W. Marx and Mead. *Contributions to a Sociology of Knowledge. 176 pp.*
Meltzer, B. N., Petras, J. W. and **Reynolds, L. T.** Symbolic Interactionism. *Genesis, Varieties and Criticisms. 144 pp.*
● **Smith, Anthony D.** The Concept of Social Change. *A Critique of the Functionalist Theory of Social Change. 208 pp.*
● **Tudor, Andrew.** Beyond Empiricism. *Philosophy of Science in Sociology. 224 pp.*

Routledge Social Science Journals

The British Journal of Sociology. *Editor – Angus Stewart; Associate Editor – Leslie Sklair. Vol. 1, No. 1 – March 1950 and Quarterly. Roy. 8vo. All back issues available. An international journal publishing original papers in the field of sociology and related areas.*

Community Work. *Edited by David Jones and Majorie Mayo. 1973. Published annually.*

Economy and Society. *Vol. 1, No. 1. February 1972 and Quarterly. Metric Roy. 8vo. A journal for all social scientists covering sociology, philosophy, anthropology, economics and history. All back numbers available.*

Ethnic and Racial Studies. *Editor – John Stone. Vol. 1 – 1978. Published quarterly.*

Religion. Journal of Religion and Religions. *Chairman of Editorial Board, Ninian Smart. Vol. 1, No. 1, Spring 1971. A journal with an inter-disciplinary approach to the study of the phenomena of religion. All back numbers available.*

Sociological Review. *Chairman of Editorial Board, S. J. Eggleston. New Series. August 1982, Vol. 30, No. 1. Published quarterly.*

Sociology of Health and Illness. *A Journal of Medical Sociology. Editor – Alan Davies; Associate Editor – Ray Jobling. Vol. 1, Spring 1979. Published 3 times per annum.*

Year Book of Social Policy in Britain. *Edited by Kathleen Jones. 1971. Published annually.*

Social and Psychological Aspects of Medical Practice
Editor Trevor Silverstone

Lader, Malcolm. Psychophysiology of Mental Illness. *280 pp.*

● **Silverstone, Trevor** and **Turner, Paul.** Drug Treatment in Psychiatry. *Third edition. 256 pp.*

Whiteley, J. S. and **Gordon, J.** Group Approaches in Psychiatry. *240 pp.*